Empowering Citizens, Engaging the Public

Rainer Eisfeld

Empowering Citizens, Engaging the Public

Political Science for the 21st Century

Rainer Eisfeld
Fachbereich 1
Osnabrück University
Osnabrück, Germany

ISBN 978-981-13-5927-9   ISBN 978-981-13-5928-6   (eBook)
https://doi.org/10.1007/978-981-13-5928-6

Library of Congress Control Number: 2018967960

© The Editor(s) (if applicable) and The Author(s), under exclusive licence to Springer Nature Singapore Pte Ltd. 2019
This work is subject to copyright. All rights are solely and exclusively licensed by the Publisher, whether the whole or part of the material is concerned, specifically the rights of translation, reprinting, reuse of illustrations, recitation, broadcasting, reproduction on microfilms or in any other physical way, and transmission or information storage and retrieval, electronic adaptation, computer software, or by similar or dissimilar methodology now known or hereafter developed.
The use of general descriptive names, registered names, trademarks, service marks, etc. in this publication does not imply, even in the absence of a specific statement, that such names are exempt from the relevant protective laws and regulations and therefore free for general use. The publisher, the authors and the editors are safe to assume that the advice and information in this book are believed to be true and accurate at the date of publication. Neither the publisher nor the authors or the editors give a warranty, express or implied, with respect to the material contained herein or for any errors or omissions that may have been made. The publisher remains neutral with regard to jurisdictional claims in published maps and institutional affiliations.

Cover image: © Emma Espejo / Getty Images

This Palgrave Macmillan imprint is published by the registered company Springer Nature Singapore Pte Ltd.
The registered company address is: 152 Beach Road, #21-01/04 Gateway East, Singapore 189721, Singapore

BOOKS BY RAINER EISFELD

English

Political Science and Regime Change in 20th Century Germany (1996, with Michael Th. Greven and Hans K. Rupp)
Pluralism. Developments in the Theory and Practice of Democracy (2006, ed.)
Political Science in Central-East Europe (2010, ed. with Leslie A. Pal)
Radical Approaches to Political Science (2012)
Political Science: Reflecting on Concepts, Demystifying Legends (2016)

German

Pluralismus zwischen Liberalismus und Sozialismus (1972; Italian ed. 1976, Croatian ed. 1992)
Sozialistischer Pluralismus in Europa (1984)
Gegen Barbarei (1989, ed. with Ingo Müller)
Ausgebürgert und doch angebräunt (1991, rev. ed. 2013)
Wild Bill Hickok. Westernmythos und Wirklichkeit (1994)
Mondsüchtig (1996 [hc], 2000 [pb]; new ed. 2012; Czech ed. 1997)
Als Teenager träumten. Die magischen 50er Jahre (1999)
Marsfieber (2003, with Wolfgang Jeschke)
Streitbare Politikwissenschaft (2006)
Mitgemacht (2015, ed.)

THE VISION

"Ultimately, IPSA supports the role of political science in empowering men and women to participate more effectively in political life, whether within or beyond the states in which they live."
International Political Science Association (IPSA): Mission Statement (2011)
"We are firmly convinced that it was the spirit of appreciating the rich potential of political science to provide ways to better attain

- peace,
- economic opportunity,
- human rights,
- participatory democracy, and, ultimately,
- individual fulfilment

that led to our task force being appointed... We hope that our report pushes political science and political scientists to realize this potential."
American Political Science Association (APSA): Report of the Task Force on Political Science in the Twenty-First Century (2011)

CHAPTER DETAILS

Part I Commitments

1. Improving the Human Condition
   The Tenets of Twenty-First-Century Political Science
   Increasingly expected to help resolve citizens' difficulties, the discipline—perceived as fragmented and method-driven—faces the challenge of becoming more relevant, more comprehensible, and (where necessary) more critical of governments, political and business elites

2. What Is the Current Human Condition?
   Today's human condition is marked by an unprecedented capacity to intervene for the good or for the bad of the species

3. Coming to Grips with Change
   The Subject Matter of Twenty-First-Century Political Science
   Political science should evolve into a topic-driven discipline focusing on causes, patterns, and the participatory implementation of political, economic, and cultural change, whose speed and extent are triggering insecurity and aggression against democratic institutions

4. Serving Citizens
   The Twenty-First-Century Political Scientist as Public Intellectual
   From past acerbic controversies among academics, it may safely be concluded that a more thoroughgoing public engagement by scholars will not automatically create a benign debating climate. Rather, a political culture for such engagement will have to be assiduously evolved

x CHAPTER DETAILS

5. The Civics of Friendly Persuasion
Alerting Citizens to Political Science and Its Public Engagement
Civic education needs to be based on curricula about citizenship, not about government. It should focus on learning democratic ways of life, including ways of coping with change

6. A Determination to Blow the Whistle
Political Science Stepping in to Avert Mendocracy
The Brexit and Trump campaigns have demonstrated that we may be on the way to mendocracy, or liars' rule. Political science should underwrite the exposure of patently false, illegal, or unethical claims and operations, by which politicians, parties, and governments may be attempting to deceive citizens and to thwart or subvert their constitutional responsibilities

Part II Issue Areas

7. Affirming Ethno-Cultural Diversity, Avoiding Tribalized Segmentation
Twenty-First-Century Political Science and the Politics of Recognition
Due to civil wars, to social plight and economic globalization, refugee and labor migration continue to be on the increase. Both for the recipient societies' minorities and for their hitherto culturally privileged majorities (the latter confronted with the challenge of accepting increasing heterogeneity), recourse to ethnicity has served as a source of social identification. Demonstrating an awareness of linkages between economic and cultural inequality and power, political science needs to advance narratives which promote mutual "recognition" and tolerance, rather than separation and conflict

8. Low Income, Inferior Education
Twenty-First-Century Political Science and Inequality of Political Resources
Unequal social resources, primarily income, wealth, and education, will unavoidably translate into unequal political resources with regard to participatory engagement and control over political agenda-setting, already now pushing democracy toward plutocracy. Reducing such disparities is of prime importance to ensure the accessibility, accountability, and—in the final instance—legitimacy of supposedly "representative" government. Political scientists should join leading economists such as Krugman, Piketty, and Stiglitz in urging tax reform and other policy changes

CHAPTER DETAILS   xi

9. Robust Regulatory Policies for Capitalism
Twenty-First-Century Political Science's Political Economy
Deregulatory state intervention and determined governmental underperformance with regard to public services have (a) been eating into the capacity of legislatures to allocate resources and (b) have deepened, if not triggered, persistent financial crises. The entrenched neo-liberal discourse has made governments and market players alike rival each other in reorganizing states as quasi-enterprise associations bent on cutting outlays. Citizens' loyalty to the state and grassroots commitment to the democratic process are thus being weakened. The pro-market trend needs to be reversed, and a reinvigorated political economy must visibly intervene in the political debate

10. Global Warming, Power Structures, and Living Conditions
Climate Politics and Twenty-First-Century Political Science
The activities of veto players among economic and political elites constraining climate policy changes in, for example, the United States, China, Russia, or India have overshadowed a more fundamental problem which is that the improvement of living conditions for hundreds of millions of poor implies, at present, an increase in CO_2 emissions. Any effective emission reduction will depend on decoupling population growth and income rise from increasing pollution.

11. Radicalization, Terrorism, Subversion of Civil Liberties
Conundrums of Twenty-First-Century Political Science
A twenty-first-century political science that focuses on peaceful conflict settlement may be facing a number of domestic and international security dilemmas. These dilemmas might not least be cast in terms of the need to develop concepts of "soft" policing and de-radicalization strategies against millennialist violence, rather than relying solely on repressive measures which threaten fundamental democratic values, without actually offering prospects of success

Part III Partisanship

12. Twenty-First-Century Political Science: Politicization of a Discipline?
A Normative Science of Democracy with Empirical Rigor
At a moment in history when the accountability of democratic governments is literally bleeding away, when the hybridization of democratic regimes in Central-East Europe is on the rise and democracies in Western Europe and North America are compromised by the erosion of democratic rules and values, political science as a science of democracy becomes inevitably partisan. It should acknowledge such partisanship, explaining aims and implications.

ACKNOWLEDGMENTS

This book will argue that the final justification for evolving political science into a discipline where problems would take priority over methods, and public relevance over sophisticated specialization, is provided by the need to face up to major issue areas of continuing democratic erosion. The work presents the first book-length study covering in detail the implications and consequences of that transformation. In the following pages, the reader may expect some determined conclusions from nearly two decades of APSA, IPSA, and PSA discussion on actual political science's disconnect with the larger public and on the discipline's doubtful relevance. But for that debate, the book could not have been conceived.

I will return to the point in a moment. But first, there is a priority list of deeply felt personal debts to repay.

The entire book would not be the same without my Canadian friend and colleague Leslie Pal, whose perceptive interventions provided a wealth of inspiration and perspective. Les and I have been collaborating for a decade: In 2008, we commenced work on a co-edited volume *Political Science in Central-East Europe: Diversity and Convergence*, which appeared in 2010 and won the distinction of being recommended as an IPSA Executive Committee selection. For the past two years, Les read and commented on every chapter, asking penetrating questions that forced me to clarify or rethink my positions. (This is not meant to imply that Les bears any responsibility for the final product.)

Leslie's unwavering confidence that I would pull the project off encouraged me to persist whenever the going got rough—and it often did. I value his continuing support the more in view of his own multiple

xiii

xiv   ACKNOWLEDGMENTS

obligations—and, I should add, of his own disposition to a more dispassionate manner of arguing.

Several ideas of this book may be traced back to a brief article entitled: "How Political Science Might Regain Relevance and Obtain an Audience: A Manifesto for the Twenty-First Century", published in the June 2011 issue of *European Political Science*. That piece (a mere six pages—rather tightly argued, I'm afraid) had been written as part of a debate on the discipline's relevance, initiated in 2008/2009 by former IPSA Secretary General John Trent at two IPSA congresses in Montréal and Santiago de Chile ("Is political science out of step with the world?"). I feel deeply indebted to John for continuing to stimulate my thinking by the evidence and the arguments which he presented.

Andrea Lenschow generously pointed me to a 2016 article in the journal *Global Environmental Politics*, which summarized major research trends regarding climate change politics. Along with Andrea's own work, that article helped me greatly in paving my access to the complexities of the issue. Serving as the department's dean for a number of years, Andrea was also instrumental in arranging for the institutional resources which the University of Osnabrück has continued to provide since my retirement. I remain most grateful for the unstinting support which she accorded my academic pursuits.

The study received its final touches from inputs by Marian Sawer, Dianne Pinderhughes, Matthew Flinders, and Leslie Pal during a roundtable debate of the book's arguments at the 2018 Brisbane World Political Science Congress. I owe a huge debt of gratitude to each of them. Marian, who with characteristic grace convened and chaired the roundtable, has enriched our discipline in a number of prominent offices, such as President of the Australasian Political Studies Association, IPSA Vice President, long-time co-editor of the *International Political Science Review*, Program Co-Chair (with Dianne) of the 2016 Poznań World Congress of Political Science. Dianne, during her historic APSA Presidency—she was the first African-American woman to serve in that capacity—commissioned a Task Force on "Political Science in the Twenty-First Century", from whose vision I quoted at the outset of this book. Matt, a former Chair of the United Kingdom's Political Studies Association, is also Founding Director of the Sir Bernard Crick Center for the Public Understanding of Politics, whose name says it all: Seeking to narrow the gap between academe and society, the Center aims at encouraging engaged citizenship on every level. About Les, nothing more needs to be written here, except that his focus on public policy and public management in turbulent times provided a perfect vantage point from which to assess the present book's approach.

Over a decade ago, by 2006, APSR editor Lee Sigelman, whose untimely death saddened the discipline three years later, saw the discipline's compartmentalization tied to the emergence of "niches", where highly specialized scholars conduct "highly particularized" research, eventually writing for "highly specialized audiences" rather than for a few specialists, but also for "many non-specialists". That same year, IPSA launched a "linkage" policy with regard to its research committees, intended to mitigate the problematic consequences of excessive specialization. Serving on the IPSA Executive Committee as Research Committee Representative from 2006 to 2012, I became involved in that effort. IPSA's 2008 Montréal conference "Political Science in the World: New Theoretical and Regional Perspectives", co-chaired by Dirk Berg-Schlosser and myself, systematically brought together delegates from research committees (27 in number) and national political science associations (23 of them) for the first time in IPSA's history. It was here that John Trent first presented his findings on the challenges calling for, as John termed it, "rejuvenating" the discipline.

Before being elected to the office of Research Committee Representative, I had chaired the Research Committee on Socio-Political Pluralism for the preceding six years. Pluralism was and remains a topic closely linked to a number of key public issues—such as disparities in political resources, deregulatory state intervention, deficiencies in public education, the rollback of organized labor, and xenophobic backlashes against immigrant minorities. Throughout the following pages, this book will urge political scientists to address those and several additional "large" questions ahead of other problems. These pages will also emphasize required redirections of the discipline's present training, research, financing, and teaching priorities.

Because such steps are certain to involve a conflict-ridden, time-consuming process, I wish to stress that every political scientist may make a start here and now, breaking new ground in her or his university, department, or study group. To illustrate that this can be both feasible and rewarding, and that support for such an endeavor may materialize from unexpected quarters, I may perhaps be excused for referring to my own professional experience which has shaped my perception of what the discipline might do.

xvi ACKNOWLEDGMENTS

In the 1974 *American Political Science Review*, Henry W. Ehrmann (1908–1994) emphasized "the breadth of historical approach and the concreteness of analysis" of my first book (in fact, my doctoral thesis) on pluralism as a potentially critical theory. Two years later, the study was, by reason of its scope, deemed suitable for an Italian translation. And Polish political scientist Stanislaw Ehrlich (1907–1997) invited me to his research committee session at the 1979 Moscow World Political Science Congress, an exercise in peaceful coexistence.

Stanislaw had founded the IPSA Study Group on Socio-Political Pluralism in 1976; two years later, it had been recognized as a Research Committee. Today, he may be more remembered for supervising in 1976 the doctoral thesis of one Jarosław Kaczyński, present chair of Poland's so-called Law and Justice Party. At the time, Stanislaw stood out by his deep-felt commitment to bridge the East-West divide within the political science community. I recall him with fondness and continuing gratitude for introducing me to the ranks of IPSA: a respected scholar, a devoted colleague, a dear friend.

The experience was repeated after the Portuguese dictatorship had been deposed by the "revolution of carnations" on the very day (April 25, 1974) my university—one of the new "red-brick" affairs built at the time across Western Germany—opened its gates to students. I took that as an omen for indicating the field to which I should turn next. Switching from reflecting on a political concept, such as pluralism, to exploring another country's social, political, and economic cleavages would be quite a change. Still, such a project would again involve historically grounded analyses, and it might lead to a major case study about the linkage of domestic politics and foreign pressures under Cold War conditions.

My resulting work brought me into contact with British historian Kenneth Maxwell (1941–), who had arrived in the United States a decade earlier. After publishing two seminal *New York Review of Books* articles in 1974/1975—"Portugal: A Neat Revolution" and, even more distinctive, "Portugal Under Pressure"—he rapidly had come to be considered a leading expert on Portuguese matters. He graciously invited me when, in the mid-1980s, he organized a number of workshops and conferences both at Columbia University and the Woodrow Wilson Center (Washington) on Portugal's current conditions and future prospects.

Bringing together leading Portuguese and American academic and political figures, and resulting in a couple of collected volumes, the frank debates during these meetings offered me unique insights and opportunities for improving my own assessments. Ken would later in his career emphasize Brazilian over Portuguese affairs (the Kenneth Maxwell Thesis Prize in Brazilian Studies at Harvard University's David Rockefeller Center for Latin American Studies is named after him), and I would also turn elsewhere. But I owe a lasting debt of gratitude to Ken, no less than to Stanislaw, for first providing me with access to the kind of informed transnational dialogue from which projects in the social sciences may immensely benefit in overcoming the confines of parochial perspectives.

Warm thanks are finally due to two anonymous reviewers and to my editor at Palgrave Macmillan, Vishal Daryanomel, for their pertinent and inspiring comments and suggestions.

PROLOGUE

"It is improbable", Herbert George Wells—commenting on the probability of social and political tendencies—predicted at the beginning of the twentieth century, "that ever again will any flushed undignified man with a vast voice, a muscular face in incessant operation, collar crumpled, hair disordered, and arms in wild activity,... talking copiously... from railway platforms, talking from hotel balconies, talking on tubs, barrels, scaffoldings, pulpits... rise to be the most powerful person in any democratic state in the world" (Wells 1901: 140).

Such hopes have been shattered both between the two great wars and once again after 1945. Not balconies and pulpits, but television and more recently social media have helped the emergence of demagogues resorting to plebiscitarian methods. Even though lacking any experience in politics and government, they have successfully appealed to voters—as noted a century after Wells by Juan Linz, expert on authoritarian systems of government—on the basis of either ample financial resources or "popularity gained outside of politics" (Linz 2007: 144). The statement instantly evokes images of a recent election in one of the world's major countries.

Political science cannot hope to immunize citizens against folly nor, for that matter, against anger or even hate. But it can attempt considerably more than it is doing at present to spread historically informed analytical thinking and careful, normatively inspired reasoning among the public. And it needs to sound the alarm, challenging mendocracy—liars' rule—toward which once venerable democracies, as evidenced by the Brexit and Trump campaigns, are presently sliding.

xix

There are, in addition to the issue just mentioned, sufficient additional reasons for such an endeavor which will be discussed below. Prominent enough among them to be singled out here, and taken up again later, rank

- the existence of cartels for manufacturing ignorance,
- the expanding production of fear,
- and—exacerbated by both—the psychologically unsettling impact of change.

"In case after case", as historians of science Naomi Oreskes (Harvard University) and Erik Conway (NASA/JPL) reported on a continuing pattern, a handful of scientists have joined forces with private corporations and think tanks funded by those industries to challenge scientific evidence, using their authority "to discredit any science they didn't like". As judged by Oreskes and Conway, these individuals had "no particular experience" in the issues under debate, but they did have influence, and they knew how to obtain media coverage for their views. The two scholars labeled them the "merchants of doubt" (Oreskes and Conway 2010: 6, 8, 9, 248, 262). Both also showed that the issue, rather than questions of science, was actually economic interests and politics—the role, and the extent, of government regulation.

When such campaigns occur, political science should go public to try and set the record straight.

By constant repetition and use in public discourse, fear has become a dominant perspective, a way "of looking at life" in our time, media sociologist David L. Altheide (Arizona State University) at the twenty-first century's outset summed up the result of his inquiries into the role of mass media for social control. Fear may come to color citizens' views on specific political issues. Thus the expanding production of fear, affecting "our culture and public order", has obvious political ramifications (Altheide 2015 [¹2002]: 3/4, 16/17, 23/24, 26).

Altheide also noted that fear provides ostensible explanations and solutions in a world perceived by many as "constantly changing and out-of-control". Again, political scientists' public interventions are urgently needed to foster more rational approaches. *In fact, helping citizens to come to grips with change—political, economic, not least cultural change—will be identified in the following pages as the core of a topic-driven twenty-first-century political science.*

British writer James Graham Ballard has, perhaps more compellingly than some social or political scientists, argued how being affected by the dramatic changes that have been occurring may motivate those who can afford such options to retreat behind gated communities, to business parks, to executive housing equipped with closed circuit television cameras, and may drive others to strike out at their increasingly "strange" environments with a violence that can include "kill[ing] someone just to feel alive" (Ballard 2004: 3, 4, 5).

If such narratives about what is presently occurring in our societies involving power, modernity, and science should make us uneasy when reading them, the sensation is only too justified. In the end, it may provide the most potent foundation for the tenacity, if not doggedness, which large numbers of political scientists will have to muster, should they indeed decide to engage the public in a determined, even bold attempt at empowering citizens. And yet, they—like others involved in comparable pursuits—might keep in mind the ray of hope to which Leonard Cohen pointed when he sang about perseverance in 1992 ("The Anthem"):

"There is a crack in everything.
That's how the light comes in."

REFERENCES

Altheide, David L. (2015 [¹2002]): *Creating Fear*. New Brunswick: Transaction Publishers.

Ballard, J. G. (2004): "Interview with the Author: J. G. Ballard talks to Vanora Bennett", in: J. G. Ballard: *Millennium People*. London: Harper Perennial, 4/5.

Linz, Juan J. (2007): "Some Thoughts on the Victory and Future of Democracy", in: Dirk Berg-Schlosser (ed.): *Democratization: The State of the Art*. Opladen/Farmington Hills: Barbara Budrich, 133–153.

Oreskes, Naomi/Conway, Eric M. (2010): *Merchants of Doubt*. New York: Bloomsbury Press.

Wells, H. G. (1901): *Anticipations. The Works of H. G. Wells*, Vol. 4 (1924). New York: Scribner.

CONTENTS

Part I Commitments	1
1 Improving the Human Condition	3
2 What Is the Current Human Condition?	15
3 Coming to Grips with Change	23
4 Serving Citizens	33
5 The Civics of Friendly Persuasion	55
6 A Determination to Blow the Whistle	65
Part II Issue Areas	81
7 Affirming Ethno-Cultural Diversity, Avoiding Tribalized Segmentation	83

xxiv CONTENTS

8 Low Income, Inferior Education 101

9 Robust Regulatory Policies for Capitalism 119

10 Global Warming, Power Structures, and Living Conditions 145

11 Radicalization, Terrorism, Subversion of Civil Liberties 159

Part III Partisanship 177

12 Twenty-First-Century Political Science: Politicization of a Discipline? 179

Index 195

ABBREVIATIONS

ABM	Anti-ballistic Missile
ANU	Australian National University
APSA	American Political Science Association
AUFTA	Australia-United States Free Trade Agreement
CCTV	Closed Circuit Television
CETA	Comprehensive Economic and Trade Agreement (Canada/European Union)
ECPR	European Consortium for Political Research
EEA	Eastern Economic Association (USA)
EU	European Union
FAS	Federation of American Scientists
FATCA	Foreign Account Tax Compliance Act
GCHQ	Government Communications Headquarters (UK)
GDR	German Democratic Republic
HUAC	House Un-American Activities Committee
ICSID	International Center for the Settlement of Investment Disputes
IPSA	International Political Science Association
ISDS	Investor-State Dispute Settlement
LSE	London School of Economics and Political Science
NAAEC	North American Agreement on Environmental Cooperation
NAALC	North American Agreement on Labor Cooperation
NAFTA	North American Free Trade Agreement
NAS	National Academy of Sciences
NSA	National Security Agency (USA)
OECD	Organisation for Economic Cooperation and Development
OSCE	Organisation for Security and Cooperation in Europe
PEGIDA	Patriotic Europeans Against the Islamization of the West (Germany)

PSA	Political Studies Association (United Kingdom)
SUNY	State University of New York
TPP	Trans-Pacific Partnership
TTIP	Transatlantic Trade and Investment Partnership (United States/ European Union)
UNICITRAL	United Nations Commission on International Trade Law

PART I

Commitments

CHAPTER 1

Improving the Human Condition

The Tenets of Twenty-First-Century Political Science

Increasingly expected to help resolve citizens' difficulties, the discipline—perceived as fragmented and method-driven—faces the challenge of becoming more relevant, more comprehensible, and (where necessary) more critical of governments, political and business elites.

"A neglect of the citizen": No less was attested to political science in its present state by 2009 Economics Nobel Laureate Elinor Ostrom. During an interview, she illustrated her criticism with the observation that once, while waiting at a meeting of the American Political Science Association (APSA), she had been asked why she was reading a book on peasants. Political science, she had been reminded, "was about presidents, parties, and Congress" (Toonen 2010: 197).

Ostrom was scheduled to be keynote speaker at the 2012 Madrid World Congress of the International Political Science Association (IPSA). Her research focus on polycentric systems of power and on the direct involvement of citizens in the governance of such systems has provided inspirations for political science, for a hopefully renascent political economy, and for climate policies (see Tarko 2017: 12/13, 53, 172; passim). Sadly, she died from cancer a few weeks before the world congress.

Any political scientist who remains unconvinced by the mere reference to a past APSA President's—and James Madison Award recipient's—reading habits could do worse than glance at the following sentences by

© The Author(s) 2019
R. Eisfeld, *Empowering Citizens, Engaging the Public,*
https://doi.org/10.1007/978-981-13-5928-6_1

3

4   R. EISFELD

António de Figueiredo, journalist and campaigner in Salazarist Portugal (de Figueiredo 1975: 10–12): "Reading and writing letters for illiterate peasants made me understand that poverty takes many cruel forms other than occasional hunger." He sensed, Figueiredo wrote, "how my intrusion must have inhibited them and saw how inarticulate they were." He also recalled his shock of discovering at an early age "that illiteracy or semi-literacy were not a product of casual neglect but part of the established social order."

Figueiredo went on to recount how, while reading to a gathering of peasants from the speeches of President Roosevelt promising freedom, a rural Republican Guard had threatened to beat him up if he persisted "in disturbing the minds of local people with that 'Communist poison'". At the time, he had determined for himself that one day he would be capable to figure out the guard's motives and the basis of his power.

As with Figueiredo, should not a similarly determined effort rank high among the concerns of political science to broaden our own and others' understanding about the ways in which citizens are being encouraged or prevented to effectively participate in their political systems? And should not such an effort include, as Ostrom insisted in her 1997 APSA Presidential address, a searching look at the knowledge and the skills which our discipline presently provides?

"All too many of our textbooks focus exclusively on leaders", Ostrom held. They do not inform future citizens "of the actions they need to know and can undertake". Nor are their moral decisions discussed. "We are producing generations of cynical citizens with little trust in one another" (Ostrom 1998: 3, 18).

The shortcoming which this admonishment called by name was unexpectedly brought into the limelight by a US legislator's derogatory assessment of the discipline. Submitting, in November 2009, an amendment to the 2010 Commerce, Justice & Science Appropriation Act, Senator Thomas Coburn (R, OK) contended that the National Science Foundation's (NSF) Political Science Program drew resources away from research which might otherwise yield "discoveries that can improve the human condition". The implication was obvious.

Coburn wished to bar the NSF from allocating—or, as he read into the record, from "wasting"—federal research money for any political science project. His motion obtained 36 votes in the US Senate, with a majority of 62 senators voting against (Eisfeld 2011: 220). Four years after his first attempt, Coburn tried again, this time choosing a time-proven approach which came close to succeeding. The "human condition" was not mentioned again. Instead, the 2013 Coburn Amendment wanted to restrict NSF political science funding to projects certified by the agency as "promoting" either national security or the economic interests of the United States.

Favored by a situation, when avoiding a government shutdown required rapidly resolving a budget stalemate between the Democratic-controlled US Senate and the Republican-led House of Representatives, Coburn managed to reach an agreement with Appropriations Committee Chair Barbara Mikulski (D, MD). Passed by acclamation (voice vote), rather than by recorded (roll call) vote, the amendment was included in the Continuing Appropriations Act of 2013, prompting the NSF to cancel the current political science grant cycle (APA 2013; Reilly 2013; Mole 2013).

After some debate, APSA responded in an equally time-honored way. The organization did not refer either to possible improvements of the human condition. Rather, it spent $48,000 in hiring the services of a Washington lobbying firm which provides "strategic communication services to clients who wish to have an impact on decision-makers": Barbara Kennelly Associates, established by a congresswoman from Connecticut who is also a political science professor. According to APSA President John H. Aldrich, someone was needed "with access to Senator Mikulski". The effort paid off: When Congress passed the omnibus appropriations bill in early 2014, the restricting amendment was omitted (Stratford 2014).

While the outcome may be considered a victory, of course it does not touch on problems posed by the state of the discipline. Soberingly enough, observations such as Ostrom's have been piling up over the past two decades. Giovanni Sartori contended in 2004 that political science—at least American-style, largely quantitative political science—"is going nowhere... Practice-wise, it is largely useless science that does not supply knowledge for use" (Sartori 2004: 786). The *New York Times* quoted Joseph S. Nye in 2009 with the assessment that the discipline may "be moving in the direction of saying more and more about less and less" (Cohen 2009). Two years later, former IPSA Secretary General John Trent, who had organized the organization's world congresses from 1973 to 1988 and again in 2000, highlighted the discipline's "retreat" from public debate: There are "few 'public intellectuals' and few connections

6   R. EISFELD

with the political class". The general result, Trent concluded echoing Ostrom, is "a sense that we are not helping citizens" (Trent 2011: 196/197).

To a considerable extent, these misgivings stem from two ongoing debates about the fragmentation (less kindly, the balkanization) of the discipline and about how much relevant work is being done in a predominantly method-driven field, whose mainstream approach has come to be "symbolized by multiple-regression equations" (Smith 1997: 254).

- Advanced fragmentation—or compartmentalization—has been tied to the emergence of "niches" where highly specialized political scientists survive by defending their "turf"—their priorities, their projects, and their responsibilities. They conduct "highly particularized" research, and they write for their own kind—for "highly specialized audiences", rather than for "a few specialists and many non-specialists" (Sigelman 2006: 475). The specialization of individual scholars has been supplemented, even fortified, by the specialization of loosely organized, research-oriented standing sections or working groups. By 2010, four national organizations alone—the British Political Studies Association, the American, German, and Russian Political Science Associations—had collectively generated no fewer than 147 such sub-groups. In many instances, there has been little or no mutual awareness of each other's projects, meetings, or publications. Cross-field research, engaging salient issue areas by cutting across traditional domains, remains underdeveloped (Eisfeld 2016: 16, 18).
- Formalized method taking precedence over substantive issues implies that problems addressed will be "fairly narrow" (due to obtainability of quantitative data), results "limited" in range, much of the work terminologically "incomprehensible" to a general public and "uninteresting" as regards content—in a word, "arcane" (Smith 2009: 2). For the sub-field of environmental policy studies—which will resurface in this book—the assessment was recently borne out by Jennifer Clapp and Peter Dauvergne, two long-time past editors of the leading journal *Global Environmental Politics*. Critical faculties are impaired, as refinement of sophisticated approaches takes precedence over examining their appropriateness for addressing salient problems. Increasingly complex modeling and statistical methods risk to disconnect scholarship from policy and issue orientation (Dauvergne

and Clapp 2016: 3). More determined critics, such as Donald Green and Ian Shapiro, have dissected what they label the "pathologies" of method-driven political science, due to practitioners' eagerness "to vindicate" their models, rather than "to understand and explain actual political outcomes" (Green and Shapiro 1994: 33; Shapiro 2002: 598).

To add insult to injury, the adopted mathematics, as will be seen below, did not always convince mathematicians.

The results of fragmentation and of method-driven, rather than problem- or topic-driven, research have tended to mutually reinforce each other. During the last decade, a succession of APSA Task Forces has taken issue with these and other presently prevailing trends.

Appointed by APSA President Theda Skocpol, a Task Force on Graduate Education in its 2004 Report to the APSA Council warned that too specialized training may lead to "unduly parochial research". Its members also emphasized that *exploring* ways in which politics can help resolve human difficulties and *communicating* to wide audiences how the study of politics may aid in better understanding "substantively important features of human life" should rank foremost among the concerns of our discipline (APSA 2004: 3, 4).

The Task Force on Political Science in the Twenty-First Century, commissioned by APSA President Dianne Pinderhughes, noted in its 2011 Report that political science is "often ill-equipped" both to address the reasons

- "why many of the most marginal members of communities… are often unable to have their needs effectively addressed by government" and
- "to develop explanations for the social, political, and economic processes that lead to groups' marginalization" in the first place.

The Report concluded that this limits the discipline's relevance "to broader social and political discourse". Therefore, new actions would have to be taken (APSA 2011: 1, 56).

A Task Force *The Double Bind: The Politics of Racial & Class Inequalities in the Americas* created by APSA President Rodney Hero (2014–2015) and incorporating a comparative approach found that, in the societies of North and South America, both "low-economic status and the incentives

8   R. EISFELD

of the party system" hamper ethno-racial minorities to translate demographic potential and civic participation "into meaningful economic gains" (Hooker and Tillery 2016: 12). Political science should further explore, by cross-disciplinary and cross-national studies, "the long-standing gaps in the life chances of whites and communities of color" (Pinderhughes 2018: 8; Hooker and Tillery 2016: 4).

Finally, a Task Force on Public Engagement set up by APSA President John H. Aldrich held in its 2016 Report *Let's Be Heard* that the discipline had a great and growing, but largely "untapped" potential to "improve lives"—depending on whether political scientists took steps to convey "more insights of greater value" on controversial topics to more people (APSA 2016: 1, 2).

The "Perestroika in American Political Science" initiative (a "movement", to the optimists) had, from 2000, certainly prepared the ground for such deliberations. Some supporters, at least, already spoke about Perestroika in terms of a broad effort (Luke 2005: 468) to make political science

- "problem-based, people-centered, and politically grounded", rather than
- "technique-based, methodology-centered and profession-grounded".

In their turn, sustained discussions among American political scientists could not fail to have a wider impact, as evidenced by two IPSA events—a 2008 Plenary Session at a conference in Montréal and subsequently a 2009 Roundtable at a World Congress in Santiago de Chile—and a 2012 UK Political Studies Association Symposium in Belfast. Matthew Flinders (Sheffield) and Peter John (University College London), whose debate had inspired the PSA Symposium, came to stress their shared view that the discipline "must engage more visibly and coherently in political and public debate" (Flinders and John 2013: 222). John Trent (Ottawa), who led both IPSA sessions and has already been quoted earlier in this chapter, concluded—having surveyed a rich array of sources—that the public may be about ripe for "humble, knowledge-based wisdom" from our discipline, after the world's affairs suffered from two decades of "misinformation and mismanagement" (Trent 2012: 91/92, 134).

These assembled arguments reveal the contours of a twenty-first-century political science which would make a sustained attempt at improving what Senator Coburn referred to as the "human condition".

Immediately, a *caveat* must be added. For such a discipline to be given even the merest chance at emerging, the "new actions" mentioned by APSA's Pinderhughes Task Force ought to include the following:

- The discipline's incentive structure needs to be revamped to a substantial extent. For academics in the early stages of their careers, the allocation of research funding, journals' prevailing publishing policies, appointment, and promotion criteria presently favor an understanding of professionalism which is biased toward quantitative, "technically sophisticated" work. Put mildly, public engagement activities are not considered "a high priority" by host and funding institutions (Flinders and John 2013: 223; Savage 2013: 198). *For the discipline to change, career incentives must change.*
- Professional training will henceforth have to include, first, the "art" of translating "arcane", "impenetrable" academic writing forms meant for other specialists into "a more direct and free-flowing" approach underlining the broader implications of research findings. Most importantly, the grasp of such an approach as *a different, but legitimate and rewarding form of scholarship* needs to be hammered home. Second, the skills future political scientists ought to acquire must show "pathways" for dealing with different kinds of media, including social media such as blogs and tweets (Smith 2009: 2; Flinders 2013: 149, 156, 162/163).
- "Problem choice is fundamental" (Calhoun 2009: 1): The way political scientists are educated should prepare and encourage them to proceed from "solving minor empirical puzzles" (Savage 2013: 191) to tackling aspects of pressing "major public issues" (Calhoun 2009: ibid). Any resulting problem- and solution-oriented agendas need, of course, to be "defined, shaped and controlled" by none other than the political science community—and, where necessary, defended against emerging governmental "New Public Management" strategies for dealing with "politically identified 'problems'" (Flinders 2018: 3): Countries such as the United Kingdom or Australia have started to link public funding to research judged as "relevant" by having a potential impact on policies for the delivery of economic growth. Governmental programs of "co-opting academics" (Flinders) through funding incentives will evidently make recalibrating the discipline's reward structures far from easy. In the future "division of labor" (Calhoun 2009: 2), as it may emerge among

10   R. EISFELD

political scientists, an increasing part of the discipline should nevertheless focus on aspects of *those* "large" questions that will surface in the book's subsequent chapters and which, it may safely be maintained, *in a rather basic sense affect the "human condition"*.

Determining that condition's present essential aspects will be the task of this book's next chapter. The third chapter will propose ubiquitous, more often than not politically induced, change that is now profoundly affecting citizens' environments, as the principal focus of twenty-first-century political science. A prominent political scientist's past assertion, according to which "modern man, in contrast [to traditional man], accepts the possibility of change and believes in its desirability" (Huntington 1968: 32), may at most be read as an ideal type, the likes of which Max Weber proposed for purposes of empirical falsification and development of finer analytical categories. Events, which have definitely falsified the "modern man" construct, will be discussed at the third chapter's outset. Only too often, the impact of economic depression, mass unemployment, war, Cold War, migratory movements, and even profound transformations of gender and sexual relations continues to result, rather than in desired change, in widespread fear and anger.

This book considers it vital that the discipline, holding out against such politically highly consequential resentments, should make a comprehensive effort at supporting citizens to better handle the ever more pervasive experience of political, cultural, and economic change affecting their lives. A twenty-first-century political science embarking on that course would, as the book's subsequent chapters will detail, commit itself to

- making ordinary citizens the "intended beneficiaries" of the knowledge it produces, acting "as an aid, refiner, extender" of lay inquiry (Lindblom 1990: 216/217, 257/258), even if this may require developing a new political culture of scholarly public engagement;
- encouraging academics to write and speak as public intellectuals seeking to advance both knowledge and human freedom, yet recognizing "the plurality of perspectives and potential incompleteness characteristic of the internal public sphere of science itself" (Calhoun 2009: 8);
- promoting a civics education that emphasizes self-government over government and informed involvement over passive spectatorship, conveying the "civic literacy" needed for weighing reasons whether

to maintain or to change one's own and the community's ways (Putnam 2003: 253; Wong 2015: 5, 8);

- blowing the whistle when politicians or governments attempt to deceive citizens, particularly when those, corporate elites and part of the media, "work hand in glove" to generate liars' rule, "mendocracy" (Perlstein 2011);
- finally, and no less importantly,
    - pinpointing the big political, economic, and socio-cultural challenges with which citizens will continue to be grappling, and which the subsequent chapter will locate more precisely in the context of the current human condition: Increasing ethno-cultural diversity; growing inequality of political resources; and underperforming governments with regard to regulatory policies; global warming—the quintessential variety of change, because it is affecting the condition of the entire planet; terrorism and its underlying causes;
    - identifying these issues as the core themes around which a major part of research, teaching, and public engagement should henceforth crystallize in an effort "to help citizens prepare themselves for various possible futures" (Hankiss 2002: 22).

In his 2002 APSA Presidential Address, Robert Putnam reminded his audience—and his profession—that alienation from the workings of the political system had increased and political participation declined over the last decades not merely in the United States, but in many other Western democracies. If one had thought, Putnam remarked, that this would have occasioned a vivid debate among political scientists about how to respond, one would "have been wrong" (Putnam 2003: 250). Engaging citizens in a joint debate about their uppermost political concerns might furnish no small part of the needed response.

References

APA [American Psychological Association] (2013): "Coburn Amendment Restricts NSF Political Science Funding", April 2013, www.apa.org/science/about/psa/2013/04/political-science-funding.aspx, accessed Sept. 12, 2016.

APSA [American Political Science Association] (2004): *Report to the APSA Council, APSA Task Force on Graduate Education.* Washington DC: APSA, files.eric.ed.gov/fulltext/ED495969.pdf, accessed Sept. 14, 2016.

12 R. EISFELD

APSA [American Political Science Association] (2011): *Political Science in the 21st Century*. Report of the Task Force on Political Science in the 21st Century. Washington DC: APSA, www.apsanet.org/portals/54/Files/TaskForceReports/TF_21stCentury_AllPgs_webres90.pdf, accessed Sept. 14, 2016.

APSA [American Political Science Association] (2016): *Let's Be Heard! How to Better Communicate Political Science's Public Value*. Report of the Task Force on Public Engagement. Washington DC: APSA, http://journals.cambridge.org/download.php?file=%2FPSC%2FPSC48_S1%2FS1049096515000335a.pdf&code=175ec04c9eeea48f9f1f376d4cb1ef35, accessed Sept. 14, 2016.

Calhoun, Craig (2009): "Social Science for Public Knowledge". *Transformations of the Public Sphere* (Essay Forum), October 10. Social Science Research Council, http://publicsphere.ssrc.org/calhoun-social-science-for-public-knowledge, accessed Sept. 18, 2016.

Cohen, Patricia (2009): "Field Study: Just How Relevant is Political Science?" *New York Times*, October 19, 2009, http://www.nytimes.com/2009/10/20/books/20poli.html, accessed Sept. 12, 2016.

Dauvergne, Peter/Clapp, Jennifer (2016): "Researching Global Environmental Politics in the 21st Century". *Global Environmental Politics*, Vol. 16 No. 1, 1–12.

Eisfeld, Rainer (2011): "How Political Science Might Regain Relevance and Obtain an Audience: A Manifesto for the 21st Century". *European Political Science*, Vol. 10, 220–225.

Eisfeld, Rainer (2016): "Specialization and Teamwork: Current Challenges to the Discipline", in: id.: *Political Science: Reflecting on Concepts, Demystifying Legends*, Opladen/Berlin/Toronto: Barbara Budrich, 14–19.

Figueiredo, António de (1975): *Portugal: Fifty Years of Dictatorship*. Harmondsworth: Penguin Books.

Flinders, Matthew (2013): "The Tyranny of Relevance and the Art of Translation". *Political Studies Review*, Vol. 11, 149–167.

Flinders, Matthew (2018): "The Politics of Impact in Political Science". Paper, 25th World Congress of Political Science (RC 33.05), Brisbane.

Flinders, Matthew/John, Peter (2013): "The Future of Political Science". *Political Studies Review*, Vol. 11, 222–227.

Green, Donald P./Shapiro, Ian (1994): *Pathologies of Rational Choice Theory. A Critique of Applications in Political Science*. New Haven/London: Yale University Press.

Hankiss, Elemér (2002): "Brilliant Ideas or Brilliant Errors? Twelve Years of Social Science Research in Eastern Europe", in: Max Kaase/Vera Sparschuh (eds.): *Three Social Science Disciplines in Central and Eastern Europe*, Berlin/Budapest: Collegium Budapest/IZ Sozialwissenschaften, 17–24.

IMPROVING THE HUMAN CONDITION   13

Hooker, Juliet/Tillery, Alvin B. (2016): *The Double Bind: The Politics of Racial and Class Inequalities in the Americas*. Report of the APSA Task Force on Racial and Social Class Inequalities in the Americas, Executive Summary. Washington: American Political Science Association 2016. https://www.apsanet.org/Portals/54/files/Task%20Force%20Reports/Hero%20Report%202016_The%20Double%20Bind/Double%20Bind%20Executive%20Summary.pdf?ver=2017-07-06-135548-510, accessed August 12, 2018.

Huntington, Samuel P. (1968): *Political Order in Changing Societies*. New Haven/London: Yale University Press.

Lindblom, Charles E. (1990): *Inquiry and Change. The Troubled Attempt to Understand and Shape Society*, New Haven/London: Yale University Press.

Luke, Timothy W. (2005): "Caught Between Confused Critics and Careerist Co-Conspirators", in: Kirsten Renwick Monroe (ed.): *Perestroika! The Raucous Rebellion in Political Science*. New Haven/London: Yale University Press, 468–488.

Mole, Beth (2013): "NSF Cancels Political-Science Grant Cycle", *Nature*, August 2, 2013, www.nature.com/news/nsf-cancels-political-science-grant-cycle-1.13501, accessed Sept. 12, 2016.

Ostrom, Elinor (1998): "A Behavioral Approach to the Rational Choice Theory of Collective Action". *APSR*, Vol. 92, 1–22.

Perlstein, Rick (2011): "Inside the GOP's Fact-Free Nation". *Mother Jones*, May/June Issue, www.motherjones.com/politics/2011/04/history-political-lying, accessed Sept. 18, 2016.

Pinderhughes, Dianne (2018): "Remaking Political Science: Reframing Democracy in the 21st Century." Paper, 25th World Congress of Political Science (RC 33.05), Brisbane.

Putnam, Robert D. (2003): "APSA Presidential Address: The Public Role of Political Science". *Perspectives on Politics*, Vol. 1, 249–255.

Reilly, Mollie (2013): "Tom Coburn Amendment Limiting National Science Foundation Research Funding Passes Senate", *Huffington Post*, March 21, 2013, www.huffingtonpost.com/2013/03/21tom-coburn-national-science-foundation_n_2921081.html, accessed Sept. 12, 2016.

Sartori, Giovanni (2004): "Where is Political Science Going?" *PS*, Vol. 11, 785–786.

Savage, Lee (2013): "A View from the Foothills: Public Engagement among Early Career Researchers". *Political Studies Review*, Vol. 11, 190–199.

Shapiro, Ian (2002): "Problems, Methods, and Theories in the Study of Politics, or What's Wrong With Political Science and What to Do About it". *Political Theory*, Vol. 30, 596–619.

Sigelman, Lee (2006): "The Coevolution of American Political Science and the American Political Science Review". *APSR*, Vol. 100, 463–478.

14 R. EISFELD

Smith, Rogers M. (1997): "Still Blowing in the Wind: The American Quest for a Democratic, Scientific Political Science". *Daedalus*, 126 (1), 253–287.

Smith, Rogers M. (2009): "The Public Responsibilities of Political Science". *Transformations of the Public* (Essay Forum). December 10, 2009. Social Science Research Council, http://publicsphere.ssrc.org/smith-the-public-responsibilities-of-political-science, accessed Sept. 14, 2016.

Stratford, Michael (2014): "In Wake of Coburn Amendment Repeal, Social Science Groups Plot Path Forward". *InsideHigherEd*, January 24, 2014, www.insidehighered.com/news/2014/01/24/wake-coburn-amendment-repeal-social-science-groups-plot-path-forward, accessed Sept. 12, 2016.

Tarko, Vlad (2017): *Elinor Ostrom. An Intellectual Biography*. London/New York: Rowman & Littlefield.

Toonen, Theo (2010): "Resilience to Public Administration: The Work of Elinor and Vincent Ostrom from a Public Administration Perspective". *Public Administration Review*, Vol. 70, 193–202.

Trent, John E. (2011): "Should Political Science be More Relevant? An Empirical and Critical Analysis of the Discipline". *European Political Science*, Vol. 10, 191–209.

Trent, John E. (2012): "Issues and Trends in Political Science at the Beginning of the 21st Century", in: id./Michael Stein (eds.): *The World of Political Science: A Critical Overview of the Development of Political Studies around the Globe, 1990–2012*. Opladen/Berlin/Toronto: Barbara Budrich, 91–153.

Wong, Alia (2015): "Why Civics Is About More than Citizenship". *The Atlantic*, September 17, 2015. http://www.theatlantic.com/education/archive/2015/09/civic-education-citizenship-test/405889/, accessed Sept. 14, 2016.

CHAPTER 2

What Is the Current Human Condition?

Today's human condition is marked by an unprecedented capacity to intervene for the good or for the bad of the species.

In her early (1958) work on the domains of man's activities, famously entitled *The Human Condition*, Hannah Arendt focused on three modes of active (as contrasted with contemplative) human life: Labor, which she defined as necessary for biological survival; work, which Arendt saw as needed to create man's collective artificial environment; and, most important to her, action—action proper, equal to human freedom and exercised as associated activity in the political, that is, the public, sphere:

> Of the three modes, action has the closest connection with the human condition of natality; the new beginning inherent in birth can make itself felt in the world only because the newcomer possesses the capacity of *beginning something new, that is, of acting.* (Arendt 1958: 9; emphasis not in original)

Such—in the highest sense—*human* activity is, of course, most fundamentally endangered when, as Arendt had earlier analyzed in her *Origins of Totalitarianism*, ideologically stipulated *inhuman* "laws" of Nature or History are executed on mankind by total regimes, whose terror forces the subjects together by a "band of iron", eradicating their capacity to act freely. Unrealistically, however, in Arendt's understanding that capacity is already corrupted when economic or social questions—issues relating to

© The Author(s) 2019
R. Eisfeld, *Empowering Citizens, Engaging the Public*,
https://doi.org/10.1007/978-981-13-5928-6_2

15

the spheres of work and labor, in other words—intrude into "authentic" politics.

In its broader meaning, the "human condition" refers to an individual's existence in his/her society, on Earth, and, in the last instance, in the universe. The notion covers social and political roles (be they ascribed or achieved), the state of available knowledge, and the range of ethical perspectives. In a chapter comprising ten succinct pages, entitled "The Twentieth Century", the unprecedented changes affecting the human condition during the past century have been summarized by an astrophysicist, Carl Sagan (1934–1996). Already 45 years ago, Sagan had noted that the rate of social and technological change had been so great "even within a human lifetime" that many people were feeling "alienated" from their own society. He had gone on to argue that time-honored political and economic attitudes, methods, and precepts were irrevocably lagging behind. The assessment made him conclude (Sagan 1973: 36, 38): "We should be encouraging social, economic, and political experimentation on a massive scale in all countries."

Or, as urged by Hannah Arendt, we should once more be trying out man's faculty to begin something new, wherein "the idea of freedom and the experience of a new beginning should coincide" (Arendt 1963: 21/22, 27).

Instead, Sagan continued at the time, the opposite seemed to be occurring. In countries such as the United States and the Soviet Union, "the official policy is to discourage significant experimentation".

Carl Sagan's contentions are singled out here for a number of reasons.

- Because of the astrophysicist's unhesitating inclusion, wherever considered "appropriate" by him (Sagan 1974: XIV), of historical, social, political reflections. Put otherwise, he determinedly chose to transcend disciplinary boundaries. As Sagan did in the field of planetary and space sciences, political science should make allowance for the debates and results of other disciplines, the sciences no less than the humanities. This book's chapter on climate politics makes the point in more detail.

If the statement should require an added explanation, it was once again provided by Hannah Arendt. Reflecting in her *Human Condition* on man's, to an ever greater extent, artificially constructed world and its more and more radically "improved" inhabitants, she concluded that this was "a political question of the first order", which could therefore "hardly be left to the decision of professional scientists or professional politicians" (Arendt 1958: 3). At least as long, she might have added, as conditions at least resembling genuine democracy exist, in which individuals may act freely, meaning in Arendt's understanding politically. In the debates surrounding such decision, political science should have a say.

- Because of Sagan's outstanding personification of the public intellectual, whose role will be pondered in the second-to-next chapter. When the National Academy of Sciences two years before his death awarded him the Public Welfare Medal, it noted that Sagan had been "enormously successful in communicating the wonder and importance of science". His 1980 TV series *Cosmos* was seen by an estimated 400–500 million viewers in over 60 countries. With international sales of some 5 million copies, the accompanying book was for a time the best-selling science book ever published in English, until surpassed by Stephen Hawking's *A Brief History of Time*. Posthumously conferring its Distinguished Public Service Award on Sagan, the National Science Foundation stated that since he had explained the relevance of science in ways the general public could fathom, "his gifts to mankind were infinite".
- Because of Sagan's commitment "to preserve and cherish" a humane world, which emerged perhaps most visibly on October 13, 1994. Delivering a public lecture at Cornell University on that day, he presented to his audience the "pale blue dot" photo taken half a year earlier by the Voyager 1 space probe before it left the Solar System, poignantly noting (Sagan 1994):

You see a dot. That's here. That's home. That's us. On it, everyone you ever heard of, every human being who ever lived, lived out their lives.

Mankind's imagined self-importance, Sagan continued, "the delusion that we have some privileged position in the universe, are challenged by this point of pale light". To him, the image underscored man's responsibility to preserve that pale blue dot, "the only home we've ever known".

To preserve our common home: During the early 1980s, work by Sagan and his collaborators (who soon became known as the TTAPS group) on the evolution of Martian global dust storms observed by Mariner and Viking probes led to the "nuclear winter" hypothesis—

18   R. EISFELD

prolonged cooling and darkening of the Earth by the distribution of smoke and dust through the atmosphere that would follow a nuclear exchange. To alert both the scientific community and the public, Sagan and his colleagues decided on a two-pronged approach. *The group's way of proceeding perfectly epitomizes the "art of translation" proposed by Matthew Flinders for political scientists bent on reducing the "level of impenetrability" of so much present work, which "cannot be overstated"* (Flinders 2013: 150, 160).

The physical models used for the group's investigation were extensively documented in the American Association for the Advancement of Science's weekly journal *Science* (TTAPS 1983). A version designed particularly for the lay reader, focusing on the climatic and biological findings obtained— devastating consequences for forests and agriculture, widespread extinction of animal species, and collapse of the food chain—was simultaneously published in *Foreign Affairs* (Sagan 1983/1984). That text included policy recommendations for reducing, by steps, the world's nuclear arsenals below the plausible "rough" threshold for triggering nuclear winter (in line with an earlier proposal by George F. Kennan), but still "adequate for strategic deterrence, if that is considered essential" (Sagan 1983/1984: 284; see also 285/286).

Indications are that the ensuing broad discussion of the climatic catastrophe possibility, which included both the US and Soviet scientists and policy-makers, may have contributed to that lessening of tensions between the Reagan and Gorbachev administrations which preceded the strategic arms reduction treaties of the late 1980s (Robock 2010: 425). Using improved climate models and now also focusing on the environmental consequences of regional nuclear conflicts—for instance, between India and Pakistan—debates on the nuclear winter danger have continued (see, e.g., Robock 2010) after the downsizing of nuclear stockpiles following the end of the Cold War.

In policy-related discussions such as these, not merely substantive arguments play a role. If the rhetoric, the style of the discourse should pander to fear, anger, prejudice, or disdain for opponents, it would erode trust in nuance, in compromise—eventually, in democracy. When, in 1990, the American Association of Physics Teachers awarded Carl Sagan its Oersted Medal, named after the nineteenth-century Danish physicist Hans Christian Ørsted, it not only lauded him for acknowledging "the responsibility of the scientist to call to the public's attention important and difficult national policy issues related to science". The organization also

WHAT IS THE CURRENT HUMAN CONDITION? 19

emphasized that Sagan, by acting "always in a thoughtful manner towards those with contrary views", had sought "to raise the intellectual and moral level of the discussion".

In 1996, Sagan, aged a mere 62, died from the effects of myelodysplasia, a rare bone marrow disease impairing production of red and white blood cells.

So what is the current human condition? A decade after mid-century, American writer Ray Bradbury had suggested an assessment (Bradbury 1962: 55): "Ambivalent man with his similar, ambivalent machines, half out of Hell, half into Heaven, stands poised for flight and wonders what he is."

Expanding on the theme in less metaphorical language, Carl Sagan substantially agreed at the twentieth century's close (Sagan 1997: 201–213). To an unprecedented extent, man had acquired the means, on the one hand, to "save, prolong, and enhance" life and, on the other hand, to destroy life:

- By 2000, 6 billion people lived on the Earth, as compared to 1.5 billion around 1900; but during the century, over 150 million were slaughtered in wars, ethnocentric "vendettas", or by "direct orders of national leaders". Such killings continue.
- Life expectancy in Western Europe and the United States is approaching 80 years (just over half that figure a century ago), but infant mortality—which in the United States is highest among industrial nations—amounts to 40,000 children per day on the planet.
- Agricultural technology and its ramifications (such as refrigeration) maintain "99.9 per cent" of human life; however, "not only on purpose but inadvertently" we continue to perform "unprecedented experiments" on the global environment, threatening our own species.
- Medical technology (including birth control methods) has "enormously improved the well-being of people", but the process has occurred particularly in the developed countries, while chemicals and radiation "have induced new diseases and are implicated in cancer".
- Innovative equipment has, while also to a quite different extent from nation to nation, "eliminated drudgery" and "enhanced the lives of many", but, not merely in the United States, real income disparities between rich and poor have been increasing "swiftly".

20 R. EISFELD

- Information and communication technology has profoundly changed culture and education, providing new tools for accessing insights of the world's civilizations and thinkers; but—again not just in the United States—what passes for literacy today is a "very rudimentary knowledge" of the own language; TV has "dumbed itself down to lowest-common denominator programming" (social media networks with user-generated content were yet in their early stages when Sagan wrote…); and citizens' "penchant for critical thinking and political action" is dwindling.

Sagan's list certainly is not exhaustive. But its key components—such as education, environment, regulation, and distribution of incomes—figure highly on a humane agenda, which a problem-driven political science might do well to move to the fore of its research, teaching, and public deliberations. An APSA Task Force in its recommendations only recently singled out "diversity, inclusiveness and inequality" as categories of analysis that should "inform each unit of study, rather than be seen as a separate or supplementary unit in the curriculum" (APSA 2011: 3).

Finally, Sagan's parting observation about citizens' waning proclivity for critical reflection and political involvement addresses a point that the profession which "knows more about democracy and effective civic engagement than any other" (APSA 2011: 56) ought to make its primary concern. Vincent Ostrom (who died a mere 17 days after his wife) wrote on the vulnerability of democracies that these are placed at risk when people perceive their relations as "being grounded on principles of command and control, rather than on principles of self-responsibility in self-governing communities" (Ostrom 1997: 4). He could have added that they are equally put at risk when people perceive an increasing number of their relationships as threatened by uncertainties which may, along with these links, also disrupt "expectations about future developments" (Ostrom 1997: 142).

Attempting to prepare individuals for such uncertainties is the strategy which political science needs to adopt if it desires to do its part in producing citizens actually willing to "deal with", even to "advance democracy" (APSA 2011: 13).

REFERENCES

APSA [American Political Science Association] (2011): *Political Science in the 21st Century*. Report of the Task Force on Political Science in the 21st Century. Washington DC: APSA, www.apsanet.org/portals/54/Files/TaskForceReports/TF_21stCentury_AllPgs_webres90.pdf, accessed Sept. 14, 2016.

Arendt, Hannah (1958): *The Human Condition*. Chicago: University of Chicago Press.

Arendt, Hannah (1963): *On Revolution*. London: Faber and Faber.

Bradbury, Ray (1962): "Cry the Cosmos". *LIFE International*, September 14, 52–62.

Flinders, Matthew (2013): "The Tyranny of Relevance and the Art of Translation". *Political Studies Review*, Vol. 11, 149–167.

Ostrom, Vincent (1997): *The Meaning of Democracy and the Vulnerabilities of Democracies*. Ann Arbor: Michigan University Press.

Robock, Alan (2010): "Nuclear Winter". *Wiley Interdisciplinary Reviews: Climate Change*, Vol. 1, May/June, 418–427, Wiley Online Library, climate.envsci.rutgers.edu/pdf/WiresClimateChangeNW.pdf, accessed Oct. 12, 2016.

Sagan, Carl (1973): *The Cosmic Connection. An Extraterrestrial Perspective*. Produced by Jerome Agel. New York: Doubleday.

Sagan, Carl (1974): *Broca's Brain. Reflections on the Romance of Science*. New York: Random House.

Sagan, Carl (1983/1984): "Nuclear War and Climatic Catastrophe: Some Policy Implications". *Foreign Affairs*, Vol. 62, 257–292.

Sagan, Carl (1994): "A Pale Blue Dot". www.bigskyastroclub.org/pale_blue_dot.html, accessed Oct. 12, 2016.

Sagan, Carl (1997): *Billions and Billions*, New York: Random House.

TTAPS [Turco, R. P./Toon, O. B./Ackerman, T. P./Pollack, J. B./Sagan, Carl] (1983): "Nuclear Winter: Global Consequences of Multiple Nuclear Explosions". *Science*, Vol. 2222 No. 4630 (23. December), 1283–1292.

CHAPTER 3

Coming to Grips with Change

The Subject Matter of Twenty-First-Century Political Science

Political science should evolve into a topic-driven discipline focusing on causes, patterns, and the participatory implementation of political, economic, and cultural change, whose speed and extent are triggering insecurity and aggression against democratic institutions.

"I stand here to plead for the study of politics in the terms of history", Harold J. Laski affirmed in his 1926 inaugural lecture at the London School of Economics and Political Science. Nothing in political studies, he went on to argue, was "rightly understood save as it is illustrated by the process of its development". And he compared the uncertain future to "a harbor which ever recedes" as men advance, using readings of history as their chart in sailing to that retreating port (Laski 1939: 35, 37, 38).

Incorporating history into political science means adopting a dynamic perspective. Such a perspective implies that change over time figures at the discipline's center stage, "shaped and constrained" (Smith 1997: 267) by the interplay of

- structure—embedded relations of power and influence
- and agency—players such as individuals, associations, political parties, social movements
- more often than not "spurred by broader economic and demographic factors".

© The Author(s) 2019
R. Eisfeld, *Empowering Citizens, Engaging the Public*,
https://doi.org/10.1007/978-981-13-5928-6_3

24   R. EISFELD

An institution, a political system, and even a constitution treated as the result of historical changes will, of course, not appear immutable. Rather, it may undergo change again.

Conceptual alternatives may be worked out by political scientists in accordance with visions of how a "good society" might be designed *and* politically attained. "Do we need, for instance, a parliamentary system?" Laski asked laconically (Laski 1939: 34). The answer he gave was: That depends on "how we define our aims", and on discovering the institutions and methods through which those aims could possibly be realized.

Acknowledging, in other words, that normative notions should play an indispensable part provides a second reason why political science needs to allot its central place to change. The discipline's paramount tenets for improving the human condition must emerge as "historically rooted" normative arguments, fortified by strong connections with empirical— quantitative—work (Smith 1997: 268/269). A regression to "more diffuse" theories with "less empirical content" (Feyerabend 1976: 212) is not implied.

However, this makes up part of the story only. To an extent which Laski in 1926 could hardly appreciate, nearly every aspect of life, including those once considered most "natural", may today be shaped by human intervention. That was the quintessence of Carl Sagan's observations on the current human condition in the preceding chapter. Or, to rephrase Marx' 11th Feuerbach Thesis: "Philosophers have hitherto only *interpreted* the world in various ways; it has become possible now to *change* it" (Krockow 1977: 14/15).

The process has been labeled the "fundamental politicization" of modern industrial society, inspired by the term "fundamental democratization" which Karl Mannheim coined during the 1930s. Mannheim referred to the new activities "of those classes which formerly only played a passive part in political life", but had been "stirred into action" during the past century (Mannheim 1940: 44). The conclusion to be drawn from fundamental politicization is that politics must henceforth be understood as "organized struggle to maintain *or to change* existing conditions" (Krockow 1977: 17). Extent of and means for attaining change offer the potential for further conflict.

Not merely has change become ubiquitous, it has also been accelerating. Cultural patterns, social standings, and professional positions have come to "feel tentative and temporary" (Krugman 2009: 125). As noted in the preceding chapter's concluding paragraph, economic, political, and cultural change, with its implied uncertainties, challenges citizens' capacity for trust in society and polity. Change is fought over by conflicting interests and elicits competing political agendas. *Both processes may trigger additional perplexed insecurity, resulting in fear and aggression—including aggression against democratic institutions, which legitimize such competition and conflict. Individuals or groups may be depicted as scapegoats, particularly when changes in social or political structure coincide with economic downturns and concomitant anxieties.*

For the more and the less recent past, these arguments about fear and aggression are borne out in an array of major industrial countries by a number of highly consequential instances.

The prolonged depression of 1873–1896, combined with the ongoing rapid transformation of a feudal order "held in veneration by many" into an industrial and urbanized class society, produced "hallucinations and irrational reactions" in Central Europe, not least in Germany and Austria: Anti-Semitism was converted into a "modern" mass movement "founded on the theory of race and blood" (Rosenberg 1943: 63/64; Rosenberg 1967: 94/95).

A generation later, the Great Depression of 1929 hit Germany on the heels of the country's traumatic defeat in the Great War, the ruin of the Empire, finally the hyperinflation of 1923. Ensuing desperation and panic prompted the German middle classes to largely vote for the Nazis (Geiger 1930; Geiger 1932: 118, 121).

Subsequent to the 1989 collapse of "actually existing socialism", when the former Warsaw Pact states emerged from sweeping system changes, harsh new political and economic realities favored nationalism as a potent mobilizing force for providing political legitimation and psychological gratifications. This was particularly the case in Russia: The psychological impact of the loss in international influence following the breakup of the Soviet Union, worsened during the 1990s by political turmoil and economic deprivation, was experienced as collective humiliation by the country's post-communist society. No more accepted than Germany's 1918 defeat during the Weimar Republic (Beyme 2016: 35), it resulted in a nationalist upsurge and fostered an authoritarian turn that has continued unabated.

In re-unified Germany, the post-1989 integration process proved "more disruptive and costly" than anticipated (OECD 1992: 10). Unemployment and underemployment (part-time work and early retirement) soared to over 30% in the new states, the former communist-ruled

German Democratic Republic (GDR). Under the double strain of reunification-induced financial burdens and increased immigration due to refugee influx, a wave of racist attacks on asylum-seekers and other foreigners erupted which, in 1992, left 17 people dead and more than 500 wounded. Responses by state governments, police, and courts—particularly in the new states—were shockingly slow to develop. The outburst created enough political pressure to make coalition and opposition parties agree on tightening the constitutional provisions on asylum by turning back asylum-seekers arriving from surrounding "safe" countries.

A quarter century later, anti-Islam and anti-foreigner resentment found a vehicle in the PEGIDA (Patriotic Europeans Against the Islamization of the West) rallies, which again started in the former GDR. The demonstrations and an increasing number of attacks on shelters signaled that a renewed wave of xenophobic prejudice may be on the rise in Germany, reacting to the government's unprecedented, if temporary, open-borders policy for refugees from Syria and Iraq.

In 2009, the Tea Party movement ("tea" as an acronym for "taxed enough already") erupted on the United States political scene against the backdrop of the 2007–2009 recession-cum-financial crisis, which in its turn had been triggered by the collapse of a credit-financed housing bubble. Grassroots disaffection and anger—fueled by conservative media and financially powerful free-market lobby groups, such as the billionaire Koch brothers' Americans for Prosperity (Mayer 2016: 170, 180/181)—over bank bail-out and federal spending legislation enacted on the initiative of the Bush and, particularly, the Obama Administration were immediate causes for the formation of Tea Party groups across the country. However, diatribes against alleged "abuse" of public assistance by illegal immigrants from Mexico and Central and Latin America stand out, as does the emphatic invocation of "Constitution"—in an "originalist", fundamentalist interpretation, "guns and religion".

In the last instance, Tea Party activists "want [their] country back"— back from changes and transformations, "bulwark against a divided present, comfort against an uncertain future" (Skocpol & Williamson 2012: 6–9, 71–72, 155; Lepore 2010: 97, 118–125). They pushed the Republican Party to the right, driving it to adopt an ever more uncompromising stance—the exact opposite of the civilizing function of politics rightly praised by Bernard Crick, namely ruling in "divided societies" by "conciliation" (Crick 1964: 140, 141). Their polarizing efforts prepared the fertile ground from which Donald Trump's 2016 Republican candidacy and subsequent US presidency could spring.

"We want our country back" also proved the UKIP (UK Independence Party) slogan that struck a chord with a decisive majority of voters in the 2016 "Brexit" referendum who asserted to be valuing "tradition and heritage". Once again too, enmity to more immigration—"controlling our borders"—turned out to be the key issue behind such pronouncements. "Getting out now will at least deprive 500 million other EU citizens of the right to come to the UK", the *Guardian* quoted a UKIP councilman (Moss 2016; Sunday Express 2016). Post-"Brexit" analyses have convincingly argued that, for many among those who voted in favor of leaving the European Union, the English national framework provided

- "a point of anchorage—a sense of identity, continuity, community",
- "a sense of status (I belong here)", and
- "a sense of power (I should be able to say what goes on here)"

in a world perceived as increasingly complex and threatening, conveying "a loss of control and a sense of anxiety" (Skey 2016). Perplexed insecurity over an incalculable future was thus compressed into a decision which meant, in effect: "Stop the world!"

A sense of lacking competence, of being overburdened by decisions which may negatively affect citizens' private and professional well-being, need, however, not necessarily lead to fear or even hate. It may also generate political apathy born from resignation, an indifference toward the political process due to perceived helplessness. In the United States 2010 midterm elections, many voters who two years before had supported the Democratic Party felt worried about their worsened economic situation and bewildered by the fiercely controversial debates about the Obama Administration's Health Care Act (whose most important provisions would only take effect by 2014). As compared to the presidential elections of 2008, voter turnout dropped by over 22 percentage points, from 63 to 40.3% (Skocpol & Williamson 2012: 161).

Regional and worldwide migration, discussed above with regard to Germany, the United States, and the United Kingdom, belong among the sweeping changes which, in recent years, have been affecting nation-states everywhere. Those changes, usually referred to by the term "globalization", have made themselves much more felt since the end of the Cold War. Before, the East-West conflict had resulted in a largely "frozen" international (geo-strategical) situation, with countries grouped according to the respective spheres of influence, and borders between the two "camps" permeable only to a limited extent. Since 1961, "the Wall"

28   R. EISFELD

between the two Germanys—which seems to have inspired Donald Trump's ideas vis-a-vis Mexico—symbolized such impenetrability.

Labor migration from Southern European countries to France and (West) Germany and immigration from former Asian and African colonies to the United Kingdom and France provided the first indications of what would follow. After 1990, spheres of influence turned from rigid to fluid. The progress of fiscal and economic globalization did not happen without political intervention; it was not merely shaped by *market players*—nationally based large enterprises spreading their subsidiaries across the globe (and changing into multinational corporations in the process) to evade high wages, encumbering taxes, and restrictive monetary policies (Hymer/Rowthorn 1970: 64, 88). Quite the contrary: It has been pro-market intervention by *governmental players*—national administrations—which pushed ongoing globalization (Cerny 1999: 19/20). In the same vein, we find governments (and terrorist militias) unleashing the wars and civil strife that, along with economic plight, religious and cultural intolerance, are producing steeply rising migrant waves.

The central aspects of those developments will be explored in more detail in later chapters. The result, however, needs to be summed up here: *In a process of accelerating change, societies both in Europe and North America are being transformed from inside and outside*, first by growing economic and financial permeation and second by migratory movements, which are resulting in increasing ethnic and cultural pluralization and diversification.

The observation additionally highlights this chapter's foremost argument: Political science in its research, teaching, and public messages must not just address changes in this or that part of polity and society. Rather, it is change in itself, *change* per se, as the fundamental analytical category and as a quickening, encompassing process, for whose implications the discipline needs to raise awareness.

A small anecdotal example taken from a 1954 science fiction novel, *Shadows in the Sun*, written by aspiring anthropologist and author Symmes Chadwick "Chad" Oliver, nicely illustrates the point. Oliver would later become Professor of Liberal Arts at the University of Texas-Austin. His novel's protagonist—another anthropologist—attempting to apply well-tested community-study techniques to a small Texas community, runs up against inexplicable data. The situation he finds himself in makes him muse on the ways most people solve the small daily problems which confront them: *by routinely resorting to past experience* (Oliver 1954: 22/23):

Should you serve grasshoppers at the next barbecue? Why, nobody does that. Shall you come home from the office, change to a light toga, and make a small sacrifice in the back yard? What would the neighbors think!

Neighbors might actually feel different today, as compared to 1954—not just putting up with such antics, but even acting likewise. Why might they comport themselves in such a manner?

- Conceivably, because roasted grasshoppers have figured among edible insects recommended by FAO, the United Nations' Food and Agriculture Organization, for their nutritional value. FAO today comprises nearly 200 member states, having counted just under 70 in 1954. Confronted by steady population increase, rising demand on food production and growing pressure on the environment, the organization for over a decade has been steadily working to raise awareness of insects as a nutritional source.
- Perchance, because small daily sacrifices—though not necessarily in the backyard—are core concepts of Hinduism. In 1954, the number of Hindu Americans had been negligible. By 2015, it amounted to 2.2 million—not least due to the Immigration Act of 1965 that had profoundly altered the national quota system, on which US immigration policy had been based since 1921.

Human-induced change may sometimes transform even *fable into fact* within no more than one or two generations. Political science should accordingly focus its efforts.

But what exactly is meant by "raising awareness" for the implications of change? A three-tier process is proposed here, by which political science should help

- change to be *accepted in principle* by individuals or groups without anger, fear, or apathy;
- change to be *judged* according to norms of equity and social justice; and
- change to be *shaped* through democratic participation reflected in public policies.

That, evidently, is the exact opposite of "acceptance" in the sense of a merely passive, in the final analysis, resigned attitude. Rather, the sugges-

30 R. EISFELD

tion made earlier is further substantiated here: Political science should help citizens to search for meaningful, discerning choices.

Sufficient open-mindedness for *accepting change in principle* belongs among citizens' capacities that must be learnt and trained by questioning one's own assumptions. The goal should consist in acquiring at least some of the qualities favorable—even if not sufficient—to the development of what has been labeled "a democratic personality". They include, for instance, the ability to resort to reflection and deliberation, rather than yielding immediately to emotional consternation; to weigh alternative goals and alternative courses of action, "taking into account the rights and obligations of oneself and others"; and to engage in "open discussion with others", searching jointly for solutions (Dahl 1989: 91, 92).

Helping evolve these qualities requires political science to take resolute issue with politicians' resort to the TINA ("There is no alternative") rhetoric. Implying that a specific decision is the only reasonable option, the stratagem's purpose—employed across Western Europe by political players such as Cameron, Merkel, or Ayrault in the context of neoliberal policies—consists in discrediting opposition "as irrational and ideologically blinded". Aiming to cut short political debates, politics are ostensibly de-ideologized (Séville 2016: 4, 9, 18, 20). Politically "paternalistic", TINA substitutes presumed expert authority for deliberation and contestation. The strategy favors a decline of political engagement, creating a "disaffected citizenry" that is the exact contrary of the open-minded public advocated here.

Accepting change in substance implies a scrutiny for guarantees that basic rights and the principles of justice remain respected and protected. It further requires careful consideration whether the existing maldistribution of social resources—such as education, income, wealth, subject of a later chapter—which already translates into grossly unequal political resources is not increased, further skewing the political process in favor of powerful minorities; or whether a specific "life world"—such as indigenous peoples' environments—may not be irrevocably and irresponsibly disrupted. Applying these criteria, citizens need to judge if the commonly applied "reform" label is not merely used as a façade for changes that would boil down to exacerbating social injustices and participatory barriers. In that case, even if prepared to accept change in principle, they may of course come to either reject or modify *specific* changes.

Accepting change by way of procedure qualifies as the intent to shape change by expressing preferences through public policies informed by a spirit of transparency and political participation. Political science should help citizens in formulating such preferences by acquiring an understanding of expected consequences "not only for oneself but for all other relevant persons as well." The intended result would consist in commencing to create and over time augmenting "a critical mass" of well-informed citizens on major issues (Dahl 1989: 112, 339).

Foreseeably, however, the discipline will have to grapple with the problem that political scientists' work might be viewed by some in the public sphere as supporting "preexisting preferences", by others as "threatening their beliefs" (APSA 2016: 11). Scholars themselves may, of course, also vie for public attention, presenting diverging views of what they consider as "truth". How to maintain credibility in the face of such possible pitfalls?

References

APSA [American Political Science Association] (2016): *Let's Be Heard! How to Better Communicate Political Science's Public Value*. Report of the Task Force on Public Engagement. Washington DC: APSA, http://journals.cambridge.org/download.php?file=%2FPSC%2FPSC48_S1%2FS1049096515000335a.pdf&code=175ec04c9eeea48f9f1f376d4cb1ef35, accessed Sept. 14, 2016.

Beyme, Klaus von (2016): *Die Russland-Kontroverse*. Wiesbaden: Springer.

Cerny, Philip G. (1999): "Globalization and the Erosion of Democracy". *European Journal of Political Research*, Vol. 36, 1–26.

Crick, Bernard (1964): In *Defence of Politics*. Harmondsworth: Penguin Books.

Dahl, Robert A. (1989): *Democracy and its Critics*. New Haven/London: Yale University Press.

Feyerabend, Paul (1976): Wider den Methodenzwang. Frankfurt: Suhrkamp.

Geiger, Theodor (1930): "Panik im Mittelstand", *Die Arbeit* 7, 637–654.

Geiger, Theodor (1932): *Die soziale Schichtung des deutschen Volkes*. Stuttgart: Enke.

Hymer, Stephen/Rowthorn, Robert (1970): "Multinational Corporations and International Oligopoly", in: Charles P. Kindleberger (ed.): *The International Corporation*. Cambridge: M.I.T. Press, 57–91.

Krockow, Christian Graf von (1977): *Herrschaft und Freiheit*. Stuttgart: Metzler.

Krugman, Paul (2009): *The Conscience of a Liberal*. New York/London: W. W. Norton.

Laski, Harold J. (1939): "On the Study of Politics (1926")", in: id.: *The Danger of Being a Gentleman and Other Essays*. London: George Allen & Unwin 1939, 32–56.

32 R. EISFELD

Lepore, Jill (2010): *The Whites of their Eyes. The Tea Party's Revolution and the Battle over American History.* Princeton/Oxford: Princeton University Press.

Mannheim, Karl (1940): *Man and Society in an Age of Reconstruction.* London: Routledge & Kegan Paul.

Mayer, Jane (2016): *Dark Money.* New York/London: Doubleday.

Moss, Stephen (2016): "'We Want Our Country Back': A Visit to the Most Eurosceptic and Europhile Places in the UK", *The Guardian*, March 14, 26. www.theguardian.com/politics/2016/mar/14/romford-aberystwyth-most-eurosceptic-europhiliac-places-uk, accessed Jan. 9, 2017.

OECD (1992): *Economic Survey: Germany.* Paris.

Oliver, Chad (1954): *Shadows in the Sun.* New York: Ballantine Books.

Rosenberg, Hans (1943): "Political and Social Consequences of the Great Depression of 1873–1896 in Central Europe", *Economic History Review* 13, 58–73.

Rosenberg, Hans (1967): *Große Depression und Bismarckzeit.* Berlin: de Gruyter.

Séville, Astrid (2016): "From 'One Best Way' to 'One Ruinous Way'? Discursive Shifts in 'There is no Alternative'", *European Political Science Review*, published online February 19, https://doi.org/10.1017/S1755773916000035, accessed Jan. 9, 2017.

Skey, Michael (2016): "'We want Our Country Back'—Stop Sneering, Start Listening", July 7, 2016. http://www.referendumanalysis.eu/eu-referendum-analysis-2016/section-8-voters/we-want-our-country-back-stop-sneering-start-listening/, accessed Jan. 9, 2017.

Skocpol, Theda/Williamson, Vanessa (2012): *The Tea Party and the Remaking of Republican Conservatism.* Oxford/New York: Oxford University Press.

Smith, Rogers M. (1997): "Still Blowing in the Wind: The American Quest for a Democratic, Scientific Political Science", *Daedalus*, 126 (1), 253–287.

Sunday Express (2016): "'We Want Our Country Back': Farage Rallies Troops Ahead of 'Independence Day' Brexit Vote", April 26, 2016. http://www.express.co.uk/news/politics/664333/We-want-our-country-back-Farage-rallies-troops-ahead-of-Independence-Day-Brexit, accessed Jan. 9, 2017.

CHAPTER 4

Serving Citizens

The Twenty-First-Century Political Scientist as Public Intellectual

From past acerbic controversies among academics, it may safely be concluded that a more thoroughgoing public engagement by scholars will not automatically create a benign debating climate. Rather, a political culture for such engagement will have to be assiduously evolved.

Sociologist Amitai Etzioni has noted that, in assuming the role of public intellectual, a scholar may be no less immune than any other person against the temptation to emotionalize or to simplify. He or she, too, runs the danger of seeking to "ingratiate" himself or herself either to "governing elites" or to the public (Etzioni 2010: 654).

After Carl Sagan and his collaborators (the TTAPS group) had published the findings that had resulted in their—earlier referred to—"nuclear winter" hypothesis, an intense scientific, political, and public discussion ensued. Emerging as a major opponent of Sagan in these debates was another public intellectual, whose role as a brilliant theoretical physicist had, since the late 1950s, been pushed into the background by his activities as "nuclear weapons expert and political advocate" (Jogalekar 2014). He was the Hungarian-born scientist Edward Teller (1908–2003) who had, in 1951, jointly with mathematician Stanislaw Ulam, invented the Teller-Ulam design which made the construction of hydrogen bombs technically possible.

© The Author(s) 2019
R. Eisfeld, *Empowering Citizens, Engaging the Public,*
https://doi.org/10.1007/978-981-13-5928-6_4

33

34   R. EISFELD

Much as Teller, "obsessed" (Jogalekar) with nuclear weapons, had in the 1950s downplayed the biological dangers of radioactive fallout as "overrated", he would now de-emphasize the climatic after-effects of nuclear war (Teller 1984; Sagan 1985). He had lobbied against the Eisenhower Administration's initiation of test-ban negotiations with the Soviet Union, even though that initiative had the support of PSAC, the President's Science Advisory Committee (chaired by MIT President James Killian), which included two of Teller's colleagues—both Nobel laureates—Hans Bethe and Isidor Rabi. Likewise, when the Partial Nuclear Test Ban Treaty concluded by the Kennedy Administration came up for ratification by the Senate, Teller had opposed the treaty on television, pointedly maintaining at a Senate hearing that in case of ratification "you would have given away the future safety of this country" (UPI 1963). Half a dozen scientists had testified differently, and PSAC had issued "a statement directly refuting" claims made by Teller (Herken [2rev]2000: 144).

The situation would repeat itself, with minor or major variations, in controversies over the Anti-ballistic Missile (ABM) Treaty, the Strategic Defense Initiative (SDI), nuclear winter, and global climate change. The major variation occurred in the SDI case. Teller himself presented the original core idea, a space-deployed X-ray laseremitting directed energy generated by a nuclear explosive, to President Reagan, while Bethe, with several fellow physicists, demolished the concept as fundamentally flawed and the envisaged system as "eas[ily]... overwhelmed or circumvented". Instead, these scientists argued in favor of a ban on space-based weapons (Herken 1987: 21/22; Bethe et al. 1984: passim).

Mathematician Jeremy Stone, who had been serving as President of the Federation of American Scientists (FAS) for three decades from 1970, in 1994 castigated Teller's "general behavior" throughout the arms race as "reprehensible", reproaching him with "using tactics of exaggeration and even smear" (Stone 1994: 2). Sagan—while admitting that his experiences with Teller had perhaps "hopelessly colored" his view of him—nevertheless made an attempt to understand what might be driving the man: "Somehow, somewhere, he wants to believe that thermonuclear weapons, and he, will be acknowledged by the human species as its savior and not its destroyer" (Sagan 1997: 274).

The examples of Bethe, Stone, and Sagan on the one hand and of Teller on the other abundantly illustrate the conundrum that any consideration of the possible or even desirable role of academics reaching out to the public must take into account. A public intellectual has been defined as one who seeks to advance both knowledge and human freedom. By playing on prevailing stereotypes about the "enemies" of freedom, a single scientist publicly respected by virtue of his work and fiercely convinced of his own views may mobilize political and media support even in the face of distinguished academic opposition.

The problem, therefore, not merely boils down to

- recruiting scholars producing "insightful and attention-attracting" studies that enable the public to understand their own and other societies "in new ways" (Gans 2009), plus
- training them in the skills required to brave public "attack politics", to withstand being "drawn into unexpected debates, misrepresented, used and abused" (Flinders and John 2013: 226).

While their engagement in public debates indeed runs the risk of "partisan politicization" (Flinders and John 2013: 225), there also remains the peril that they may willingly opt for politicization, motivated by reasons such as those listed by Etzioni. At the very least, a constellation in which public intellectuals hold contrary views due to divergent interpretations of data and situations may result in heated debates, whose manner and progress may mislead, rather than enlighten, citizens' perceptions of the issues addressed.

These observations, of course, also apply to political studies. A few pertinent cases, as well as the conclusions which suggest themselves, will subsequently be set out. To clarify the antagonists' positions, somewhat extensive quotations may be necessary here and there.

During the period from the mid-1950s to the late 1960s, a singular type of public intellectual had emerged in political science: fairly uncontested, because they were capable of generating the complementary "master tales" of pluralism and totalitarianism which were adequate to the height of the Cold War. Robert Dahl (1915–2014) in the case of pluralism and Hannah Arendt (1906–1975) and Carl Joachim Friedrich (1901–1984) with regard to totalitarianism may be considered prominent examples. Their narratives did not merely come to dominate the discipline—they were transformed into "public philosophies", which public players grew accustomed to invoke routinely both as guideline and as justification for their policies (Lowi 1967; Lowi 1979: 51 ss.).

Portraying "capitalist democracy in a favorable light, and [giving] it a little theoretical apparatus", pluralism with its connotations of multiple power centers and gradualist reform provided what has been aptly termed a "legitimating discourse" (Merelman 2003: 9–11, 18, 50/51). The concept also "discriminated nicely between this system and other systems with which we as a nation were in rivalrous relations".

Regarding those systems, the notion of totalitarianism as put forward by Arendt and Friedrich, with its implications of paramount ideology and ruthless terror, figured of course as pluralism's nightmarish twin.

However, by 1966, Arendt, after prolonged uncertainties, had arrived at the judgment that the period of total rule in the Soviet Union should be limited to the years 1928–1953, having ended with Stalin's death just as "totalitarianism came to an end in Germany with the death of Hitler". In its place, Arendt argued, a one-party dictatorship—reprehensible enough in its methods—had emerged (Arendt 1979: XXXVII).

Friedrich, in contrast, stuck to the opinion, at the price of watering down his own defining criteria, that the Warsaw Pact states' "totalitarian character" had remained untouched. In 1969, reversing every earlier argument, Friedrich even alleged that Stalin's and Hitler's regimes were "nowhere near" typical totalitarian dictatorships. On the contrary, they needed to be considered as "extreme aberrations" (quoted in Lietzmann 1999: 145/46).

While the Cold War was thawing, the "armies of the night" (Mailer) were converging on Washington in protest against ever more massive bombing in Vietnam, and Lyndon Johnson's envisioned "Great Society" succumbed to the escalating costs of the Vietnam War, the pluralist concept also underwent a transformation by its leading exponent. Indicting pluralism's egalitarian shortcomings, Robert Dahl proceeded to propose a determined effort at further democratization: a spill-over of democratic norms onto economy and society, the "enfranchisement" of blue- and white-collar employees resulting in industrial self-government (Dahl 1982: 199, 204; Dahl 1989: 327 ss., 331/332). Charles Lindblom, who had collaborated with Dahl on the 1953 study *Politics, Economic, and Welfare*, was no less peremptory in parting with the original pluralist approach (Lindblom 1977).

For a superficially "harmonious" society in "supposedly peaceful times"—the mid-1950s—(Merelman 2003: 3, 4), pluralism had provided a "benign" view of the political process (Lindblom 1982: 9, 16), with totalitarianism as a suitably malevolent counterpart. Under the impact of political events, the conceptual consensus dissolved. Subsequently, several competing approaches emerged, none of which "enjoys as broad acceptance" as pluralism did (Merelman 2003: 277). Attempts at building on pluralism but giving it a critical twist, also failed to do the job. Chantal Mouffe's "agonistic pluralism" provides one example: democratic politics being viewed as "trying to defuse the potential antagonism that exists in human relations", transforming "antagonism into agonism" (Mouffe 2000: 15, 16). Another instance is furnished by Andrew McFarland's process theory termed "neopluralism" and including—in addition to multiple elites from interest groups—social movements, policy networks, political entrepreneurs, and governmental agencies (McFarland 2004: 60/61).

The existence of approaches stressing different regime features and competing for explanatory strength implies the emergence of a correspondingly large number of scholars competing with, or possibly challenged by, their academic peers, when attempting to fulfill the role of public intellectuals. The instances subsequently described may shed further light on these issues and should also serve to clarify another salient point:

> Disciplines are not, and should not be, considered, "autonomous" in the sense that they may erect walls around their respective turf, inside which only scholars of the same calling might be permitted to evaluate prevailing standards or published conclusions. Debates on a particular topic should consequently not be expected to remain restricted to specialists of the same field. Rather, public controversies may well play out in a "cross-boundary" fashion.

Books and articles by Samuel Huntington (1927–2008), a "Cold War liberal with a conservative cast of mind" (Hodgson 2009), have continued to elicit public controversies—from *The Soldier and the State* (1957) through *Political Order in Changing Societies* (1968) and *The Clash of Civilizations* (1996) to *Who Are We?* (2004). They also brought Huntington positions as advisor to the US Department of State, the Carter Administration, to Brazil's repressive military dictatorship and South Africa's apartheid regime. For both countries, he advocated "controlled", "orderly" democratization "from above" (on South Africa, see Marks and Trapido 1989: 28/29; on Brazil, Skidmore 1988: 164–167. See also Huntington's own observations in his APSA Presidential Address on the "masterpiece" of Brazilian transition to democracy, in which "political science played a modest role": Huntington 1988: 7). His first two books had laid the groundwork for these options.

38   R. EISFELD

In *The Soldier and the State*, Huntington contended that the earlier primary question: "What pattern of civil-military relations is most compatible with American liberal democratic values?" had been superseded by the "more important" issue: What pattern would "best maintain the security of the American nation?" Liberal US society needed to be defended by a "realistic and conservative" military establishment whose ethic emphasized the weakness, the evil, and the irrationality in man's nature. Today, Huntington concluded, America could "learn more from West Point than West Point from America" (Huntington [2]1985: 3, 63, 79, 466).

Political Order in Changing Societies rated political order or its absence, the difference between "effective" and "debile" political systems, as "the most important political distinction among countries". To Huntington, differences "between democracy and dictatorship" mattered less than "organization, effectiveness, stability" (Huntington 1968a: 1). His "functionalist" approach surfaced again during the same year, when Huntington opined in a *Foreign Affairs* article that "in an absent-minded way the United States in Viet Nam may well have stumbled upon the answer to 'wars of national liberation'". According to Huntington, that "effective response" amounted to what he termed "forced-draft urbanization and modernization" diminishing the Viet Cong's "rural constituency".

The means to realize the goal, albeit by "drastically and brutally speed[ing] up" history, consisted in—here Huntington borrowed a phrase from another writer—"the 'direct application of mechanical and conventional power'". If that application, Huntington continued, took place "on such a massive scale as to produce a massive migration from countryside to city", the Maoist-inspired rural revolution would be "undercut by the American-sponsored urban revolution". The process, however, needed time. Therefore, "peace in the immediate future must be based on accommodation". This Huntington considered "not unreasonable", once it became evident that the Viet Cong's strategy "cannot succeed" (Huntington 1968b: 650, 652, 653, 655).

Huntington did not spell out in detail that the "massive" application of power, whose higher historical significance he emphasized, had since 1965 involved saturation bombing of presumed Viet Cong countryside strongholds (including the use of B-52 aircraft as conventional bombers), artillery barrages to prepare "search and destroy" missions, the designation of "free-fire zones", and the widespread use of herbicides and defoliants. These operations had dislocated, during the three years 1965/1966/1967, a wave of 2.1 million registered refugees (Subcommittee 1975: 4).

Huntington admitted that the "social costs" had been "dramatic and often heart-rending", conditions in the refugee camps "at times been horrendous" (Huntington 1968b: 649). But he remained fascinated by the instrument of historically important "forced-draft urbanization" which he thought to have identified as an answer to "wars of national liberation" *in general*. That instrument's continued use would, or so Huntington believed, not just blunt the Viet Cong's support, but "rapidly" bring every "country in question out of the phase in which a rural revolutionary movement can hope to generate sufficient strength to come to power" (Huntington 1968b: 652).

Unsurprisingly, Huntington's position was attacked in the *New York Review of Books* by a fellow academic, whom the editors of *Foreign Policy*— the very journal which had published Huntington's text—would, by 2005, select as the world's preeminent public intellectual: the radical Vietnam War opponent ("an obscenity") and MIT linguist/cognitive scientist Noam Chomsky (1928–). When Huntington claimed that, in his response, Chomsky had "mutilate[d] the truth in a variety of ways with respect to [his] views and activities on Vietnam", Chomsky replied by quoting extensively from Huntington's article, concluding: "He expresses no qualms, no judgment at all about such methods (which clearly involve 'war crimes' as defined by Nuremberg Principle VI, for example)" (*New York Review of Books* 1970).

By that time, Chomsky's work had already transformed linguistics, and he had received honorary doctorates from the Universities of London and Chicago. His essays criticizing US involvement in Vietnam and the subservience of "liberal" intellectuals to power, published in the *New York Review of Books*, were contributing to the growth of sustained opposition against the Vietnam War. Huntington's own academic career, however, remained quite unaffected by the incident.

That would change a decade and a half later, when his afore-mentioned book *Political Order in Changing Societies* was challenged on grounds of defective scholarship, rather than from ethical concerns. *Political Order* included, partly based on other work, several mathematical equations pertaining to presumed relationships between social mobilization/political participation/political institutionalization, supplemented by a classification of racist (apartheid) South Africa as a "satisfied society" (Huntington 1968a: 55). A 25-year old Boston graduate student, Ann Koblitz, found the equations algebraic nonsense. When her objections met with no response in class, she consulted her husband, Harvard Mathematics

40   R. EISFELD

Instructor Neal Koblitz. (At present, Ann Koblitz is Professor of Women and Gender Studies at Arizona State University; her husband is a Professor of Mathematics at Washington University.)

In a 1981 article entitled "Mathematics as Propaganda", Neal Koblitz found Huntington guilty of "mathematical quackery", charging that he invoked nonsensical equations for the purposes of achieving "mystification, intimidation" through creating "an impression of precision and profundity". Five years later, Huntington was nominated to the National Academy of Sciences by the NAS Section on Social and Political Sciences. Section Chair Julian Wolpert (Princeton) now hit back, accusing Koblitz to have himself used "a phony semblance of spurious algebra" for compiling an "irresponsible" piece "which somehow got past a peer review process of 'scientists'". That response incensed a Yale mathematician, Serge Lang (1927–2005), who had been elected to the NAS the previous year (which meant he would be expected to vote on Huntington's membership), and had earlier engaged in a years-long dispute with political sociologist Seymour Martin Lipset over the allegedly "prejudiced" questions in a survey which Lipset had distributed to the US professoriate (Sykes 1988: 208–211; Lang 1998: 131–134, 223–228).

Under NAS rules, nominations may be formally challenged. This is what Lang proceeded to do. Koblitz' assessment was circulated by him among Academy members, along with his own conclusion that Huntington had produced "pseudo-science". When the dispute became public, Huntington defended himself by asserting that, when his study had been made "in the early 1960s, there had been no major riots, strikes, or disturbances" in South Africa. Lang reminded him—and the public—that a decade of black protest, both non-violent civil disobedience and violent rioting, had culminated in the Sharpeville massacre of March 21, 1960 when South African police, opening fire at a crowd of black protesters, had killed half a hundred people and injured many more. Huntington also downplayed his use of mathematical symbols as "simply a shorthand way of summing up a complicated argument", not intended "as a rigorous quantitative tool". Lang countered by quoting, from some twenty pages of *Political Order*, mathematical symbols indeed suggesting rigorous quantitative tools, and by pointing out that Huntington's "comparative quantitative analyses" had been included in the reasons for his nomination (Sykes 1988: 213, 217; Lang 1998: 34/35, 60–68).

Huntington's nomination in 1986 failed to secure the require two-thirds majority. When he was re-nominated a year later, "he was the only one of the 62 nominees to be turned down" (Sykes 1988: 213). As a consequence, Lang found himself violently attacked. FAS President Jeremy Stone, mentioned earlier in connection with Teller, wrote of a "campaign" against Huntington that reminded him "of the political effects of the McCarthy campaigns". Economics Nobel laureate Kenneth Arrow even more bluntly maintained that, in Lang's case, "the McCarthyite tendencies [were] clear". Where Stone held that "only political scientists can, and should, stand in judgment on the 'scholarship' of other political scientists", Karl W. Deutsch wrote to Lang that he found his "attempt pernicious" to "establish" himself "as a mathematician in control of the field of political science" (Lang 1998: 114, 117, 119, 136).

Lang responded no less firmly. "McCarthy waged his campaigns without documentation", he wrote, "by throwing around the generic label 'communist' in a charged atmosphere". He objected to any purported similarity with his carefully detailed attempts to inform others about "defects" in Huntington's scholarship. Lang also contended that it was precisely unchecked disciplinary autonomy—"unaccountable to others who may look into the way that discipline is practiced by some of its members"—which promoted the "balkanization" of science. The responsibility of an informed vote, he added, was borne out by the NAS rule which required members to vote on all candidates proposed by all sections (Lang 1998: 80/81, 120).

Lang's arguments may be considered valid. The accepted understanding of McCarthyism includes demagogic, unsubstantiated vilification. The charge to allegedly resort to "McCarthyism" has been used, not merely in the United States, as a weapon to try and deter scholars from publicly broaching unpleasant current or past malpractices involving particular individuals.[1] And, as mentioned above, relevant public controversies may be expected to evolve in a "cross-boundary" fashion: Challenges may originate from academics whose expertise—in, for example, linguistics or

---

[1] In 2011, this book's author found documentary proof that Theodor Eschenburg (1904–1999), one of West German political science's "founding fathers", had been involved as a textile industry cartel manager during the Nazi regime in the forced "Aryanization" of Jewish firms. After he started publishing his findings, one of Eschenburg's former students, journalist Sybille Krause-Burger, called the author a "burial ground McCarthy" in her newspaper column—admittedly the most inventive epithet ever to have been leveled at him.

42   R. EISFELD

mathematics—touches on the methods or conceptual approaches (their validity, their accuracy) of another discipline—for example, political science, or whose broader ethical commitment may move them to raise objections if they should conclude that fundamental principles have been violated.

Lang had reproached Huntington for dealing in "political opinions passed off as science" (Lang 1998: 31 ss.). Two decades later, when Huntington's theses on *The Clash of Civilizations* and on American identity (*Who Are We?*) had appeared in essay and book form, two prominent public intellectuals placed these works essentially in the same category: Sociologist and international affairs expert Amitai Etzioni (1929–) and Columbia literary theorist and cultural philosopher Edward Said (1935–2003).

In his review essay, Etzioni charged *Who Are We?* with merely having "the appearance of scholarship", while in fact belonging among the sort of "ideological tracts" which "appeal to, reinforce, and help to legitimate one form of prejudice or another". Etzioni identified fear and mounting threat as the "ideological slant" running through many of Huntington's works, from which an advocacy of "nationalism, militaristic regimes, and an earlier America" would be derived, "in which there was one homogeneous creed and little tolerance for pluralism" (Etzioni 2005: 477, 483, 485). Edward Said, with regard to *The Clash of Civilizations*, also labeled Huntington an ideologist, "recklessly" resorting to "vast abstractions" such as Islam and the West providing "little self-knowledge or informed analysis" (Said 2001: 11, 14).

The alarmist pattern stressed by Etzioni's review indeed links *Clash* to *Who Are We?*: "Resurgence" of Islamic civilization in the former, Mexican immigration and "Hispanization" in the latter case as the principal problems faced by "the West", respectively the United States. Both works moreover argued substantially in sync. Warnings of "Mexican demographic expansion"—by which "in due course, the results of American military expansion in the nineteenth century could be threatened and possibly reversed"—already surfaced in *Clash* (Huntington 2002 [1996]: 206). So did the "American Creed" with its combination of individual liberty, political equality, and economic opportunity as an alleged pillar of Western civilization, whose end a rejection of that Creed would effectively imply (Huntington 2002: 305, 307). Throughout *Who Are We?*, the Creed, a product of America's "Anglo-Protestant settler society", was subsequently invoked as "a force for good in the world" (Huntington 2005:

XVIII, 39, 41, 59–80). Both books portrayed multiculturalists as the villains of the piece. In *Clash*, their "divisive siren calls" constituted an "immediate and dangerous challenge" to the "United States as we have known it" and, "effectively", to "Western civilization" (Huntington 2002 [1996]: 305, 307). *Who Are We?* viewed multiculturalism as "basically an anti-Western ideology", which along with globalization and immigration, "battered American consciousness" (Huntington 2005: 4, 173). The pervading twin anxieties of the Cold War years—aggression from without, subversion from within—were re-emerging in new clothes.

Huntington had published his original 1993 *Foreign Affairs* essay "Clash of Civilizations?" (with a question mark) as a critical response to a very different diagnosis of post-1989 global politics which his erstwhile student Francis Fukuyama had submitted. That "vision" had first been presented by Fukuyama in another (1989) essay entitled: "The End of History?" (also including a question mark), then more assertively in a 1992 book which resembled Huntington's book-length version of his thesis in omitting the original question mark. In a somewhat triumphalist stance prompted by the "heady days of 1989" (his term), Fukuyama had claimed that "the triumph of the Western idea"—economic and political liberalism—might be equated with "the final form of human government", the "end point" of mankind's ideological evolution (Fukuyama 1989: 3, 4). The former RAND analyst and deputy director of the US State Department's policy planning staff had hastened to add that liberalism's victory was as yet incomplete in the "material world". Conflicts such as terrorism and wars of national liberation would certainly continue "to fill the pages of *Foreign Affairs*". So would conflicts between what Fukuyama a bit stiltedly referred to as states still "stuck in history", as between those and the lucky ones "at the end of history". But with regard to "ideological pretensions of representing different and higher forms of human society", the dice were supposed to have been cast in favor of liberalism (Fukuyama 1989: 12, 17).

After having expanded his thesis into a book, Fukuyama would several times amend it without, however, modifying its core statement. A mere three years after *The End of History* (without question mark) had come out, Benjamin Barber remarked laconically that Fukuyama had not anticipated the extent to which the "infotainment telesector" had changed both economic and political realities. In the place of victorious liberalism, Barber diagnosed a "global theme park", a "McWorld" tied together by communications, entertainment, and commerce whose *leitmotif* was increasingly reduced to "I want, I want, I want" and "Gimme, gimme, gimme". That world of cosmopolitan commerce, he contended, was challenged by what he termed "Jihad", fear in the face of change and uncertainty coupled with "self-sacrificing zealotry" whose proponents gathered around a variety of "sharply imagined ethnic, religious, and racial identities". What McWorld and Jihad had in common, however, was waging war on "that conscious and collective human control under the guidance of law we call democracy" (Barber 1995: 4–6, 93, 164, 215).

To sum up the narrative at this point, an exemplary array of public intellectuals' names—Huntington, Chomsky, Lang, Etzioni, Said, Fukuyama, Barber—and a no less exemplary sequence of acerbic controversies support the conclusion: The problem to be solved will not be limited to mobilizing many more political scientists

- to serve as "credible sources of reliable information", conveying to their audiences more insights in ways that are "more meaningful, memorable, and actionable to more people" (APSA 2016: 1, 2, 4);
- to "frame new questions", develop "fresh perspectives", "highlight ignored values", challenging assumptions that had been taken "for granted" (Putnam 2003: 251);
- to "engage more visibly and coherently in political and public debate" (Flinders and John 2013: 222).

All those tasks indeed need to be tackled. But too often the underlying assumption seems to be that the new engagement will emerge—if at all—as a largely conflict-free process, accompanied by political scientists' mutual applauding and back-slapping. That attitude surfaces most visibly if the last of the preceding three observations, made by Matthew Flinders and Peter John, is quoted in full:

Political science must engage more visibly and coherently in political and public debate.

An even approximately homogeneous political science, however, is nowhere in sight. Rather, there exists—just as among "ordinary" humans— a huge variety of academically trained individuals with diverging judgments about the present political, social and economic status quo, or—as outlined in the third chapter—about the desirable directions, extent, and instruments of debated changes.

Defining, as was done above, a public intellectual as one who seeks to advance both knowledge and human freedom does not help either. Again, intellectuals may have quite different ideas about how best to advance human freedom through the progress of knowledge.

Responsibly and systematically engaging various audiences in a manner from which both the discipline and the public may benefit will not happen without observing some rules of the game. *In other words, it will require assiduously developing a political culture for such interventions, a code of good practice not unlike codes for good scientific conduct which have increasingly been adopted.* Controversies—the statement bears repeating—will be unavoidable, debates will abound. To aid a public, for whom "the growth in specialized knowledge has made it extremely difficult" to evaluate "claims made by public intellectuals" (Posner [2]2003: 388), such rules should be few and succinct, to wit:

> Public intellectuals should offer only clearly reasoned arguments. Their pronouncements should allow for complexity. They should identify viable alternatives.

To flesh out these maxims:

Public intellectuals should offer only clearly reasoned arguments
A Smithsonian Institution study on the evolution of the "flying saucer" myth has diagnosed in segments of society "a widespread rejection" of analytical thinking (Peebles 1994: 287). Already in the past, that attitude proved a fertile ground for the emergence of political mistrust, suspicion, and conspiracy theories. More recently, in the wake of the 2007–2009 Great Recession, the 9/11 attacks, the Iraq and Syrian wars, of the anti-terrorism (anti-ISIS) military campaigns and of substantial forced migratory movements from Latin America, North Africa, and the Near East, a reenactment has been occurring of what Robert Griffith had labeled already a generation earlier, in an award-winning work (Griffith 1970), the "politics of fear" during the McCarthy years:

Political decision-makers, in order to "promote social control of citizens", and in concert with many of the foremost mass media, have kept pursuing "an expanding politics of fear" which came to "inform everyday life behavior". By appeals to emotions and stereotypes, citizens' beliefs are "being constructed and manipulated" (Altheide 2006: 15/16, 18). Gradually, a public discourse dominated by fear may result in providing a

46   R. EISFELD

perspective of ostensible "knowledge" about a world perceived "as constantly changing and out-of-control", preventing citizens from questioning specific policies or political measures (Altheide [2]2015 [[1]2002]: 4, 23, 26).

Carl Sagan has pointed out that often it will be exactly the "niches" left by "sparse and poor popularizations" of scholarly work in the natural and the social sciences, which will be filled by "magical" world views, making citizens "routine and comfortable practitioners as well as victims of credulity" (Sagan 1997: 9, 17). It is in those hitherto abandoned niches that rational, topically relevant, stylistically accessible public-oriented writing (Isaac 2015b) by political scientists particularly needs to weigh in. Not least their existence requires the establishment of incentives and of professional training capacities for scholars from the start of their careers to encourage the dissemination of research results among wider non-academic audiences (Savage 2013: 198).

If controversies should result, any sort of personal vilification—possibly topped by accusations of allegedly "McCarthyist" tactics, as in the Lang/Huntington affair—should be absolutely out of the question. That includes even severe cases of previous defamatory attacks from interested quarters. Such instances, when "not just the message" was misrepresented for ideological reasons, but the "messengers" themselves became "victims of vicious personal attacks" (Oreskes and Conway 2012: 2, 265), will briefly be discussed below.

If they occur, scientists—whether as public intellectuals or "just" as fellow academics—need to stand up, patiently but forcefully rebutting false allegations, soberly repudiating slanderous defamations. Unfortunately— "garbage", by being ignored, "does not just go away" (Oreskes and Conway 2012: 265).

In his advocacy of a more public, carefully reasoned political science, Jeffrey Isaac—long-time editor of APSA's *Perspectives on Politics*—cited as an example the journal's September 2015 issue on the grossly neglected issue "American Politics of Policing and Incarceration". In his editorial, he emphasized that "police brutality, incarceration, and repression are not limited to authoritarian regimes. They also play an important role in the functioning of polyarchal, so-called democratic regimes." Isaac classified these policies as "seriously constrain[ing... and] distort[ing]... the functioning of 'democracy' in the United States", concluding that a national debate about the "carceral state" is needed which, however, "is likely to come up against some serious obstacles". By *precise analyses* of the system's many interacting features (persistent racial disparities, economic gains for business corporations *and* rural communities, a general emphasis on revenue, militarization of policing, legal limits on police accountability), but also by "*new forms of scholarly praxis* designed to publicize and to contest abuses", political science might *in an exemplary fashion* contribute to bringing the topic "to the forefront of public attention" (Isaac 2015a: 610/611, 615/616).

Public intellectuals' pronouncements should allow for complexity
The rule is, first and foremost, intended to rebut "man on horseback" expectations. In a wider sense, these relate to popular hopes that a "strongman"—not necessarily a military figure, rather H. G. Wells' "man with a vast voice, a muscular face in incessant operation"—might "put things right", providing simple authoritarian answers to troubling problems, where democratic politics are experiencing difficulties in arriving at satisfactory solutions by compromise. Public intellectuals should feel an obligation to expose such hopes as *magical* thinking, unsuited to twenty-first century societies, usually resulting in the suppression—rather than the solution—of conflicts. Citizens run the risk that the price to be paid will involve curtailment of civil liberties (particularly for minorities), removal of the regime from public scrutiny, ensuing arbitrariness and corruption.

In their attempts at unraveling specific issues for public audiences, political scientists need to acknowledge that in complexity a threat "to cut policy elites loose from effective control" by citizens is always inherent (Dahl 1989: 335). America's punitive policies, just referred to, provide a case in point. Their various local, state and federal, social, political, and financial components add up to "an interlocking system, grounded in historical path dependencies and possessing a reinforcing 'logic' of [its] own" (Isaac 2015a: 611). That is exactly what complexity entails, whose impact as a rule will tend to increase with the "sheer number of policies" (Dahl 1989: 336). Any public utterances calling into question a system such as the "carceral state" need to address these various dimensions. Otherwise salient issues and players would not receive the attention which is essential if any progress in the direction of dismantling the system is to be achieved.

Allowing for complexity must not be confused with invoking uncertainty. Pointing out that a specific problem may be too "complex" to be reduced to a few simple factors and consequently exploring the issue in depth is the very opposite of producing doubt or, more fundamentally, of manufacturing ignorance. For studies in such purposeful engineering of doubt, uncertainty, or ignorance, not least for (ab)use as a political instru-

48   R. EISFELD

ment—"We rule you, if we can fool you" (there is an evident link here to the issue of mendocracy, discussed later in the book)—the term "agnotology" was coined by Irish social historian Iain Boal whom his Stanford colleague Robert Proctor had prodded for a suitable word (Proctor 2008: 11, 27). Proctor was grappling with a problem which may well beset future public intellectuals from the ranks of political science in their turn, involving as it does confrontation among academics over both substance and professional ethics.

By 2005, he was one of three historians having testified, in cases such as *U.S. v. Philip Morris Inc. at al.*, against the U.S. tobacco industry's attempt to influence depiction of the history of drug use (including smoking)—while "at least thirty-six" fellow historians had testified in favor of the industry. A number of scholars from academic institutions such as Yale or Oxford, whose names have surfaced, were each paid up to nearly or over half a million dollars over the years for testifying and/or "friendly" publishing efforts, without disclosing business funding (Proctor 2008: 16).

Where "friendly" publishing is concerned, complexity again comes into play. As Proctor has contended, scholars recruited by the tobacco industry did not deliberately misrepresent, falsify, or fabricate historical data. Rather, they arrived at the desired purposes by confining their research: *Not* exploring topics "that could show the industry in a disadvantageous light" resulted in the omission of facts and tie-ins (Proctor 2004: 1174/1175). Unfortunately, the "Tobacco strategy" of "merchandising doubt", pursued by a limited number of scientists "joining forces with think tanks and private corporations" and guided by industry lawyers and public relations experts, provided a model for challenging scientific evidence on further contemporary issues (Oreskes and Conway 2012: 6, 9).

Exactly why did issues such as tobacco, acid rain, or global warming serve as focal points for prolonged "doubt-mongering campaigns" (Oreskes and Conway 2008: 76, 2012: 262)? Because, as science historians Naomi Oreskes (San Diego, now Harvard) and Eric M. Conway (JPL) explained in their 2008 article "Challenging Knowledge" and their 2010 book *Merchants of Doubt* (filmed in 2014 under the same title by award-winning producer/writer/director Robert Kenner), these campaigns were not really about science, but about governmental regulation. Shaped by their Cold War careers (not unlike Edward Teller), the protagonists "viewed regulation as the slippery slope to Socialism". Free-market fundamentalists by conviction, they have continued "opposing any kind of restriction on the pursuit of market capitalism, no matter the justification" (Oreskes and Conway 2008: 77, 80).

Highlighting, according to its own presentation, "market-based solutions for regulatory goals", the Mercatus—Market—Center at George Mason University has served, since its inception in the mid-1980s, as one of several academic beachheads for espousing anti-regulatory ideas. Largely funded by the oil refinery-based conglomerate Koch Industries, and closely linked to the Cato Institute, a free-market think tank also established by the Koch brothers—billionaire co-owners of Koch industries, who already surfaced in this book's third chapter—a decade earlier, the Mercatus Center's position included opposing air pollution regulation. Shortly before joining (from 1998 to 2007) the Center as an economist, Susan Dudley, currently professor at George Washington University, claimed that "by blocking the sun, smog cut down on cases of skin cancer". Efforts by the Environmental Protection Agency (EPA) to reduce pollution ("caused in part", as *The New Yorker* staff writer Jane Mayer pointed out, "by emissions from oil refineries") would, according to Dudley, "cause up to eleven thousand additional cases of skin cancer each year". Dudley's assertion was embraced by the District of Columbia Circuit Court in a 1999 ruling on EPA measures, and it took the US Supreme Court to overrule the decision (Mayer 2016: 153, 154).

Promoted in the United States by a "charitable-industrial complex" (a label used by Jane Mayer in her investigative book *Dark Money*) of corporate lobby groups, foundations, think tanks, and institutes, free-market fundamentalism has evolved into an enormously successful "wealth defense movement" (Mayer 2016: 377). An "article of faith" (Oreskes and Conway 2012: 249), it has no place for complexity, such as considering the environmental and social costs of private enterprise. Not least for that reason, public intellectuals need to expose laissez-faire economics as the hidden agenda behind attacks on well-established insights, in the abovementioned, as in similar, instances. (Such as when present US Vice President Mike Pence, contending that "smoking doesn't kill", in 2009 as a member of the House of Representatives voted against a bill that allowed Congress to regulate tobacco. Or when Pence, as Indiana governor, in 2015 signed a bill that loosened the terms of the state's Clean Indoor Air Act [Schumaker 2016]).

50   R. EISFELD

Public intellectuals should identify viable alternatives
That maxim relates directly to the third chapter. If the discipline's focus is on political, economic, or cultural changes and their participatory implementation, the elaboration and discussion of alternative aims and means automatically come to mind. And if politics are being studied in the terms of history, as quoted at that chapter's outset, room needs to be left for both continuities and transformations—in other words, path dependence and contingency.

Path dependence refers to former events or decisions which continue to shape long-run political structures or patterns of attitude and behavior. Contingency implies that political decisions "might have been taken differently, or not have been made at all" (Greven 2000: 27).

Path dependences are, of course, anything but immutable. Consider the case of Germany: During the eighteenth, nineteenth, and early twentieth centuries, German society (particularly, but not merely in Prussia) came to be shaped "from above" by command, control, and subordination. Due to that long-term experience, repeated through successive generations, the orientation of the average individual to the political system even after World War II for nearly two decades remained that of the "subject" (Almond and Verba [4]1972 [[1]1963]: 7, 19, 38, 429). From the mid-1960s onward, however, the cultural pattern commenced to change toward "participant" or "citizen" orientation, due to more "liberal" styles of socialization in family and school, increased activity in voluntary associations (both paralleling generational change), socio-economic modernization including female "emancipation", last but not least successful performance of the parliamentary-democratic political system (Conradt 1980: 251–265).

If such transformations may considerably reduce or even annul path dependence over time, contingency implies that decisions are subject to change on short notice, that they may be altered or revised. Combating political apathy, indifference, and resignation, or even anger, frustration, and rage—all of which, as indicated in the third chapter, often originate from perceived subjective helplessness—public intellectuals should accustom citizens to contingency. They should be explaining alternatives, including public policies, insisting that change may indeed be shaped. By providing information and reasoned assessments, they should try to "tame"—which, of course, is different from "control"—contingency (Palonen 1999: 6/7), particularly serving those citizens who, because of disadvantages in education, status, and income, may feel overwhelmed, incapable of choosing between alternatives by judging potential consequences.

Resignation, indifference to political alternatives, and frustration about government characterize individuals who may be labeled "apolitical". To restore part of their civil dignity to these prospective audiences, to alleviate the feeling that they have been abandoned by their governments, should rank among the major tasks of political scientists as public intellectuals. Otherwise—and if measures such as those discussed in Chaps. 8 and 9 should fail to be enacted—groups will persist (or even gain in numbers) to whom opting for Brexit, or voting for Donald Trump, may seem meaningful choices.

REFERENCES

Almond, Gabriel A./Verba, Sidney ([4]1972 [[1]1963]): *The Civic Culture*. Princeton: Princeton University Press.

Altheide, David L. ([2]2015; [1]2002): *Creating Fear*. New Brunswick: Transaction Publishers.

Altheide, David L. (2006): *Terrorism and the Politics of Fear*. Landam/Oxford: AltaMira Press.

APSA [American Political Science Association] (2016): *Let's Be Heard! How to Better Communicate Political Science's Public Value*. Report of the Task Force on Public Engagement. Washington DC: APSA, http://journals.cambridge.org/download.php?file=%2FPSC%2FPSC48_S1%2FS1049096515000335a.pdf&code=175ec04c9eeea48f9f1f376d4cb1ef35, accessed November 2, 2016.

Arendt, Hannah (1979): *The Origins of Totalitarianism*. New York: Harcourt Brace Jovanovich.

Barber, Benjamin R. (1995): *Jihad vs. McWorld*. New York/Toronto: Random House.

Bethe, Hans A./Garwin, Richard L./Gottfried, Kurt/Kendall, Henry W. (1984): "Space-based Ballistic-Missile Defense". *Scientific American*, Vol. 251, No. 4, 39–49.

Conradt, David P. (1980): "Changing German Political Culture". In: Almond, Gabriel A./Verba, Sidney (eds.): *The Civic Culture Revisited*. Boston/Toronto: Little, Brown & Company, 212–272.

Dahl, Robert A. (1982): *Dilemmas of Pluralist Democracy*. New Haven: Yale University Press.

Dahl, Robert A. (1989): *Democracy and its Critics*. New Haven: Yale University Press.

Etzioni, Amitai (2005): "The Real Threat: An Essay on Samuel Huntington". *Contemporary Sociology*, Vol. 34, 477–485.

Etzioni, Amitai (2010): "Reflections of a Sometime-Public Intellectual". *PS*, Vol. 43, 651–655.

52 R. EISFELD

Flinders, Matthew/John, Peter (2013): "The Future of Political Science". *Political Studies Review*, Vol. 11, 222–227.

Fukuyama, Francis (1989): "The End of History?" *The National Interest*, No. 16, 3–18.

Gans, Herbert J. (2009): "A Sociology for Public Sociology". *Transformations of the Public Sphere* (Essay Forum), September 3. Social Science Research Council, http://publicsphere.ssrc.org/gans-sociology-for-public-sociology, accessed Sept. 29, 2016.

Greven, Michael Th. (2000): *Kontingenz und Dezision*. Opladen: Leske & Budrich.

Griffith, Robert (1970; 2nd ed. 1988): *The Politics of Fear. Joseph R. McCarthy and the Senate*. Lexington: University Press of Kentucky.

Herken, Gregg (1987): "The Earthly Origins of Star Wars". *Bulletin of the Atomic Scientists*, Vol. 43 No. 8, 20–29.

Herken, Gregg (2rev2000): *Cardinal Choices. Presidential Science Advising from the Atomic Bomb to SDI*. Stanford: Stanford University Press.

Hodgson, Godfrey (2009): "Samuel Huntington. Obituary." *The Guardian*, January 1. https://www.theguardian.com/world/2009/jan/01/obituary-samuel-huntington, accessed Sept. 9, 2016.

Huntington, Samuel P. (2 1985; 1 1957): *The Soldier and the State*. Cambridge/ London: Belknap Press of Harvard University Press.

Huntington, Samuel P. (1968a): *Political Order in Changing Societies*. New Haven/London: Yale University Press.

Huntington, Samuel P. (1968b): "The Bases of Accommodation". *Foreign Affairs*, Vol. 46, 642–656.

Huntington, Samuel P. (1988): "One Soul at a Time", *APSR*, Vol. 82, 3–10.

Huntington, Samuel P. (1993): "The Clash of Civilizations?" *Foreign Affairs*, Vol. 72 No. 3, 22–49.

Huntington, Samuel P. (2002 [1996]): *The Clash of Civilizations and the Remaking of World Order*. London: The Free Press.

Huntington, Samuel P. (2005): *Who Are We?* London: The Free Press.

Isaac, Jeffrey C. (2015a): "The American Politics of Policing and Incarceration", Editorial, *Perspectives on Politics* Vol. 13, 609–616.

Isaac, Jeffrey C. (2015b): "A Political Science Public Sphere", *The Plot (Politics Decoded) Newsletter*, October 1. http://www.the-plot.org/2015/10/01/a-political-science-public-sphere/, accessed 11/5/2016.

Jogalekar, Ashutosh (2014): "The Many Tragedies of Edward Teller", *Scientific American*, January 15. https://blogs.scientific.american.com/the-curious-wavefunction/the-many-tragedies-of-edward-teller, accessed 9/25/2016.

Lang, Serge (1998): *Challenges*. New York: Springer.

Lietzmann, Hans J. (1999): *Politikwissenschaft im "Zeitalter der Diktaturen"*. Opladen: Leske + Budrich.

SERVING CITIZENS   53

Lindblom, Charles E. (1977): *Politics and Markets*. New York: Basic Books.
Lindblom, Charles E. (1982): "Another State of Mind. Presidential Address, APSA, 1981". *APSR* Vol. 76, 9–21.
Lowi, Theodore J. (1967): "The Public Philosophy: Interest-Group Liberalism". *APSR*, vol. 61, 5–24.
Lowi, Theodore J. (1979): *The End of Liberalism*. New York: W. W. Norton.
Marks, Shula/Trapido, Stanley (1989): "South Africa Since 1976: An Historical Perspective", in: Johnson, Shaun (ed.): *South Africa: No Turning Back*. Bloomington/Indianapolis: Indiana University Press, 1–51.
Mayer, Jane (2016): *Dark Money*. New York/London: Doubleday.
McFarland, Andrew S. (2004): *Neopluralism*. Lawrence: University of Kansas Press.
Merelman, Richard M. (2003): *Pluralism at Yale*. Madison/London: University of Wisconsin Press.
Mouffe, Chantal (2000): *Deliberative Democracy or Agonistic Pluralism*. Political Science Series, Vol. 72. Vienna: Institute for Advanced Studies. http://nbn-resolving.de/urn:nbn:de:0168-ssoar-246548, accessed October 2, 2016.
New York Review of Books (1970): *A Frustrating Task*. Letter by Samuel P. Huntington; reply by Noam Chomsky, February 26. www.nybooks.com/articles/1970/02/26/a-frustrating-task, accessed October 10, 2016.
Oreskes, Naomi/Conway, Eric M. (2008): "Challenging Knowledge. How Climate Science Became a Victim of the Cold War". In: Robert N. Proctor/Londa Schiebinger (eds.): *Agnotology. The Making and Unmaking of Ignorance*. Stanford: Stanford University Press, 55–89.
Oreskes, Naomi/Conway, Eric M. (2012): *Merchants of Doubt*. London. Bloomsbury.
Palonen, Kari (1999): "Contingency in Political Theory". In: Finnish Yearbook of Political Thought, Vol. 3, 5–10.
Peebles, Curtis (1994): *Watch the Skies! A Chronicle of the Flying Saucer Myth*. Washington/London: Smithsonian Institution Press.
Posner, Richard A. (^{2}2003 [^{1}2001]: *Public Intellectuals. A Study of Decline*. Cambridge: Harvard University Press.
Proctor, Richard N. (2004): "Should Medical Historians be Working for the Tobacco Industry?" *The Lancet*, Vol. 363, 1174–1175.
Proctor, Richard N. (2008): "Agnotology. A Missing Term to Describe the Cultural Production of Ignorance (and its Study)". In: Robert N. Proctor/Londa Schiebinger (eds.): *Agnotology. The Making and Unmaking of Ignorance*. Stanford: Stanford University Press, 1–33.
Putnam, Robert D. (2003): "APSA Presidential Address: The Public Role of Political Science". *Perspectives on Politics*, Vol. 1, 249–255.
Sagan, Carl (1985): "On Minimizing the Consequences of Nuclear War". *Nature*, Vol. 317, October 10, 485–488.

54   R. EISFELD

Sagan, Carl (1997): *The Demon-Haunted World. Science as a Candle in the Dark.* London: Headline Book Publishing.

Said, Edward W. (2001): "The Clash of Ignorance". *The Nation*, Vol. 273, No. 12, 11–14.

Savage, Lee (2013): "A View from the Foothills: Public Engagement among Early Career Researchers". *Political Studies Review*, Vol. 11, 190–199.

Schumaker, Erin (2016): "Remember When Mike Pence Said Smoking doesn't Kill?" *Huffington Post*, October 28. http://www.huffingtonpost.com/entry/mike-pence-said-smoking-doesnt-kill_us_58121434e4b064e1b4b0bf93, accessed April 26, 2017.

Skidmore, Thomas E. (1988): *The Politics of Military Rule in Brazil, 1964–1985.* New York: Oxford University Press.

Stone, Jeremy (1994): "Conscience, Arrogation and the Atomic Scientists". *F.A.S. Public Interest Report*, Vol. 47, No. 4, 1–18. www.fas.org/faspir/pir0894.html, accessed Sept. 28, 2016.

Subcommittee to Investigate Problems Connected with Refugees and Escapees of the United States Senate Committee of the Judiciary (1975): *Humanitarian Problems in South Vietnam and Cambodia: Two Years after the Cease-Fire.* Washington: U. S. Government Printing Office.

Sykes, Charles J. (1988): *ProfScam: Professors and the Demise of Higher Education.* Washington: Regnery Gateway.

Teller, Edward (1984): "Wide-Spread After-Effects of Nuclear War". *Nature*, Vol. 310, August 23, 621–624.

UPI (1963): *1963 Year in Review. Nuclear Test Ban Treaty.* http://www.upi.com/Archives/Audio/Events-of-1963/Nuclear-Test-Ban-Treaty/, accessed September 25, 2016.

CHAPTER 5

The Civics of Friendly Persuasion

Alerting Citizens to Political Science and Its Public Engagement

Civic education needs to be based on curricula about citizenship, not about government. It should focus on learning democratic ways of life, including ways of coping with change.

Maintaining or changing their ways in a fundamental, even vital sense: That is the challenge confronting a family of "Friends" (commonly referred to as Quakers) during the American Civil War in the 1956 William Wyler movie *Friendly Persuasion*. Starring Dorothy McGuire and Gary Cooper, the film stands out on several counts, all of which are notable, even if not all were benign:

- It depicts the uprooting of a pacifist Quaker family's hitherto peaceful life by the invasion of enemy troops, which forces every family member to reconsider whether under any circumstances it may be "right" to resort to violence.
- Originally planned early after World War II, the film with its professed sympathies for pacifism was deferred for years, as it fell under the shadows of the first and second "Hollywood Hearings" (1947/1951), then of the Korean War. Conducted by the House Un-American Activities Committee (HUAC), the hearings were intended to ferret out artists with presumed Communist ties or sympathies.

© The Author(s) 2019
R. Eisfeld, *Empowering Citizens, Engaging the Public*,
https://doi.org/10.1007/978-981-13-5928-6_5

55

56   R. EISFELD

- When Gary Cooper reportedly wanted his role changed to that of a "fighting" family patriarch, because his public expected him "to do something", the original novel's author Jessamyn West is said to have responded that he would in fact be doing something—he would "refrain". His audience would observe "a strong man refraining". In an eventual compromise, Cooper disarms a Confederate soldier after a struggle, but lets him go unhurt. In another compromise, the family's oldest son—played by Anthony Perkins—decides to fight, fires his gun once, and then is injured.
- For the 1957 Annual Academy Awards, *Friendly Persuasion* received nominations in six categories: Best Picture, Best Director (William Wyler), Best Supporting Actor (Anthony Perkins), Best Adapted Screenplay (Michael Wilson), Best Original Song (Dimitri Tiomkin), and Best Sound Recording. Screenwriter Michael Wilson (1914–1978) was disqualified for the Award proceedings, because his name had been omitted from the movie's credits. He had already received an Academy Award in 1952, but HUAC named him an unfriendly witness, and Hollywood's movie studios subsequently blacklisted him.
- Wilson emigrated to France for a decade, continued to write or collaborate without credit on scripts for Hollywood films, and would go on to win another (1958) Academy Award for *Bridge on the River Kwai*. That award was posthumously given to his widow in 1985.
- At a 1988 state dinner in Moscow, Ronald Reagan handed Mikhail Gorbachev a copy of the 1956 film, toasting "the art of friendly persuasion... the hope of holding out for a better way of things" (Kraemer 2015: 205).
- Michael Wilson's writing credits for *Friendly Persuasion* were finally restored in 1996 (Dmohowski 2002: 507).

Why would the fortunes of the film and its script writer merit being included in reflections on the future of civics education and, moreover, in a civics course of the kind that will be advocated here?

Any response to the question needs to briefly address three problems which are likely to beset attempts at introducing a twenty-first-century civics even more than the project of a twenty-first-century political science.

Political expediency. In its final report (often referred to as the "Crick Report"), the Advisory Group on Citizenship set up in 1997 by the

United Kingdom's Secretary of State for Education, unanimously and unequivocally ranked teaching *controversial* issues as "the very essence of what constitutes a worthwhile education". Other than mere training, the group affirmed, education requires "the development of further qualities of mind beyond retentive memory": reasoning skills, respect, fairness, empathy (Crick Report 1998: 57).

However, the report also cautioned that controversial issues may be causing speculations about bias or even indoctrination (ibid.: 58). Others have noted that precisely for that reason, efforts to ramp up civic education may have floundered because the subject matter is likely to consist of "politically touchy" issues, something with which "politicians are wary of dealing" (Wong 2015: 5). Depending on political orientations, this may prove particularly relevant if the educational focus, as advocated here, is on change:

While "controversial issues", precisely in view of that emphasis, are "the very issues most important for students to discuss" (Gerson et al. 2011: 14), curricula sticking to traditional values and approaches are apt to stand a better chance of being considered favorably than ventures into new—let alone contested—socio-cultural or analytical terrain. The argument may be viewed as particularly salient in the case of the United States, considering the extent to which "culture war" debates about symbols, ideals, and values have, since the 1980s/1990s, "permeated the politics of education" in that country (Wolbrecht and Hartney 2014: 611, 613).

Competition from STEM: With increasing political support for the early acquisition of skills in the fields of science, technology, engineering, and mathematics, the debate has been picking up speed whether STEM-centered curricula may be edging out civics or even, more generally, arts, humanities, and social sciences. One partial response has consisted in a number of initiatives to include art and design among STEM subjects, changing the acronym to STEAM. Retired US Supreme Court Justice Sandra Day O'Connor (appointed by Ronald Reagan) and former Democratic US Senator John Glenn, the erstwhile astronaut, have recently recommended a similar solution for civic education: "While we fully support the vast resources committed to promote STEM subjects, we seriously question the cost of doing so at the expense of the humanities." Citizenship, O'Connor and Glenn insisted, needs to be taught with the same "devotion" applied to instill scientific knowledge. Both affirmed their belief that it should be "integrated with these subjects" (O'Connor and Glenn 2015). The Crick Report, it should be added, already listed contexts such as the ethical issues raised by scientific progress, statistics, data handling, investigation of opinion polls, or the examination of electoral systems as examples where integration with science, mathematics, and information and communications technology might be achieved (Crick Report 1998: 53, 54).

Whittling down to "government": Not just in the United States, civics courses have been "gradually replaced" by courses in government, "mostly inspired by political science" (Putnam 2003: 253)—by a political science mainstream, that is, which has been emphasizing the "management" of parliamentary/presidential and party government. The shift "from active involvement to passive analysis" has been labeled "powerful"—"not how *we* can influence public life, but who else has influence" (Putnam 2003: ibid.; emphasis added). This tallies with earlier observations by another APSA president in her 1997 Presidential Address, quoted at the outset of the first chapter.

Doubtlessly, the workings of democracy should be taught and need to be understood. But it amounts to a truism that they may be learnt in different ways. A language and a curriculum primarily devoted to "government" tend to neglect relationships established so that people may learn to "govern themselves for themselves" (Ostrom 1997: 34). Vincent Ostrom, from whose book *The Meaning of Democracy and the Vulnerability of Democracies* the preceding quote is taken, goes on to argue in favor of being taught, by arrangements of education, the ways of active, rather than passive, citizenship: "On our way to becoming adults, we may otherwise lose the moral understanding and knowledge" appropriate to living in a democratic society (Ostrom 1997: 26).

APSA's formerly annual, now biennial Teaching and Learning Conferences, held since 2004, have sought to combine an emphasis on active learning tools—such as project-based learning, games, simulations, or role-playing exercises—with a focus on community engagement, attention to underrepresented or marginalized groups, the why's and how's of nurturing values of citizenship, equality, and democracy. In a further encouraging development, APSA, PSA, ECPR, and the British International Studies Association are organizing their first Joint International Teaching and Learning Conference for 2019. Under the heading "Teaching Politics in an Era of Populism", the conference aims to explore—and, hopefully, meet—the challenges raised by the proliferation of a political "culture" in which "expertise and established standards of evidence are devalued" (APSA 2018)—a theme reverberating through this book. Curriculum construction in a period "of rapid and sometimes dramatic political change" will be a major issue to which the forum will direct its attention.

In somewhat exemplary fashion, *Friendly Persuasion*, both the film and the way it fared, demonstrate how a civics curriculum might take into account hurdles such as those listed and still arrive at effectively addressing civic shortfalls. On that many-layered score, *Friendly Persuasion* may be considered to have an edge over the more recent (2016), also much-lauded *Hacksaw Ridge*. Directed by Mel Gibson, historically largely accurate, the biographical war drama recounts how a young lad brought up as a pacifist Seventh-day Adventist enlists at the outbreak of World War II as a conscientious objector refusing to carry weapons, but willing to serve as a combat medic. During training, he suffers persecution and ridicule. In the battle of Okinawa, he manages to rescue several dozens of injured soldiers under enemy fire and is himself wounded. After the war, he receives the Medal of Honor as the first conscientious objector. The movie was judged as both "harrowing" and "inspiring", like *Friendly Persuasion* a tribute "to the courage of remaining true to one's convictions".

While *Friendly Persuasion*'s plot has traditional connotations—family, faith, farming—the film also offers a modern narrative, raising the question whether to alter or to maintain basic values in a changing (and challenging) social environment. Partly bowing to the prevailing mood of the mid-1950s in the pivotal scenes referred to above, it does not fundamentally disavow a pacifist stance, but makes compromises whose scope may be subject to debate.

The movie's emphasis on civility, trust, and compassion moreover managed to serve as a link between domestic and international affairs when, in his second term as President, Ronald Reagan decided to switch policies vis-à-vis the Soviet Union from a pattern of denouncing "the evil empire" to an attempt at nuclear arms limitation negotiations. Reagan's 1988 toast which, as briefly described above, included handing over a videotape of the film to Gorbachev, in a small but telling way signified the relationship of trust which the two men had built between them. That relationship, in its turn, may be considered to have contributed its part to the 1987 INF (Intermediate-Range Nuclear Forces) Treaty, the first genuine agreement on partial nuclear disarmament between the two states.

A major casualty of blacklisting, the film's writer—Michael Wilson— "never recovered his professional standing". He continued to work "under the table" in the Hollywood black market, although for lower pay (Buhle

60   R. EISFELD

and Wagner 2003: X; Dmohowski 2002: 498, 505). Wilson did not live to see the Writers Guild of America finally restore his credit for *Friendly Persuasion* after 40 years. In 1947, the Hollywood Association of Motion Picture Producers had resolved to take "positive" action by "eliminating any subversives", specifically referring to "unfriendly" HUAC witnesses (Schrecker 1994: 216). Six years later, the Association concluded an agreement with the Screen Writers Guild which, again referring to HUAC "or any similarly duly constituted" committee, relieved producers from the obligation to credit uncooperative writers (Dmohowski 2002: 500/501).

A civics curriculum including *Friendly Persuasion* as a case study of a movie "deeply embroiled in the politics of the Hollywood blacklist" (Dmohowski 2002: 491), of these maneuvers' ramifications and not least of the film's screen portrayals and their impact (Reagan: "powerfully acted and directed") may benefit—again in an exemplary fashion—from the analyses of a historically informed political science.

Such studies first show how McCarthyism—as defined in the previous chapter—came into "full swing" before the senator from Wisconsin entered the scene, owing to a deeply rooted sense of unease dating back to the 1917 Russian revolution "that something malignant and foreign" might be "contaminating the nation". They demonstrate the way HUAC, converted (after its inception in 1938) into a standing House committee in 1945 and aided by John Edgar Hoover's FBI, established a pattern of anti-Communist investigation on which McCarthy merely needed to capitalize. The analyses subsequently illustrate how and why the political climate slowly changed, not least due to the "Warren Court's" 1956/1957 reversal of previous Supreme Court decisions (Morgan 2003: 61, 525, 541 ss.)—excepting the legacy of the "loss of China" demagoguery, which "helped freeze" US foreign policy toward East Asia for two decades (Halberstam 1992 [¹1972]: 105/106, 115 ss.). HUAC (where Richard Nixon's political career had begun) was finally abolished by the House of Representatives in 1975.

The studies further indicate that, while governments and legislatures set the political agenda, the role of private employers—such as labor unions, universities, newspapers, radio and TV stations, and the motion picture industry—was instrumental in spreading the "obsession" through society (Schrecker 1994: 20, 40). This also meant, and there is one more important lesson, that individual acts of courage could and did contribute to terminating McCarthyist malpractices. In the case of the Hollywood blacklist, that happened when Otto Preminger and Kirk Douglas

THE CIVICS OF FRIENDLY PERSUASION   61

announced in 1960 that they had hired and were crediting blacklisted screenwriter Dalton Trumbo (1905–1976) for, respectively, the films *Exodus* and *Spartacus*. Most importantly, the analyses document that the last 40 years saw an immense number of partly controversial, partly extended scholarly interpretations of the McCarthyist period. They testify as much to "the discovery of new sources and the rereading of old ones" (Schrecker 1994: 255), as to the fact that—once again—carefully reasoned arguments should not be expected to exclude diverging judgments, even if there has been increasing agreement on two points:

- McCarthyism in the broader sense was—as briefly indicated already in the previous chapter—a movement of "fear", both in the sense of building on wide-spread anxieties and of sowing additional fear by its demonizing of a perceived enemy (Morgan 2003: XIV; Schrecker 1998: Ch. 4: "They Are Everywhere").
- The movement had a familiar additional political component: "Desperate to regain political power", the Republican Party "used the anguish and distress" feeding McCarthyism (Morgan 2003: 525, citing Hubert Humphrey).

The vast available body of scholarly work on this, as on many other controversial issues, may—and that is the salient point—produce curricular materials that serve to initiate and sustain calmer, more substantial debates, tolerant of complexity and diversity, respectful of others' perspectives. Because citizens increasingly tend to "access media that reinforce their own prior beliefs", and to talk to other people who do likewise, the need to increase the attention given in school-based civic learning to discussing controversial political issues has rightfully been assessed as "dramatic" (Gould 2011: 27/28). Current public political debates have, on the other hand, been judged "vacuous and sometimes vicious", including "outright falsehoods", and marked (not least due to the effects of social media) by a wide-spread "decline in civility" (Gerson et al. 2011: 9, 12). Referring to both the Trump and the Brexit campaigns, the problem will be discussed in detail below.

Debating controversial issues from a variety of scholarly perspectives should additionally prepare students for the prospect that, in attempting to cope with important aspects of their further lives under conditions of continuing rapid social and cultural change, publicly engaged political

62   R. EISFELD

scientists will be available, on whose views they might draw if they should desire. Former APSA Director Michael Brintnall has affirmed his organization's resolve to "advance *and reshape* the commitment" to education in civic engagement (Brintnall 2013: XII; italics added). In the same recent APSA volume, Alison Rios Millett McCartney (Towson University, Maryland) not merely warned that, if political science neglects to energetically pursue the avowed aim of encouraging students' "confidence, knowledge, skills, and motivations to maintain a dynamic, vibrant democracy", the discipline will "lose existing momentum much as political scientists in the 1920s and 1930s did" (McCartney 2013: 14).

McCartney pointedly added a second warning which has already surfaced in these pages: Should political science fail to evolve an academic culture—including an appropriate "reward structure"—valuing its own professionals' civic engagement, it cannot "genuinely promote" such engagement in its students (McCartney 2013: 17).

It may be considered a safe bet that, in order to accordingly educate political scientists, administrators, school teachers, and in the last instance students, the "art of friendly persuasion" praised by Ronald Reagan in his Moscow toast will be direly needed.

A decidedly different reaction, however, is required from the profession acting in concert through its associations and from large numbers of scholars acting individually in those cases where political language is being used to disorient, to destabilize, and to destroy—

- to disorient citizens by proffering "alternative facts" (Trump adviser Kellyanne Conway),
- to destroy political trust by spreading "fake news",
- to destabilize democratic institutions by the systematic lying of leading political figures, parties, and governments.

References

APSA (2018): "Teaching Politics in an Era of Populism." Joint International Teaching and Learning Conference 2019. https://www.apsanct.org/TEACHING/Teaching-in-Political-Science/Joint-International-Teaching-Conference, accessed October 27, 2018.

Brintnall, Michael (2013): "Foreword". In: Alison Rios Millett McCartney/ Elizabeth A. Bannion/Dick Simpson (eds.): *Teaching Civic Engagement: From Student to Active Citizen.* Washington: American Political Science Association, XI–XII.

THE CIVICS OF FRIENDLY PERSUASION   63

Buhle, Paul/Wagner, Dave (2003): *Hide in Plain Sight. The Hollywood Blacklistees in Film and Television, 1950–2002*. New York: Palgrave Macmillan.

Crick Report (Final Report of the Advisory Group on Citizenship 1998): *Education for Citizenship and the Teaching of Democracy in Schools*. London: Qualifications and Curriculum Authority.

Dmohowski, Joseph (2002): "The Friendly Persuasion (1956) Screenplay Controversy: Michael Wilson, Jessamyn West, and the Hollywood Blacklist." *Historical Journal of Film, Radio and Television*, Vol. 22, 491–514.

Gerson, Michael et al. (2011): "Civic Common Sense", in: Jonathan Gould (ed.): *Guardian of Democracy. The Civic Mission of Schools*. Annenberg Institute for Civics at the University of Pennsylvania/Campaign for the Civic Mission of Schools, 9–15.

Gould, Jonathan (ed., 2011): *Guardian of Democracy. The Civic Mission of Schools*. Annenberg Institute for Civics at the University of Pennsylvania/Campaign for the Civic Mission of Schools.

Halberstam, David (1992 [[1]1972]): *The Best and the Brightest*. New York: Ballantine Books.

Kraemer, Sven F. (2015): *Inside the Cold War from Marx to Reagan*. Lanham/London: University Press of America.

McCartney, Alison Rios Millett (2013): "Teaching Civic Engagement: Debates, Definitions, Benefits, and Challenges." In: Alison Rios Millett McCartney/Elizabeth A. Bannion/Dick Simpson (eds.): *Teaching Civic Engagement: From Student to Active Citizen*. Washington: American Political Science Association, 9–20.

Morgan, Ted (2003): *Reds. McCarthyism in Twentieth-Century America*. New York: Random House.

O'Connor, Sandra Day/Glenn, John (2015): "Teaching Better Civics for Better Citizens". *Wall Street Journal*, May 12. http://quest.icivics.org/news/wall-street-journal-op-ed-teraching-better-civics-better-citizens-abstract, accessed Jan. 28, 2017.

Ostrom, Vincent (1997): *The Meaning of Democracy and the Vulnerability of Democracies*. Ann Arbor: University of Michigan Press.

Putnam, Robert D. (2003): "APSA Presidential Address: The Public Role of Political Science". *Perspectives on Politics*, Vol. 1, 249–255.

Schrecker, Ellen (1994): *The Age of McCarthyism*. Bopston/New York: Bedford/St. Martin's.

Schrecker, Ellen (1998): *Many Are the Crimes. McCarthyism in America*. Princeton: Princeton University Press.

Wolbrecht, Christina/Hartney, Michael T. (2014): "'Ideas About Interests': Explaining the Changing Partisan Politics of Education." *Perspectives on Politics*, Vol. 12, 603–630.

Wong, Alia (2015): "Why Civics Is About More Than Citizenship". *The Atlantic*, September 17. www.theatlantic.com/education/archive/2015/09/civic-education-citizenship-test/405889, accessed Jan. 28, 2017.

CHAPTER 6

A Determination to Blow the Whistle

Political Science Stepping in to Avert Mendocracy

The Brexit and Trump campaigns have demonstrated that we may be on the way to mendocracy, or liars' rule. Political Science should underwrite the exposure of patently false, illegal, or unethical claims and operations, by which politicians, parties, and governments may be attempting to deceive citizens and to thwart or subvert their constitutional responsibilities.

In the *Toronto Star* November 4, 2016, issue, the daily's Washington Bureau Chief, Daniel Dale, published a fact-checked list of 560 false claims uttered or tweeted by Donald J. Trump during his presidential campaign in the six weeks between September 15 and October 30 of that year. *Star* reporter Tanya Talaga added an attempt at examining the falsehoods for patterns (Dale and Talaga 2016). According to the list, Trump repeatedly and falsely claimed, for instance, that

- the US murder rate was the highest in 45 years, particularly refer-ring—again falsely—to cities such as Baltimore, Chicago, New York, Washington DC;
- the United States had two million criminal illegal immigrants;
- neither education nor jobs existed in the US "inner cities";
- over 50% of African-American youth were unemployed;
- Hispanic poverty had increased dramatically under the Obama administration.

© The Author(s) 2019
R. Eisfeld, *Empowering Citizens, Engaging the Public*,
https://doi.org/10.1007/978-981-13-5928-6_6

As in his campaign assertions about Mexico supposedly exporting drug dealers and rapists to the United States, or Hillary Clinton allegedly favoring open borders "with the Middle East", Trump's untruths pandered to xenophobia in general, and to white fears specifically—that all good, that is, white, citizens were potential victims. In proceeding thus, Trump was able to capitalize on the "politics of fear" discourse (discussed in Chap. 4), which had emerged after 9/11. He defeated Clinton 62:33 in counties with at least 85% white; 65:30 in counties with a 97% or more US-born population; and 70:27 in counties where 20% or more of residents described their ancestry as "American". He won over 70% of the vote in rural counties with less than 20,000 residents, and in counties where less than 20% of the population had a degree, he again received seven in ten votes (Bloomberg 2016).[1]

Xenophobic fears were likewise fueled in the United Kingdom by falsehoods which the "Vote Leave" organization, chaired by Labour MP Gisela Stuart und Conservative Justice Secretary Michael Gove, spread during 2016. Four weeks before the June referendum, "Vote Leave" distributed a poster depicting a British passport flipped open like an inviting door, into which footprints led. The text read: "Turkey (population 76 million) is joining the EU. Vote Leave, take back control." In fact, Turkey's accession to the European Union was and is nowhere in sight, with not even half of the *acquis communautaire* chapters requiring negotiation opened since 2005, just one (science and research) provisionally closed, and several blocked by Cyprus. Nonetheless, in "coordinated statements" (Boffey and Helm 2016), Gove and Penny Mordaunt, Armed Forces Minister of State at the UK Department of Defense, maintained over the weekend before the poster's launch that Turkey's inhabitants would move "here freely when they join the EU soon" (Mordaunt)—"as soon as 2020" (Gove).

Mordaunt also had an additional message, warning about "high crime rates, problems with gangs and terror cells" in Turkey and other potential EU candidates (Baron 2016). "Vote Leave" immediately pitched in on

---

[1] On February 21, 2017, the *Washington Post* published a Fact Checker team analysis, according to which Trump as President had continued making "false or misleading" statements, to the extent of making 133 such claims during his first 35 days in office. The *Post* concluded that "Trump ha[d] changed nothing in his approach to the truth since being elected president." The most frequent statements—24—concerned immigration (Cillizza 2017; Kessler 2017).

both counts, emphasizing alleged consequences of Turkey's birthrate—"we can expect to see an additional million people added to the UK population"—and ratcheting the alleged security threat from "far higher" crime and "more widespread" gun ownership up: The government would "not be able to exclude Turkish criminals from entering the UK" (Boffey and Helm 2016). A compilation of front page headlines from *Daily Mail, Daily Express, Daily Telegraph,* and *Sun* demonstrated that the "xenophobic message" was seized upon and "systematically" aggrandized further by the four tabloids (Barnett 2016: 47).

The additional assertion that "the strain on Britain's public services" would increase was intended, like a variety of similar claims, to evoke an association with "Vote Leave's" most notorious poster: "We send the EU £350 million a week. Let's fund our NHS [National Health Service] instead. Take Control on 23 June." The claim was publicly rejected as "misleading" (a "gross figure" used "in contexts that imply it is a net figure") four weeks before the referendum by Sir Andrew Dilnot, Chair of the UK Statistics Authority, a non-governmental body accountable to Parliament. He pointed to the rebate which Margret Thatcher had obtained in 1984, and to other EU payments received by Britain (UK Statistics Authority 2016). However, one week before the referendum, a survey by Ipsos MORI, Britain's second largest market research organization, found that 47% of the public still believed the figure, while 14% did not know (Stone 2016a). *Almost half the British population either disbelieved, or turned a deaf ear to, the country's chief statistician's attempt to put across the difference between a gross and a net figure.*

Attempts at explaining these attitudes have concluded that

- on a fundamental emotional level, the "Vote Leave" campaign succeeded in evoking "a sense of dread of the future" (Crines 2016: 61), contrasting it with the promise of an alternative future, over which some "control" might be regained (Berry 2016);
- where fact checks refuted outrageous claims, citizens resisted corrections inconsistent both with prior beliefs and with additional hopes which the Leave side's "potent rhetorical mix of nostalgia, grievances and imagined destiny" had ignited (Banducci and Stevens 2016: 22; Parry 2016: 63).

On the day after the referendum, UKIP (United Kingdom Independence Party) leader Nigel Farage disowned the "Vote Leave" pledge that £350m

68   R. EISFELD

a week would be spent on the health service, which he had endorsed two weeks before the referendum, as "a mistake"—"it wasn't one of my adverts, I can assure you" (Stone 2016b). By the time, however, the mixture of "distortions, half-truths and outright lies" (Barnett 2016: 47) had taken the intended effect, as exemplified by the statement of a Residents' Association chair in Stoke-on-Trent (dubbed "Brexit capital of Britain" after 69.4% had voted in favor of 'Leave'), according to which immigration had been "the big issue": Purportedly, it was "putting too much pressure" on public services (Corrigan 2017). Once again, the emphasis on change, the message that things in the United Kingdom had gotten "worse", played a crucial role in shaping attitudes and voting patterns (Goodwin and Milazzo 2017: 452).

In their joint analysis of the referendum campaign's "fig leaves and fairy tales", a team of political scientists from London, Southampton, and Sheffield chose the epithet "mendacity"—more precisely, a "degree of mendacity" which, if it were to become commonplace, would "badly damag[e]" one of the "crucial foundations of our democratic system" (Renwick et al. 2016: 31). Five years earlier, the American historian and journalist Rick Perlstein had, when writing about the Republican Party's stratagems long before the advent of Donald Trump, used the sobriquet "mendocracy", or liars' rule. Perlstein had, at the time, already won wide acclaim by his works on American conservatism. In a piece subtitled "How political lying became normal", published in the progressive magazine *Mother Jones*, Perlstein argued that the "absurdly doctored stories and videos" manufactured by right-wing ideologues not just continued to fool mainstream media. They literally flourished under the "protective bubble" of a media definition of "civility" evolved during the 1980s which "privileged 'balance' over truth-telling—even when one side was lying".

That regime of "liars and their [media] enablers now work[ing] hand in glove", Rick Perlstein concluded, "I call a mendocracy" (Perlstein 2011).

The emergence of cartels for manufacturing ignorance, discussed in Chap. 4, certainly played a part in preparing the ground for systematic political mendacity. The cartels' strategies of "merchandising doubt", resorting to the plain denial of facts for ideological reasons, had struck a chord with the anti-regulation Republican Party, putting it "on a collision course with science" (Oreskes and Conway 2012: 67, 240).

The larger story, however, is more complex and extends beyond the Republican Party.

A DETERMINATION TO BLOW THE WHISTLE   69

Publication of the *Pentagon Papers* (to which this chapter will return) revealed the machinations of a Democratic administration. The *Papers* documented the existence of "an inner U. S. government": the apparatus surrounding the president, for whom the "enemy" was their country's media, the judiciary, even Congress. Led by a Democratic president, that apparatus "sneak[ed] the country" into the Vietnam War, manipulating lawmakers, the public, and the press (Halberstam 1993 [¹1972]: 409, 619, 655, partly quoting *New York Times* journalist Neil Sheehan).

- During the 1960s, President Lyndon Johnson lied to hide or down-play successive steps in the escalation of the Vietnam War.
- In the early 1970s, President Richard Nixon lied to protect himself, his advisers, and their instruments, the White House "plumbers", who had bungled the Watergate break-in. With impeachment for multiple abuses of power imminent, Nixon resigned. A number of "the president's men" were sentenced to prison terms.
- In the late 1980s, President Ronald Reagan, according to two House and Senate Committees, "favored or at least tolerated an environment" in which the arms-for-hostages deal labeled Iran-Contra Affair could unfold "in deception and disdain of the law". In this context, Reagan repeatedly gave public statements that "were wrong". On the exact extent of his involvement, the shredding of documents by officials left the record "incomplete" (Congressional Committees 1987). For domestic and international reasons, both committees trod reluctantly—whereas in Nixon's case they had proceeded vigorously—during their investigation to determine Reagan's precise role (Hersh 1990: 46). Reagan's Secretary of Defense, two National Security Advisers (one conviction vacated on appeal), an Assistant Secretary of State, and other staff were indicted or convicted, but (preemptively) pardoned by Reagan's successor George H. W. Bush, who had been vice president at the time of the Iran-Contra Affair.
- In the late 1990s, President Bill Clinton lied not about political matters, but—both to the public and in a lawsuit deposition—with regard to an extramarital affair. However, he perjured himself in the process. The House of Representatives initiated his impeachment, but Clinton was acquitted by the Senate.
- During the early 2000s, President George W. Bush, for the purposes of justifying an invasion of Iraq, resorted—in the words of former

CIA division chief Tyler Drumheller—to an "unprecedented" manipulation of intelligence about weapons of mass destruction (WMD) allegedly held by Saddam Hussein's regime, and about equally alleged links of the regime to the Al Quaeda terrorist group: "The public was misled" (Drumheller 2006: 4, 87).

In a 2008 study, the Center for Public Integrity—a nonpartisan watchdog group accepting contributions from neither corporations nor labor unions, supported by the Ford Foundation and other charities—together with the Fund for Independence in Journalism reported that Bush in the run-up to the invasion had made, during two years, 260 false statements regarding such weapons and/or ties. Increased by hundreds more from the Secretaries of State and Defense, the Vice President, the National Security Adviser, and other top officials, these contentions were, as the Center—not unlikely retired spy Drumheller—concluded, "part of an orchestrated campaign" that aroused public opinion. The administration led the nation to war "under decidedly false pretenses" (Center for Public Integrity 2008).

As regards the comportment of the United Kingdom's Blair government, a fundamentally similar pattern emerged from Sir John Chilcot's 2016 Iraq Inquiry Report, even if Tony Blair was originally more hesitant and had urged Bush to involve the United Nations. When submitting to Parliament, in September 2002, a Joint Intelligence Committee (JIC) dossier on Iraq, Prime Minister Blair added a signed foreword, in which he wrote (Blair 2002):

- "What *I believe* [italics added] the assessed intelligence has *established beyond doubt* [italics added] is that Saddam has continued to produce chemical and biological weapons, that he continues in his efforts to develop nuclear weapons, and that he has been able to extend the range of his ballistic missile program."
- "*I am in no doubt* [italics added] that the situation is serious and current, that he has made progress on WMD… The document discloses that his military planning allows for some of the WMD to be ready within 45 minutes of an order to use them. *I am quite clear* [italics added] that Saddam will go to extreme lengths…"

In contrast, Sir John Chilcot, a member of the British governmental advisory body known as Privy Council, emphasized in his presentation of the Inquiry Report: "The assessed intelligence had *not* established 'beyond doubt' either that Iraq had continued to produce chemical and biological weapons or that efforts to develop nuclear weapons continued." Regarding the judgments in the Prime Minister's statement and in the JIC dossier, Sir Chilcot concluded that they had been presented "with a certainty that was *not* justified" (Chilcot 2016: 5, 6; italics added). The Inquiry Report's executive summary considered it "unlikely" that Parliament and the public would have "distinguished between the authority of the judgements in the Foreword and in the dossier". In restrained British prose, the summary added that the Prime Minister's "deliberate" selection of a formulation "which grounded the statement in what Mr. Blair believed" indicated a "distinction" between those beliefs and the Intelligence Committee's "actual judgments" (quote in Edwards 2016).

But it was Blair's foreword, particularly the "ready within 45 minutes" claim, which set the tone for the media reporting that followed and may be compared to the Brexit case: "45 Minutes from Attack" [*Evening Standard*], "Brits 45 Minutes from Doom" [*Sun*], "He's Got 'em—Let's Get Him" [*Sun*] (Culloty 2016).

Later, before the Chilcot inquiry, the government retreated to the position that the claim had referred to battlefield weapons, rather than to long-range missiles—which, considering the WMD context sketched by Blair, seemed pretty labored.

Before long, both analysts and satirists came to insist that the acronym WMD really stood for "weapons of mass *deception*". In 2003, Sheldon Rampton and John Stauber, at the time co-editors of *PR Watch*—published by the liberal advocacy group Center for Media and Democracy—wrote a book bearing that very title on the Bush administration's tactics of securing support for the invasion of Iraq. Similarly, a year later John Dean in a work entitled *Worse than Watergate* attested Bush "high deception" in "mislead[ing] Congress and the American people" into war against Iraq. Having served earlier as White House Counsel to Nixon for three years, Dean had become heavily implicated in the president's attempted cover-up of the Watergate break-in. He cooperated with the prosecutors and, when convicted, had to serve only four months' time.

In 1971, Dean had received from one of the then-president's operatives a so-called Nixon's Enemies List including 20 names—among which journalists figured as a minority. The list's purpose was, as Dean explained at the time in a written memorandum, to "use the available federal machinery to screw our political enemies".

In February 2017, Donald Trump, while continuing to make unsubstantiated claims (such as allegedly having been wiretapped by the Obama administration), turned the tables and accused a number of media of spreading fake news, denouncing them as enemies of the public on Twitter: "The FAKE NEWS media (failing @nytimes, @NBCNews, @ABC, @CBS, @CNN) is not my enemy, it is the enemy of the American People!" (Grynbaum 2017).

Sharply critical of George W. Bush, Dean expressed even stronger reservations about Donald Trump's—as compared to his former chief—more "obsessive vengefulness" and "reflexive dishonesty". Dean stated he did not think that "Nixon even comes close to the level of corruption we already know about Trump" (Coppins 2017).

Politicians' sporadic bending of the truth changing into sustained mass deception amounts to a continuing assault on citizens' informed political participation, the very core principle of democracy. The perpetual and purposeful feeding of false information poisons participation at the roots and reduces democratic procedure to an empty husk. Present political science has been focusing to a large extent on the "management" of parliamentary and party government—on "good governance" through rule of law, transparency, and administrative efficiency (a rather "Bismarckian" notion which has more to do with the Rechtsstaat ideal than with democracy). Currently, the discipline is not sufficiently prepared nor, perhaps, sufficiently equipped to deal with the ongoing transition from democracy to mendocracy (which would, for instance, take it much deeper into media studies). However, it ought to develop the required capacities.

This becomes apparent when considering two attempts by scholars to respond, respectively, to the Brexit mendacity and to Trump's falsehoods.

An Open Letter on "propagating falsehoods at public expense", signed by some 250 British academics from the country's political studies, economics, and law departments, appeared in the *Telegraph*'s Opinion pages nine days before the referendum. Coordinated by Alan Renwick from the University College of London's Constitutional Unit, it could hardly have commenced more forcefully: "A referendum result is democratically legitimate only if voters can make an informed decision. Yet the level of misinformation in the current campaign is so great that democratic legitimacy is called into question." Subsequently, however, the text tapered off. It took both sides to task for "making misleading claims", urged the media "to focus more fearlessly on challenging deliberate misinformation", and called for reviewing—*after* the referendum—"ways to strengthen campaign truthfulness without curtailing legitimate free speech" (Open EU Referendum Letter 2016).

As might have been feared, no change of tone occurred in the public debate. The letter failed in its essential purpose for at least three reasons: It came too late, it was too balanced, and it did not form part of a more comprehensive effort.

- With just over one week to go before the referendum was set to take place, the initiative could hardly be expected to make a noticeable impact. The debate's standards—if one wishes to refer to them by that term—were, by that time, pretty much fixed. In contrast, the first of a number of public statements needed to have been launched once the deceitful trend of the campaign became discernible. This, in its turn, would have required a political studies discipline wherein the idea of determined intervention in public debates had already gained wide acceptance.
- The letter castigated the aforementioned £350m-a-week-payment-to-the-EU 'Leave' claim as "a blatant falsehood". In contrast, the 'Remain' assertion according to which over three million British jobs were linked to EU exports fell under the verdict "in line with independent analyses, but not all would go in case of Brexit". The two campaign statements, quite evidently, represented different levels of mendacity. Yet the text reproached "both sides" equally with "making misleading claims".

Among the letter's signatures was that of Matthew Flinders, then chair of the Political Studies Association. In a post-referendum assessment published by the Bernard Crick Centre for Understanding Politics, Flinders minced his words much less, writing that "emotive arguments", such as "control" or "power", had been directed against "the other", identified as "'immigrants" or "'foreigners". The scientist rightly labeled the Brexit campaign's political calculation "alarmingly simple: 'emotive claim + identified folk devil = Leave success'" (Flinders 2016).

A conception of "scholarly impartiality", or the desire to garner as many signatures as possible, may have prompted the letter's authors to opt for a "balanced" version. In contrast, it would have been imperative to put the xenophobic content of the "Vote Leave" organization's claims in the sharpest possible spotlight, the way Flinders did subsequently.

74   R. EISFELD

Proceeding thus would not have implied remaining silent on the "Remain" campaign's deficits. When the *Toronto Star* counted 104 false claims by Trump during the three televised presidential debates, the newspaper also mentioned 13 such claims on Clinton's part (Dale and Talaga 2016). But the disparity was so huge that the report's unmistakable focus remained on the falsehoods committed by one side. The lesson to be learnt from the Brexit case is that the open letter's authors should have proceeded likewise.

- In line with the conception outlined earlier in this book, a sustained effort by political scientists on individual and organizational levels would have been called for in order to realistically exert influence on the referendum campaign's tone and substance. The effort ought to have included social media, radio and TV appearances, and public speaking engagements. Such engagements might, for instance, have exposed to necessary ridicule the incongruous pronouncement: "People in this country have had enough of experts" by none other than expert Michael Gove, who had studied at Oxford and was serving as Justice Secretary. They might have ridiculed intolerance and ethnic prejudice by creatively adapting tales such as that used by Harold Laski when he had addressed, decades earlier, public meetings for the Labour Party (Martin 1953: 60).

The story told by Laski pictured an American gentleman from the Deep South who had come to Washington on a political assignment and was introduced by the president to Booker T. Washington, then the most famous of American blacks. According to Laski, the gentleman said later: "What was I to do? I couldn't call a nigger Mister, and I couldn't call him nigger without insulting the President of the United States. So I compromised and called him Professor."

In any case, in the United Kingdom an academics' Open Letter did call for ways to strengthen campaign truthfulness. In the United States, a message by a renowned political sociologist proposed establishment of an American Committee for the Defense of Democracy (ACDD). Shielding the American democracy "from assaults by the Trump Administration", resisting the "Trump catastrophe" were the avowed purposes of Amitai Etzioni's proposal. According to Etzioni, the ACDD should have a sharply limited agenda: Protecting the right to vote, the freedom of the press, and the courts' independence; stopping "the abuse of public office for private gains". He wanted the ACDD, which he imagined launching as a dues-paying association, to serve as organizational core for an eventual social movement. Other causes—such as women's rights, identity politics, or environmental issues—should be left to other associations (Etzioni 2017). The fault with Etzioni's plan is that the ACDD might well be perceived not as an "overarching" (Etzioni) association, but as one more advocacy group alongside, for instance, the National Urban League (blacks) or the Human Rights Organization (lesbians/gays). Due to Etzioni's suggestion that it should issue an annual score evaluating democratic actions by office-holders and candidates, it might even be confused with ADA, the long-established Americans for Democratic Action—a group which publishes annual voting scores. Moreover, a newly created committee would need indeterminate time to build the writing and speaking potential for intervening publicly, to achieve prestige, and to establish an effective organizational capacity, which the political science profession, its departments, and associations already have.

On the level of individually engaged scholarship, the discipline's inherent possibilities are indicated by John Trent's self-published 2015 brochure entitled *Harper's Canada—Read This Before You Vote*. Trent, it will be remembered, is the former IPSA Secretary General, to whose prominence in the ongoing debate on the state of political science this book's Chap. 1 attested. In his booklet, he also identified himself to readers as a "political and social activist" (he might have added that he has been a long-time Liberal Party supporter). His book contended in considerable, if admittedly "selective", detail (backed up by references which he put on his website) that Stephen Harper's Conservative administration, "governing with a mixture of centralization, secrecy and authoritarianism", had "attack[ed] the democratic bases" of Canada's political institutions. In concluding, he submitted suggestions for the country's "necessary renewal", focusing on the strengthening of civil society, a reduction of economic inequalities, environmental protection, and engaging with Canada's Native Peoples (Trent 2015: 6, 11, 51, 58–62).

On an associational level, a few first steps toward the desired goal may also be discerned, even if they occurred after the event—in this case, after President Trump's executive order of January 2017 banning citizens from seven countries from entry into the United States for three months. The American Political Science Association, for instance, "condemned" the order, calling on Trump to rescind it "immediately". Discerning a "lack of full regard for liberal democratic norms and practices", APSA did not

76   R. EISFELD

mince words either in underscoring political scientists' authoritative work: The organization urged the President and the officials of his administration to consider "scholarly understandings of the strengths and foundations of the United States' political system and political culture", when making decisions that may affect both (APSA 2017).

Where the current chapter's heading therefore emphasizes the desired emergence in the discipline of a determination "to blow the whistle", the term is used in the wider sense of outside experts, such as political scientists, sounding the alarm, alerting the public, rather than in the narrower meaning of insiders (employees) revealing malpractices. The ethical grounds, however, are identical, and in both cases the focus is on remedying grossly immoral abuses or patently false claims by politicians, parties, or government agencies (or, for that matter, by business corporations). Political science should therefore energetically support initiatives for comprehensive, effective whistleblower protection laws, such as urged by an overwhelming majority of the European Union's parliamentary representatives (European Parliament 2017).

In fact, the discipline may take its inspiration from an early whistleblower in the term's narrower connotation, Daniel Ellsberg, and from the US Supreme Court ruling in the *Pentagon Papers* case. Ellsberg, with a PhD in economics, worked for the Rand Corporation as a strategic analyst from 1959 to 1964, then joined the Department of Defense as Special Assistant for three years, returning to Rand in 1967. Because he had come to consider the United States' military involvement in Vietnam a crime, he concluded that he should "expose and resist it", seeking "moral and political change". Ellsberg revealed to the *New York Times* and to other newspapers those documents and analyses on US decision-making relating to Vietnam, which became known as the *Pentagon Papers*. The hope which he then expressed applies as well to our time and profession: That "truths that changed me could help [others] free themselves" (Ellsberg 1972: 1, 40. It should be noted that NSA whistleblower Edward Snowden, to whose disclosures Chap. 11 will refer in more detail, has been labeled "a post-9/11 Ellsberg".).

After the *New York Times* had started publishing the *Pentagon Papers* in 1971 (followed by the *Washington Post*), the Nixon Administration sought a permanent restraining order from the courts, invoking reasons of "national security". When the government's attempt was quashed by the Supreme Court, opinions by the concurring judges emphasized the danger of "perpetuating bureaucratic errors" through secrecy in government.

To protect the values of democratic government, the "informed and critical public opinion" of an "enlightened citizenry" was needed (*Pentagon Papers* 1971: 655, 657). The *New York Times*, in commenting, summarized the decision to the effect "that when the Government has been devious with the people, it will find no constitutional sanction for its efforts to enforce concealment by censorship" (*Pentagon Papers* 1971: 650).

Daniel Ellsberg's above-quoted hopes—expressed by him in almost biblical terms (John 8:32)—and the federal judges' dicta encapsulate the case for political science's public engagement to try and avert present trends toward liars' republics.

The case against mendocracy concludes the discussion of basic arguments in favor of political science evolving into a topic-driven discipline committed to help resolving citizens' difficulties over dealing with comprehensive changes. Within that framework, the book now turns to those issues that were identified in Chap. 1 as core themes around which a major part of the profession's research, teaching, and public engagement should henceforth crystallize.

References

APSA [American Political Science Association] 2017: *Statement.* January 30. http://www.apsanet.org/portals/54/goverance/APSA-statement-eo-immigration.pdf, accessed March 23, 2017.

Banducci, Susan/Stevens, Dan (2016): "Myth versus Fact: Are We Living in a Post-Factual Democracy?" In: Daniel Jackson/Einar Thorsen/Dominic Wring (eds.): *EU Referendum Analysis 2016: Media, Voters and the Campaign*, Poole: CSJCC Bournemouth University, 22.

Barnett, Steven (2016): "How Our Mainstream Media Failed Democracy". In: Jackson/Thorsen/Wring (eds.): *EU Referendum Analysis...*, op. cit., 47.

Baron, Thomas (2016): "Vote Leave: Stop Offending Turkish People to Further Your Own Agenda". *Independent,* May 26. http://www.independent.co.uk/voices/vote-leave-stop-offending-turkish-people-to-further-your-own-agenda-a7047836.html, accessed Feb. 23, 2017.

Blair, Tony (2002): "Foreword to the Dossier on Iraq", Sept. 24. https://www.theguardian.com/world/2002/sep/24/Iraq.speeches, accessed March 13, 2017.

Bloomberg (2016): "The Voters Who Gave Trump the White House". November 9. https://www.bloomberg.com/politics/graphics/2016-how-trump-won, accessed Feb. 23, 2017.

78   R. EISFELD

Berry, Mike (2016): "Understanding the Role of the Mass Media in the EU Referendum". In: Jackson/Thorsen/Wring (eds.): *EU Referendum Analysis...*, op. cit., 14.

Boffey, Daniel/Helm, Toby (2016): "Vote Leave Embroiled in Race Row over Turkey Security Threat Claims". *Guardian*, May 21. https://www.theguardian.com/politics/2016/may/21/vote-leave-prejudice-turkey-eu-security-threat, accessed Feb. 23, 2017.

Center for Public Integrity (2008): *Iraq: The War Card—False Pretenses*. https://www.publicintegrity.org/2008/01/23/5641/false-pretenses, accessed March 11, 2017.

Chilcot, Sir John (2016): *Statement*. July 6. http://www.iraqinquiry.org/uk/media/247010/2016-09-06-sir-john-chilcots-public-statement.pdf, accessed March 13, 2017.

Cillizza, Chris (2017): "Donald Trump's Streak of Falsehoods Now Stands at 33 Days". *Washington Post*, February 21. https://www.washingtonpost.com/news/the-fix/wp/2017/02/21/donald-trumps-unbroken-streak-of-falsehoods-now-stands-at-33-days/?utm_term=.688213b2fea2, accessed Feb. 23, 2017.

Congressional Committees Investigating the Iran-Contra Affair (1987): *Majority Report (Findings and Conclusions)*, November 18. https://www.brown.edu/Research/Understanding_the_Iran_Contra_Affair/h-themajorityreport.php, accessed March 11, 2017.

Coppins, McKay (2017): "'He Is Going to Test Our Democracy as It Has Never Been Tested'". *The Atlantic*, January 17, 2017. https://www.theatlantic.com/politics/archive/2017/01/john-dean-interview/513215, accessed March 15, 2017.

Corrigan, Phil (2017): "Will Brexit Be a Key Issue for Voters in the Stoke-on-Trent Central By-Election?". *Stoke Sentinel*, February 17. http://www.stokesentinel.co.uk/people/PhilCorrigan/profile.html, accessed Feb. 19, 2017.

Crines, Andrew S. (2016): "The Rhetoric of the EU Referendum Campaign." In: Jackson/Thorsen/Wring (eds.): *EU Referendum Analysis...*, op. cit., 61.

Culloty, Eileen (2016): "After Chilcot, Remember the Media's Propaganda War". *FuJo Institute for Future Media & Journalism*, July 8. www.fujomedia.en/chilcot-news-media, accessed March 15, 2017.

Dale, Daniel/Talaga, Tanya (2016): "Donald Trump: The Unauthorized Database of False Things". Toronto Star, November 4. https://www.thestar.com/news/world/uselection/2016/11/04/donald-trump-the-unauthorized-database-of-false-things.html, accessed Feb. 16, 2017.

Drumheller, Tyler (with Elaine Monaghan, 2006): *On the Brink: An Insiders Account of How the White House Compromised American Intelligence*. New York: Carroll & Graf.

Edwards, Jim (2016): "'Not an Accurate Description of the Intelligence': What the Chilcot Report Says About Whether Blair Lied About WMD". *Business Insider Deutschland*, July 6. http://www.businessinsider.de/iraq-qar-chilcot-report-did-tony-blair-lie-about-wmd-2016-7?r=UK&IR=T.

Ellsberg, Daniel (1972): *Papers on the War*. New York: Simon & Schuster Pocket Books.

Etzioni, Amitai (2017): "What We Need Is A Committee For The Defense Of Democracy". *Huffington Post*, February 23. http://www.huffingtonpost.com/entry/needed-the-committee-for-the-defense-of-democracy_us_58ac5ef1e4b029c1d1f88f0d, accessed March 23, 2017.

European Parliament (2017): "MEPs Call For EU-Wide Protection For Whistle-Blowers", February 14. http://www.europarl.europa.eu/news/en/news-room/20170210IPR61823/meps-call-for-eu-wide-protection-for-whistle-blowers, accessed March 24, 2017.

Flinders, Matthew (2016): "Post-Truth, Post-Political, Post-Democracy...". Sir Bernard Crick Centre, July 3. www.crickcentre.org/blog/post-truth-post-political-post-democracy, accessed March 23, 2017.

Goodwin, Matthew/Milazzo, Caitlin (2017): "Taking Back Control? Investigating the Role of Immigration in the 2016 Vote for Brexit". *British Journal of Politics and International Relations*, Vol. 19, 450-464.

Grynbaum, Michael (2017): "Trump Calls the News Media the 'Enemy of the American People'". *New York Times*, February 17. https://www.nytimes.com/2017/02/17/business/trump-calls-the-news-media-the-enemy-of-the-people.html, accessed March 17, 2017.

Halberstam, David (1993 [¹1972]): *The Best and the Brightest*. New York: Ballantine Books.

Hersh, Seymour M. (1990): "The Iran-Contra Committees: Did They Protect Reagan?", *New York Times Magazine*, April 29, 46-47, 61-67. http://www.nytimes.com/1990/04/29/magazine/the-iran-contra-committees-did-they-protect-reagan.html?pagewanted=all, accessed March 11, 2017.

Kessler, Glenn (2017): "100 Days of Trump Claims". *Washington Post*, February 21. https://www.washingtonpost.com/news/fact-checker/wp/2017/02/21/100-days-of-trump-claims/?utm_term=.bea791697a98, accessed Feb. 23, 2017.

Martin, Kingley (1953): *Harold Laski (1893-1950). A Biographical Memoir*. London: Victor Gollancz.

Open EU Referendum Letter (2016): "Both Remain and Leave Are Propagating Falsehoods at Public Expense". *Telegraph*, June 14. http://www.telegraph.co.uk/opinion/2016/06/13/letters-both-remain-and-leave-are-propagating-falsehoods-at-publ/, accessed March 18, 2017.

Oreskes, Naomi/Conway, Eric M. (2012): *Merchants of Doubt*. London. Bloomsbury.

Parry, Katy (2016): "The Toxicity of Discourse: Reflections on UK Political Culture Following the EU Referendum". In: Jackson/Thorsen/Wring (eds.): *EU Referendum Analysis...*, op. cit., 63.

Pentagon Papers (1971): Documents as Published by the *New York Times*. New York: Bantam Books.

Perlstein, Rick (2011): "Inside the GOP's Fact-Free Nation". *Mother Jones*, May/June issue. http://ww.motherjones.com/politics/2011/04/history-political-lying, accessed March 6, 2017.

Renwick, Alan/Flinders, Matthew/Jennings, Will (2016): "Calming the Storm: Fighting Falsehoods, Fig Leaves and Fairy Tales". In: Jackson/Thorsen/Wring (eds.): *EU Referendum Analysis...*, op. cit., 31.

Stone, Jon (2016a): "Nearly Half of Britons Believe Vote Leave's False '£350 Million a Week to the EU' Claim". *Independent*, June 16. http://www.independent.co.uk/news/uk/politics/nearly-half-of-britons-believe-vote-leaves-false-350-million-a-week-to-the-eu-claim-a7085016.html, accessed Feb. 23, 2017.

Stone, John (2016b): "Video Evidence Emerges of Nigel Farage Pledging EU Millions for NHS Weeks Before Brexit Vote". *Independent*, June 25. http://www.independent.co.uk/news/uk/politics/brexit-eu-referendum-nigel-farage-nhs-350-million-pounds-live-health-service-u-turn-a7102831.html, accessed Feb. 23, 2017.

Trent, John E. (2015): *Harper's Canada*. Self-Published.

UK Statistics Authority (2016): *Statement on the Use of Official Statistics on Contributions to the European Union*. May 27. https://www.statisticsauthority.gov.uk/news/uk-statistics-authority-statement-on-the-use-of-official-statistics-on-contributions-to-the-european-union/, accessed Feb. 23, 2017.

PART II

Issue Areas

CHAPTER 7

Affirming Ethno-Cultural Diversity, Avoiding Tribalized Segmentation

Twenty-First-Century Political Science and the Politics of Recognition

Due to civil wars, to social plight and economic globalization, refugee and labor migration continue to be on the increase. Both for the recipient societies' minorities and for their hitherto culturally privileged majorities—the latter confronted with the challenge of accepting increasing heterogeneity—recourse to ethnicity has served as a source of social identification. Demonstrating an awareness of linkages between economic and cultural inequality and power, political science needs to advance narratives which promote mutual "recognition" and tolerance, rather than separation and conflict.

When American economist/sociologist Jeremy Rifkin contended a decade and a half ago that the European Dream was "eclipsing" the American Dream, he added a warning: Agreeing with numerous other analysts, he identified a European "immigrant dilemma" which might impair the dream and even "undo" Europeanization (Rifkin 2004: 247, 250).

Rifkin, who belongs among the widely visible public intellectuals discussed in Chap. 4, has written profusely on change—mainly on changes affecting the economy and the labor force. The American Dream was defined by him as the classical upward mobility story ("from rags to riches"), suffused with material self-interest, work ethic, individual success in the marketplace, and unilateral exercise of power. In contrast, Rifkin described the European Dream as centering on quality of life, social

© The Author(s) 2019
R. Eisfeld, *Empowering Citizens, Engaging the Public,*
https://doi.org/10.1007/978-981-13-5928-6_7

83

capital, sustainable development, and global cooperation (Rifkin 2004: XII, 3, 266, 383).

Europe's "immigrant dilemma" was spelled out by Rifkin in political and demographic terms:

- On the one hand, Europe's fertility rates are the lowest "of any region in the world", and the continent's population is aging fast. According to projections, the demographic situation is bound to drastically affect, within the next 30 years, Europe's global economic competitiveness, tax revenue, and welfare—foremost retirement—budgets. Without strong immigration, Rifkin argued, the European project would "die" (Rifkin 2004: 254, 255).
- On the other hand, as amply illustrated by examples (Germany, the United Kingdom) in this book's preceding chapters, resentment toward immigrants has been growing throughout Europe. "Whether justified or not, many—not all—Europeans feel beleaguered by immigration, and their angst is not likely to abate anytime soon" (Rifkin 2004: 252, 255).

The economic—and socio-political—future of the United States is no less "tied to nonwhites" (Maharidge [2]1999: 48), even if in a somewhat different manner:

- Due to the birth, immigration, and workforce participation rates of Hispanics (Latinos), the composition of the US labor force is projected to change "dramatically" over the next decades: By 2050, the non-Hispanic whites' share is expected to drop around 50%, while the Hispanic share will grow to one quarter (Lee and Mather 2008: 6).
- Among the US working class, defined for statistical purposes as working people with less than a bachelor's degree and presently constituting about two-thirds of the civilian labor force, the shift will occur even earlier: The "browning of the working class", with "people of color" becoming a majority and once again driven by Hispanics, is projected to happen by 2032. The cohort including workers aged 25 to 34 years should make the transition three more years earlier (Wilson 2016: 3, 7).

There has been anti-immigrant backlash in the United States, particularly in the Latino context (Abrajano and Hajnal 2015: 17/18, 152/153).

That backlash did not start just recently, and it did not merely take the form of Donald Trump's campaign rhetoric, or of a number of voting patterns that contributed to giving him the presidency. With a succession of citizen-generated initiatives, multiethnic California led the way from the late 1970s to the mid-1990s. That statement refers to Propositions 13 (tax rollback), 184 ("three-strikes-and-you're-out"), 187 (illegal immigrants ineligible for public benefits), 209 (ending affirmative action in state government), and 227 (English-only).

However, Proposition 187 was found unconstitutional five years later. And by 2016, Proposition 58 was passed, allowing for bilingual education again. The continuing change in the composition of the state's population, Hispanics' increasing political mobilization, plus a growing realization of the extent the immigrant workforce contributes to California's economic performance played a role in Proposition 227's repeal.

Fear and resentment did not simply disappear, however; to a considerable extent, they have "move[d] east" in the country (Early and Richman 2016). And indicators continue to reflect significant economic inequalities between ethnic groups. The Economic Policy Institute (a think tank focusing on the needs of low- and middle-income workers in economic policy discussions), which published the above-quoted report on the changing ethnic composition of the US working class, has emphasized a need for reforms not merely with regard to the criminal justice system—a subject earlier touched upon in this book—but also in the fields of early childhood education, higher minimum wages, and equal pay for equal work (Wilson 2016: 1). By 2015, one-in-five blacks and less than one-in-six Latinos, but two-in-five whites of age 25–29 had completed four years of college. Unemployment rates among Latinos were almost 1.5 times, among blacks more than double the rate for white Americans. Hispanic households were twice, black Americans almost three times as likely to live in poverty as non-Hispanic white households, respectively, white Americans (US Congress 2015a: 1–3, 2015b: 1, 4/5). De facto housing and educational segregation directed at Hispanics, if less visible, have additionally been emerging as a sustained pattern (Santiago 1996: 131, 151).

During 1968, the National Advisory Commission on Civil Disorders had characterized racial—black—ghettos as an "environmental jungle", with a prevailing "culture of poverty" that resulted from "unemployment and family disorganization". The Commission also concluded that white society was "deeply implicated in the ghetto. White institutions created it, white institutions maintain it, and white society condones it" (NAC 1968:

2, 262). Such entrenched structures may take generations to cede to changes, even if political mobilization had carried, by 2017, one black US President and, among members of the 115th Congress, 4 Hispanic, 3 Afro-American Senators, 46 black, and 34 Latino Representatives into office.

It would be difficult to ignore the racist legacy of the United States, deriving from slavery and from the country's nineteenth century wars of conquest against Mexico and Spain. Europe, however, displays no less ugly legacies, stemming either from Western Europe's colonial past or from East-Central Europe's ethnically grounded varieties of nationalism which came into their own between the two world wars. During the 1970s, ethnicity turned into a renewed source of potential conflicts, as an increasing number of individuals in many countries began to insist again on the "salience of ethnic-based"—as against class-based, "which of course continue to exist"—forms of social identification (Glazer and Moynihan 1975: 3, 7). Now, with social inequalities and economic insecurities (subject of Chap. 9) mounting in the already multiethnic, multireligious, multicultural societies which immigration is continuing to pluralize further, ethnicity is being rediscovered on an even vaster scale as a source of identity, of imagined "certainty in an uncertain world" (Durando 1993: 26).

In Central-East Europe, "virtually all aspects of the transition from Communism to democracy" displayed "ethno-cultural dimensions which cannot be ignored" (Kymlicka 2001: XII). Most conspicuous among these, of course, were the decade-spanning civil wars in Serbia and Croatia which after 1991 shocked the world with their levels of brutality. The atrocities of "ethnic cleansing" dramatically disproved the hopes pronounced a decade and a half earlier, when cautious optimism in assessing societal levels of toleration had still seemed indicated: "A multi-lingual and multi-ethnic society like Yugoslavia may exhibit considerable frictions between its constituent units, but those frictions will not necessarily threaten the existence of the society itself" (Weale 1985: 26).

Armenia, Georgia, Moldova, Ukraine also experienced ethnically driven conflicts, in which Russia has been intervening and which continue to linger—Karabakh, Abkhazia, South Ossetia, Transnistria, Crimea, the Donbass region. Czechoslovakia, in 1993, split over the question how to satisfy the demands of the Slovaks as the largest minority group. Slovakia's population, for its part, includes sizable Hungarian and Roma minorities. The overall Central-East European situation has been summed up as follows:

While the numerical proportion of the region's ethno-cultural minorities has considerably declined since the 1930s, the social, economic and political problems associated with their existence have not abated proportionally (Liebich 2002: 117).

Not just in Central-East Europe, or in the United States, but also in Western Europe ethnic and cultural heterogeneity has of course long predated the onset of recent migratory movements. From the 1960s, West European governments for decades failed to depart from piecemeal responses and to pursue any consistent national program of integrating refugees and immigrant workers. A variety of country-specific barriers—including a legacy of colonialism for the Netherlands, France, and the United Kingdom—impeded, and due to their long-term effects continues to hamper, a politics of effective inclusion. Several major examples will be briefly reviewed:

- In Belgium and (West) Germany, immigrant workers from Southern Europe, North Africa and Turkey were imported by the millions under bilateral blanket agreements during the 1960s. Due to high birth rates and increasing settlement of family members, their numbers continued to increase. Legal traditions of citizenship based on ethnicity (*ius sanguinis*), implying national self-definition as a community of descent, worked to obstruct the development of concepts both for a long-term immigration policy and for integrating those foreigners already in place.

In Belgium, changes toward replacing ethnicity by the birthplace principle (*ius soli*) were introduced in 1984. As regards implementation of succeeding policies, however, the characterization "laissez-faire" by analysts keeps cropping up, resulting in educational segregation, rising poverty and youth unemployment rates. Particularly in the Brussels region, second or third generation immigrants "face many of the same socioeconomic challenges their parents faced in the 1960s and '70s, only now with an increased sense of pessimism" (Williams et al. 2016).

In Germany, successive conservative-liberal governments continued to insist that Germany was "not a country of immigration". The obstinately maintained tradition of *ius sanguinis* contributed to the afore-mentioned wave of post-unification xenophobic violence in the early 1990s. After the advent of the red-green coalition government in 1998, more liberal citizenship legislation was introduced, but became a sharply divisive issue, until a watered-down law substituting *ius sanguinis* by *ius soli* went into effect.

- In France, with a Muslim population of around 10%—under French *laicité* laws, no official numbers are available—an estimated 30–40% of prison inmates are Muslims. (Bowman [2017]. Bowman directs the Adam Smith Institute, a London-based think tank. The prodigious figure of 70%, which has been widely reported—see, e.g., Moore [2008]—is most probably false.) The disproportionate representation among incarcerated persons closely resembles that of African-Americans in the United States, who make up 12% of the general, but 35% of the prison population, with "more young black men in prison than in college" (Sagan 1997: 207). In 2015, French Prime Minister Manuel Valls castigated "territorial, social, ethnic apartheid" in the country. Referring to the suburban "ghettos" and the "stigma" of their inhabitants, he contended that "social misery" was augmented by "daily discrimination because of surname, or color of skin, or even being a woman" (Valls 2015).

Ghettoization—stigmatization—discrimination: No social scientist could have used more precise terms than the head of the French government. The diagnosis refers to the concentrations of immigrants in the *cités HLM*—large rent-controlled concrete housing complexes in the metropolitan suburbs (*banlieues*). In these segregated communities, poverty—not least due to low school achievement and high youth unemployment rates—and an embittered sense of exclusion, particularly among young men, more often than not continue to prevail. Subsequent to Algeria's achievement of independence in 1962, but also due to favorable economic circumstances in France, hundreds of thousands of immigrants had arrived from the Maghreb states. Initially lodged in shantytowns, they and their families increasingly (were) moved to the *habitations à loyer modéré (HLM)* constructed en masse since the mid-1950s.

When immigrants were the first to become unemployed during the 1970s severe recession, the *cités HLM* started to evolve from symbols of modern building into underprivileged areas (Tissot 2008: 2). In spite of recurrent riots—the most severe in 2005, resulting in the proclamation of a national state of emergency—neither comprehensive nor sustained public programs have effectively addressed the underlying pattern of ethnic discrimination, including often-reported police harassment.

- In the Netherlands, post-World War II immigration flows during both the 1950s and the 1970s originated from Indonesia (formerly Dutch East Indies), Surinam, and the Netherlands Antilles, during the 1960s and 1970s from Morocco and Turkey under bilateral labor recruiting agreements resembling those concluded by Belgium and West Germany. The immigrants encountered the complex social and political arrangements of Dutch group-based accommodation, which had evolved over many decades. The main segments of that pillarized (*verzuilt*) system—which started to come apart after the 1960s due to decreasing importance of traditional cleavages, but of whose attitudes and procedures many would seem to have per-sisted—were Protestants, Catholics, Social Democrats, and Liberals.

Each involved group, enjoying considerable autonomy in the management of its internal affairs, had its own political parties, trade unions and other associations, schools and universities, radio stations, and newspapers. Proportional standards in political representation, civil service appointments, and allocation of financial resources figured prominently as additional "consociational" features. So did elite predominance, the arcane character of political negotiations—and a large measure of political immobilism (Lijphart 1968: 111, 129, 131), which has been identified as "the gravest problem" (Lijphart 1977: 51): Similar to Germany, but for different reasons, it took Dutch governments until 1998 to acknowledge that the Netherlands were a country of immigration (van Meeteren et al. 2013: 114, 118).

Inspired by the traditions of *verzuiling*, Dutch immigrant policy emphasized "self-organization" and "education in minorities' own languages" through establishment of Muslim (and Hindu) schools, association-building and "political consultation facilities for migrant communities". However, due to the fragmentation of these communities, plus the policy's failure after the 1970s economic downturn to meet problems of increasing immigrant joblessness—in particular, of youth unemployment—the envisaged Muslim "pillar" that might have functioned as an effective partner in the system, failed to materialize (van Meeteren et al. 2013: 118).

90   R. EISFELD

Both the bitterness of second-generation Muslims, feeling deprived of promised equal opportunities, and Dutch resistance to multicultural approaches began to intensify. The murder, by a Moroccan-Dutch Muslim, of film director and vehement Islam-critic Theo van Gogh in 2004 and death threats against his collaborator, Somali-born feminist Ayaan Hirsi Ali (who, after a prolonged controversy about the validity of her Dutch citizenship, left the Netherlands for the United States), had a particularly detrimental impact in fueling a "culture of distrust" among the Dutch majority. The ensuing political polarization changed integration policy "severely", grounding it in a pronouncedly "assimilistic" approach (van Meeteren et al. 2013: 118, 119).

- In the United Kingdom, post-World War II decolonization and favorable labor market conditions attracted hundreds of thousands of immigrants from India, Pakistan, Bangladesh, and the West Indies. As Commonwealth citizens, they enjoyed unrestricted entry, until the British Nationality Act of 1981—foreshadowed by the Commonwealth Immigrants Act of 1962—created a distinct British citizenship (Voicu 2009: 73/74). During subsequent decades, the complete eviction of Indians from Uganda and the civil war in Somalia brought more Asians and Africans to England. High unemployment, poverty, urban deprivation, and perceived police harassment sparked recurrent, often severe racial rioting across the country during the late 1950s, much of the 1980s and the early 2000s. Political responses included increasingly restrictive immigration and asylum laws, on the one hand, and repeated anti-discriminatory race relations and police accountability legislation, on the other hand. Still, Muslims who make up not quite 5% of the England/Wales population, presently account for 14.4% of prison inmates (Shaw 2015).

Following the 2004 enlargement of the European Union by admitting Poland, Hungary, the Czech Republic, Slovakia, and four more Baltic/Balkan countries, labor migration to the United Kingdom from Central-East Europe surged (as it did, but less so, to the Netherlands). Widespread perceptions that these immigrants were reducing the wages and job chances of British-born workers contradicted empirical evidence (Wadsworth et al. 2016: 1; passim). Fueled by the "Leave" campaign, concerns over immigrants nevertheless contributed massively—as was demonstrated in Chap. 6—to the result of the Brexit referendum.

To sum up: Quite evidently, immigration has its political, its economic, and its cultural sides. There is a need that cannot be emphasized strongly enough, for coherent and consistent programs on each level to be discussed, enacted, and evaluated, which tie in with measures on every other level. A few selected instances from each field must suffice to indicate the extent and character of the issues to which political scientists should accord high priority.

POLITICS

- As illustrated by "problem" boroughs in every single European country briefly examined above (and by additional riots in several), *the local—communal—level* is the level which largely decides on the success or failure of integration—while immigrant policy is often "determined and funded at the national level" (OECD 2006: 11). Rather than top-down policies, integration pacts between federal, state (province), and local agencies seem strongly indicated. (In a later chapter, the urban level will also prove pivotal for climate change, i.e. low-carbon, development policies.)

Political scientists, if not entire departments, should go public with proposals for such pacts, whose implementation they would be prepared to accompany and to evaluate. The pacts would provide federal/state funds to establish local structures and appoint competent local personnel for providing advice, support, and mentoring in the fields of social assistance, housing, schooling, and labor market access. They would mandate the development of round-table concertation and cooperation procedures involving—along with local and regional authorities and migrants—native-born citizens, local volunteers, school boards, religious leaders (both native-born and immigrant), trade unions, Chambers of Commerce and local employers (see also below), NGOs including possible nascent immigrant associations (see also OECD 2006: 12/13). Competently staffed committees might, in frequent meetings, address specific economic and cultural issues.

Integration pacts could, in short, be designed to (re-)introduce communal social capital: goodwill, reciprocity, trust. "Mingling" on every level, arriving not only at "mixed" schooling, but also at "mixed" housing, should figure among the foremost goals.

92   R. EISFELD

- A necessary corollary consists in robust, resolutely enforced legal guarantees against discriminatory treatment in the public and private spheres. "Universal rights", as Eleanor Roosevelt (who chaired the United Nations Commission authoring the 1948 Universal Declaration of Human Rights) reminded every new generation, begin in "the world of the individual person: the neighborhood he lives in; the school or college he attends; the factory, farm or office where he works" (Roosevelt 1948). Everyday discriminatory practices, particularly in the treatment of adolescent job applicants from immigrant families, ought to be included regularly in the agenda of integration pact concertation talks. They should additionally be discussed on an equally regular basis between national governments, employers' associations, trade unions, and the CEOs of large business corporations. Again, political science should provide support by empirical studies, recommendations, and monitoring programs.
- Robert Peel, in the early nineteenth century, conferred the assignment on the newly established London Police Force ("bobbies") to prevent crime and disorder by "secur[ing] public respect" and the public's willing cooperation. Only the minimum degree of physical force was to be used, and service offered to all members of society "without regard to their race or social standing" (Peel 1829). Evidently, Peel's instructions to the police have acquired a surprising modernity—even timelessness—under circumstances vastly different from those of his period. Building the sort of consensual ties between police and the citizens' community regardless of "race or social standing", which Peel considered imperative—*and in whose favor political scientists ought to argue*—would require today that police forces develop intercultural "literacy" (Pickering et al. 2008: 102, 108), and that their ethnic composition should at least resemble that of the various local communities. This means that they would need to include a "sufficient" number of officers with minority—immigrant—roots *on every hierarchical level*.

The latter principle's importance was recognized when the Northern Ireland peace process was negotiated: For reducing possible future bias toward Protestants, 50% of the province's police officers were to be recruited from Catholic and other confessions. A single figure, however, should suffice to indicate the magnitude of the present task: According to a report by the British Parliament's Home Affairs Committee, the United

Kingdom's police would need to recruit 17,000 officers with minority roots over the next decade to be representative of the British population's composition expected for 2024 (Evans 2015). Ethnic minorities now make up 5.5% of British police officers, but 14% of the UK population (House of Commons 2016: 3, 4). Ratios in the Netherlands are not too dissimilar: Ethnic minorities represented 7% of the Dutch police force by 2010, but 21.4% of Dutch society in 2014 (Çankaya 2015: 389). For France, the past efforts at hiring officers from ethnic minorities have been characterized as mere "half-measures" (Hargreaves 2004: 238).

Against that not-too promising backdrop, political scientists should urge to further proceed from the awareness that it would be "extremely shortsighted" to ignore the effect that the police have "on public attitudes toward law, government, force, arms, corruption, and civic responsibility." Indeed, as has been emphasized by a preeminent scholar in the field of policing research, "the police, of all criminal justice agencies, are the most pervasive and influential" (Bayley 1977: 234). The issue will resurface below in the chapter on counter-terrorism and civil liberties.

CULTURE

- It is now generally recognized that obligatory training in the immigration country's official language, including tests within determined periods, is indispensable for providing immigrants with meaningful work and life perspectives. It is less often realized that acquiring bilingual capability constitutes—and should be emphasized as such— an enormous step toward reconciling acculturation with the continuing expression of cultural peculiarities.

An equally compulsory civics integration program is also increasingly acknowledged as a crucial supplement of language training. The program's courses should stress

- constitutional values, rights, and responsibilities;
- ways of active social and political citizen involvement;
- the ethnic, cultural, and religious composition of the receiving society, along with the importance of respect and toleration in relations between these groups.

Once more, political science may contribute by suggesting such programs *in accordance with the principles of civics education (emphasizing citizenship rather than government)* laid out in Chap. 5.

- The general speeding-up of social and cultural change noted in Chap. 3 has also included religious creeds. "Both the factual presence and the awareness of religious diversity will continue to grow for an unforeseeable length of time" (Schmidt-Leukel 2016: 7). Claims by religious minorities to be granted special treatment, avoidance of the discrimination of certain lifestyles by specific religions, effective guarantees for individuals to "opt out" by adopting ideas and practices running counter to their religious and cultural heritage rank among the many thorny issues on which politics and political science will have to focus much greater attention than presently.

ECONOMICS

- As evidenced by earlier parts of this chapter, immigrant unemployment, particularly youth unemployment, have emerged as a common scourge across Western Europe. In an area where cultural habits and work situation unavoidably intersect, programs are urgently required for flexibly integrating language training, vocational education, on-the-job training and upskilling measures (see already OECD 2008: 252). The importance of the concertation procedures outlined above in matters relating to employment—not least regarding everyday discriminatory practices—can hardly be overemphasized.
- Deliberately diversifying hiring procedures for police officers, as discussed above, may be subsumed under affirmative action programs. Affirmative action has served as an instrument "to catch up", to advance education and employment opportunities for members of groups which have been in the past discriminated against because of gender, ethnic origin, or religion. They have come to be viewed as "disadvantaged" because, as a consequence of discriminatory university admission and hiring practices, they have been "underrepresented in significant positions in society" (Crosby 1994: 15). In a political science sense, such practices have resulted from inequalities in political resources—a topic which will resurface in Chap. 8—resulting in "power asymmetries" (Eberhardt and Fiske 1994: 204).

Affirmative action has been most widely practiced in Canada—where it includes individuals of indigenous descent—and the United States. In the latter country, it has been attacked politically and in the courts as alleged "reverse discrimination". On a limited scale—frequently on local levels, "narrowly targeted as to job and group" (de Vries and Pettigrew 1994: 183)—affirmative action programs have also been tried out in the Netherlands. There is a dire need for comparative studies and informed political science discussion of the role which affirmative action elements might possibly play in Western Europe, with reducing youth unemployment as the overriding objective.

Two conclusions seem unavoidable in concluding this chapter:

- West European countries are still in the early stages of developing considered strategies for the societal inclusion of millions of immigrants.
- The United States finds itself on the verge of a probable increase in aggressive anxieties that "threatens ever-greater racial tension" (Abrajano and Hajnal 2015: 21, 216), after the emergence of whites as "the coming minority" will have penetrated the collective consciousness. In its May/June 2017 issue, the influential magazine *Foreign Affairs* printed an unusually dire warning by three political scientists, two American, one Canadian: "Few democracies have survived transitions in which historically dominant ethnic groups lose their majority status. If American democracy manages to do that, it will prove exceptional indeed" (Mickey et al. 2017: 29).

On both continents, moreover, the political climate has become additionally charged by the threat of further Islamist terrorist acts. Still,

- domestic responses by "sanctuary" cities and counties and by courts to President Trump's successive executive orders introducing travel bans targeted at Muslims,
- no less than the rejection, by voters, of anti-immigration contenders in the 2017 Dutch parliamentary, the 2016 Austrian, and the 2017 French presidential elections

have shown that the impact of xenophobic diatribes, though considerable and frightening, may yet be contained.

96   R. EISFELD

The more pressing is the need for political science to intervene by in-depth studies—normatively driven, empirically grounded—in experiences with immigration and immigration policies, effectively summarized for public debate. Such studies could help to put in a better perspective the plethora of political, economic, and cultural challenges which have emerged across the entire European continent, in the United States, and in Canada. They could, it may be hoped, also help to deal with them more reasonably, more flexibly, more equitably.

The argumentative thrust of these studies ought to be the exact opposite of Samuel Huntington's appeal to anxieties in his "ideological tract" (Etzioni) *Who Are We?* discussed earlier. Huntington, it will be remembered, invoked the "American Creed", which he portrayed as having emerged during the frontier period's "settler society", as a pillar of civilization *that should persist unchanged*, but was now being "undermined" by threatening "Hispanization". In contrast, political science should—on condition that cultural "tribalization" can be avoided (Sartori 1997: 60/61, 62)—endorse the inherent "worth of diversity": cultural "multiplicity" in the sense of a "cross-fertilized" culture as a humane perspective inherent in further change.

REFERENCES

Abrajano, Marisa/Hajnal, Zoltan L. (2015): *White Backlash. Immigration, Race, and American Politics*. Princeton/Oxford: Princeton University Press.

Bayley, David H. (1977): "The Limits of Police Reform". In: David H. Bayley (ed.): *Police and Society*, Beverly Hills/London: Sage, 219–236.

Bowman, Sam (2017): "Are 70% of France's Prison Inmates Muslims?" Adam Smith Institute, March 29. https://www.adamsmith.org/blog/are-70-of-frances-prison-inmates-muslims, accessed April 19, 2017.

Çankaya, Sinan (2015): "Diversity Policies Policing Ethnic Minority Police Officers". *European Journal of Policing Studies*, Vol. 2, 383–404.

Crosby, Faye J. (1994): "Understanding Affirmative Action". *Basic and Applied Social Psychology*, Vol. 15, 13–41.

Durando, Dario (1993): "The Rediscovery of Identity". *Telos*, No. 97, 117–144.

Early, David E./Richman, Josh (2016): "Twenty Years After Prop. 187, Attitudes Toward Illegal Immigration Have Changed Dramatically in California." *Mercury News*, November 22. http://www.mercurynews.com/2014/11/22/twenty-years-after-prop-187-attitudes-toward-illegal-immigration-have-changed-dramatically-in-california, accessed April 7, 2017.

Eberhardt, Jennifer L./Fiske, Susan T. (1994): "Affirmative Action in Theory and Practice". *Basic and Applied Social Psychology*, Vol. 15, 201–220.

Evans, Martin (2015): "Police Need to Recruit 17,000 More Black Officers to Reflect Society". *Telegraph*, June 30. http://www.telegraph.co.uk/news/uknews/law-and-order/11707007/Police-need-to-recruit-17000-more-black-officers-to-reflect-society.html, accessed May 1, 2017.

Glazer, Nathan/Moynihan, Daniel P. (eds., 1975): *Ethnicity*. Cambridge/London: Harvard University Press.

Hargreaves, Alec G. (2004): "Half-Measures: Anti-discrimination Policy in France". In: Herride Chapman/Laura L. Frader (eds.): *Race in France*. New York/Oxford: Berghahn Books, 227–245.

House of Commons (2016): *Police Diversity*. Home Affairs Committee, First Report of the Session 2016–17. https://www.publications.parliament.uk/pa/cm201617/cmselect/cmhaff/27/27.pdf, accessed May 4, 2017.

Kymlicka, Will (2001): "Preface". In: Will Kymlicka/Magda Opalski (eds.): *Can Liberal Pluralism Be Exported? Western Political Theory and Ethnic Relations in Eastern Europe*. Oxford: Oxford University Press, XII-XVII.

Lee, Marlene A./Mather, Mark (2008): "U. S. Labor Force Trends." In: *Population Bulletin*, Vol. 63 No. 2 (June), 3–18. http://www.prb.org/pdf08/63.2uslabor.pdf, accessed April 7, 2017.

Liebich, André (2002): "Ethnic Minorities and Long-Term Implications of EU Enlargement". In: Jan Zielonka (ed.): *Europe Unbound*. London: Routledge, 117–136.

Lijphart, Arend (1968): *The Politics of Accommodation*. Berkeley/Los Angeles: California University Press.

Lijphart, Arend (1977): *Democracy in Plural Societies*. New Haven/London: Yale University Press.

Maharidge, Dale (^{2}1999 [^{1}1996]): *The Coming White Minority. California, Multiculturalism, and America's Future*. New York: Vintage Books.

Meeteren, Masja van/Pol, Sanne van de et al. (2013): "Destination Netherlands: History of Immigration and Immigration Policy in the Netherlands". In: Judy Ho (ed.): *Immigrants*. New York, Nova, 113–170.

Mickey, Robert/Levitsky, Steven/Way, Lucan Ahmad (2017): "Is America Still Safe for Democracy?" *Foreign Affairs*, Vol. 96 No. 3, 20–29.

Moore, Molly (2008): "In France, Prisons Filled With Muslims". *Washington Post*, April 29. http://www.washingtonpost.com/wpdyn/content/article/2008/04/28/AR20080428025602.html?sid=ST2008042802857, accessed April 19, 2017.

NAC [National Advisory Commission on Civil Disorders] (1968): *Report*.

OECD (2006): *From Immigration to Integration. Local Solutions to a Global Challenge*. Paris: Organisation for Economic Cooperation and Development, Local Economic and Employment Development.

OECD (2008): *Jobs for Immigrants*. Vol. 2: *Labour Market Integration in Belgium, France, the Netherlands, and Portugal*. Paris: Organisation for Economic Cooperation and Development.

Peel, Robert (1829): *Sir Robert Peel's Principles of Law Enforcement*. https://www.durham.police.uk/About-Us/Documents/Peels_Principles_Of_Law_Enforcement.pdf, accessed May 2, 2017.

Pickering, Sharon/McCulloch, Jude/Wright-Neville, David (2008): "Counter-Terrorism Policing: Towards Social Cohesion." *Crime, Law and Social Change*, Vol. 50, 91–109.

Rifkin, Jeremy (2004): *The European Dream*. Cambridge: Polity Press.

Roosevelt, Eleanor (1948): "Where Do Universal Rights Begin?" https://www.thoughtco.com/eleanor-roosevelt-universal-declaration-of-human-rights-3528095, accessed April 26, 2017.

Sagan, Carl (1997): *Billions and Billions*, New York: Random House.

Santiago, Anna M. (1996): "Trends in black and Latino Segregation in the Post-Fair Housing Era: Implications for Housing Policy". *Berkeley La Raza Law Journal*, Vol. 9, 131–153.

Sartori, Giovanni (1997): "Understanding Pluralism." *Journal of Democracy*, Vol. 8, 58–69.

Schmidt-Leukel, Perry (2016): "Religious Pluralism in Thirteen Theses". *Modern Believing*, Vol. 57, 5–18.

Shaw, Danny (2015): "Why the Surge in Muslim Prisoners?" *BBC News*, March 11. www.bbc.com/news/uk-31794599, accessed April 20, 2017.

Tissot, Sylvie (2008): "'French Suburbs': A New Problem or a New Approach to Social Exclusion?" *Working Paper Series* # 160 (10 pp.), Center for European Studies, https://halshs.archives-ouvertes.fr/halshs-00285025/document, accessed April 20, 2017.

U.S. Congress (2015a): Joint Economic Committee, Democratic Staff: *Economic Challenges in the Black Community*. April 14. https://www.jec.senate.gov/public/_cache/files/eb7a5e6e-db59-452e-8736-0603bef2d2c8/economic-challenges-in-the-african-american-community-4-14.pdf, accessed May 8, 2017.

U.S. Congress (2015b): Joint Economic Committee, Democratic Staff: https://www.jec.senate.gov/public/_cache/files/96c9cbb5-d206-4dd5-acca-955748e97fd1/jec-hispanic-report-final.pdf, accessed May 8, 2017.

Valls, Manuel (2015): "Manuel Valls évoque 'un apartheid territorial, social, ethnique' en France." *Le Monde*, January 20, http://www.lemonde.fr/politique/article/2015/01/20/pour-manuel-valls-il-existe-un-apartheid-territorial-social-ethnique-en-france_4559714_823448.html, accessed April 20, 2017.

Voicu, Anca (2009: "Immigration and Immigration Policies in UK." *Romanian Journal of European Affairs*, Vol. 9, No. 2, 71–86.

Vries, Sjiera de/Pettigrew, Thomas F. (1994): "A Comparative Perspective on Affirmative Action: *Positieve Actie* in The Netherlands". *Basic and Applied Social Psychology*, Vol. 15, 179–199.

Wadsworth, Jonathan/Dhingra, Swati et al. (2016): *Brexit and the Impact of Immigration on the UK*. London School of Economics, Centre for Economic Performance. http://cep.lse.ac.uk/pubs/download/brexit05.pdf, accessed April 20, 2017.

Weale, Albert (1985): "Toleration, Individual Differences, and Respect for Persons". In: John Horton/Susan Mendus (eds.): *Aspects of Toleration*. New York: Methuen, 16–35.

Williams, Aaron/Kaeti Hinck et al. (2016): "How Two Brussels Neighbourhoods Became a 'Breeding Ground' for Terror". *Washington Post*, April 1. https://www.washingtonpost.com/graphics/world/brussels-molenbeek-demographics/, accessed April 19, 2017.

Wilson, Valerie (2016): "People of Color Will Be a Majority of the American Working Class in 2032". Economic Policy Institute, June 9. http://www.epi.org/publication/the-changing-demographics-of-americas-working-class/, accessed April 7, 2017.

CHAPTER 8

Low Income, Inferior Education

Twenty-First-Century Political Science and Inequality of Political Resources

Unequal social resources, primarily income, wealth, and education, will unavoidably translate into unequal political resources with regard to participatory engagement and control over political agenda-setting, already now pushing democracy toward plutocracy. Reducing such disparities is of prime importance to ensure the accessibility, accountability, and—in the final instance—legitimacy of supposedly "representative" government. Political scientists should join leading economists such as Krugman, Piketty, and Stiglitz in urging tax reform and other policy changes.

As if palpable tendencies toward mendocracy in the United States and the United Kingdom were not enough, a World Bank inequality specialist attested to the former country that it was sliding from democracy toward "plutocracy", for it "empower[s] the rich politically to a much greater extent than the middle class or the poor" (Milanovic 2016: 194, 199). Nota bene, this was written before Donald Trump's cabinet assumed office.

Former lead economist in the World Bank's Research Department for almost two decades, Branko Milanovic contended that the "obsolescent and restrictive nature" of the American political system and its "slant in favor of the rich" would be intensely scrutinized, if the United States were a recent democracy. However, the system's tradition of two centuries

© The Author(s) 2019
R. Eisfeld, *Empowering Citizens, Engaging the Public,*
https://doi.org/10.1007/978-981-13-5928-6_8

101

works as a powerful psychological barrier against such scrutiny (Milanovic 2016: 203).

While the observation certainly holds true, it should first be remembered that the United States did only recently become an unmitigated democracy with full adult suffrage and broad protection of civil and political liberties: The "single-party, authoritarian enclaves" in the states of the former Confederacy, including "significantly unfree civic spheres", were not dismantled until the early 1970s, when the civil rights movement and the federal government "managed to stamp out authoritarianism" in the South (Mickey et al. 2017: 20, 22, 23). The layer of democratic political culture may thus be flimsier than commonly presumed.

A second cultural process, which took place during the same past half century, must be taken into account. Amounting to what has been described as a religious "Southernization" of the United States (Egerton 1974: 195; Shibley 1991: 160, 162), it involved a profound shift in religious dominance from mainline to evangelical Protestantism. During a period when US society combines continuing high religiosity with "discrepancies between rich and poor seldom seen in American history", devout evangelicals, favoring personal piety over social justice, "have not worked to stem the growth of inequality" (Putnam and Campbell 2010: 14–17, 230, 257/258). As a primary impulse, the feeling "of direct personal access to God" (Hofstadter 1966: 55/56) has eclipsed earlier evangelical voices, promoting a more egalitarian society. The same aspiration has caused an increase in number of Bible study groups, whose members presently include around 25% of US adults. Compared to other self-help groups, their focus has been more on members' personal concerns and less on civic engagement (Wuthnow 2004: 99). That attitude may, once again, *not* provide the most reliable bulwark against a slide into more profoundly authoritarian patterns of policy-making.

But the straw breaking the camel's back may well be the ongoing "advocacy explosion" (Berry and Wilcox [5rev]2009: 15): the comprehensive replacement, by "professionally led policy advocacy groups", of grass-roots, face-to-face, cross-class associations which had once served as schools for democratic citizenship. As forcefully argued by Theda Skocpol, evangelical Protestants engaging in voluntary associations could be evolving into an atypical species. The rest of civic America is meanwhile transformed into an ensemble of professionally directed groups employing media consultants and pollsters, focused on computer-directed fund-raising from foundations and business elites. Ordinary members may become "a nonlucrative

LOW INCOME, INFERIOR EDUCATION   103

distraction" in a civic world where the wealthiest and best-educated Americans are, again, "much more privileged" and which is, consequently, "very oligarchical" (Skocpol 2004: 105, 133/134, 135).

Quite possibly mutually reinforcing, these trends figure among the key issues which political science needs to explore more fully and to keep in the public focus more consistently. Economists recently writing about growing income inequality, such as Thomas Piketty, have been less reticent than political scientists in affirming "that the risk of a drift toward oligarchy is real and gives little reason for optimism about where the United States is headed" (Piketty 2014: 514). A notable exception is Larry Bartels from Princeton who, in concluding a robust study on America's partisan patterns of income development and equally partisan politics (calling the available evidence "striking and sobering"), not only refrained from mincing words, but added an adequate touch of irony: "Our political system seems to be functioning not as a 'democracy' but as an 'oligarchy'. If we insist on flattering ourselves by referring to it as a democracy, we should be clear that it is a starkly unequal democracy" (Bartels 2008: 287).

Economists Paul Krugman and Joseph Stiglitz, both Nobel Laureates, had preceded both Milanovic and Piketty in arguing along the same lines. The captions of their articles spoke for themselves: "Oligarchy, American Style" (Krugman 2011) and, even more suggestively, "Of the 1%, by the 1%, for the 1%" (Stiglitz 2011). Another decade earlier, political and economic commentator Kevin Phillips had warned that "market theology and unelected leadership" were displacing politics and elections. Either meaningful democratic politics would be brought back to life, or wealth would be likely to cement "plutocracy by some other name" (Phillips 2002: 422). Oligarchy and plutocracy were on their way of establishing themselves as respectable analytical terms for America's possible political future. Stiglitz followed his brief comment with a 2012 book-length study on *The Price of Inequality*, where he stressed that the disproportionate political influence wielded by the top 1% of income earners—mostly corporate executives—was "eviscerating" American democracy (Stiglitz 2012: 136).

Long a political science commonplace, the contention that unequal social resources—such as income, education, and status—translate into unequal political resources has, as will be demonstrated in a moment, recently undergone impressive empirical testing (Solt 2008; Gilens and Page 2014). Against the backdrop of the democratic premise that "adult human beings are entitled to be treated as political equals" (Dahl 2006: 1),

104   R. EISFELD

it follows that the reduction of disparities in control over political resources should be considered of prime importance for ensuring the broad accessibility, accountability, and, in the final instance, legitimacy of supposedly "representative" government.

In contrast, Robert Dahl, writing by the early 1960s, conceded even at the time that the political system offered "unusual" opportunities for "pyramiding" such resources into "a sizable political holding", that is, a structure of influence and power. Dahl did not then seriously question such maldistribution, still holding, as he did, to the belief that "probably no resource is uniformly most effective in American politics" (Dahl 1961: 227; Dahl 1967: 378). Over the subsequent two decades, he and Yale colleague Charles Lindblom would turn more skeptical and radical in their critique of institutional rigidity and political inequality: Indicting egalitarian shortcomings resulting from economic constraints, they came to diagnose a "privileged position of business", and of "corporate executives in particular".

The privilege involved the capacity to either distort public policies, or (should undesirable measures nevertheless be legislated) to contract out from under the effects of unwelcome legislation (Dahl 1982: 40 ss.). Corporate enterprise thus "restrict[s] polyarchal rules and procedures [i.e. those approximating democracy] to no more than a part of government and politics" and "challenge[s] them even there". The role of business, Lindblom concluded, is not merely that of another interest group (Lindblom 1977: 170, 190). By 2006, Dahl classified political inequalities among American citizens as "unacceptably large". And he judged a scenario, which he sketched in some detail, in which political inequality in the United States would further increase substantially, as "rather likely"—even if "not inevitable" (Dahl 2006: 78, 98, 104). A decade later, Milanovic, invoking economic, social, and political factors, much more pessimistically forecast "a 'perfect storm' of rising inequality" for the United States. The political component of the process he described was that advancing concentration of income would further reinforce the political power of the rich, making "pro-poor policy changes in taxation, funding for public education, and infrastructure spending even less likely than before" (Milanovic 2016: 181).

Economic inequality has been rising by bounds in North America and many West European countries during the last decades. In the United States, however, the magnitudes involved have been "enormous", with the United Kingdom "following this trend" (Piketty and Saez 2013: 458,

461; Milanovic 2016: 75/76; Atkinson 2015: 20/21. The late Anthony Atkinson, doyen of inequality studies, was mentor to Thomas Piketty). In France, between 1983 and 2015, 20% of income growth went to the top 1% of the income pyramid; an identical amount accrued to the entire bottom 50%. In Canada, the same 1% took roughly 30% of income gains from 1997 to 2007 (Piketty 2017; Conference Board of Canada 2017). In the United Kingdom, between 1979 and 2007, the top 1% share of the national income went up from 6 to 14.5%, that of the top 0.1% from 1.3 to 6.5%. Over the ten years from 1997 to 2007 alone, income for those 0.1% grew by 64.2%, but by just 7.2% for the bottom 50% (High Pay Commission 2011a: 22, 2011b: 22). The independent UK High Pay Commission commented that "Britain now has a gap between rich and poor that rivals that in some developing nations". At present trends, by 2035, 14% of the national income would accrue to the top 0.1%, a level of disparity last "seen in Victorian England" (High Pay Commission 2011b: 7, 24).

The second part of that late-nineteenth-century period was known in America as the "Gilded Age", and historical comparisons with regard to glaring income inequalities have alluded to the present United States as a "new" or "second" Gilded Age (Krugman 2007; Bartels 2008; Eichler and McAuliff 2011; Beddoes 2012). The "explosion" (Piketty 2014: 294) of inequality in the United States has been demonstrated by a variety of indicators. Robert Dahl chose 1979 and 2000 average income ratios for the *top* 1% and the *bottom* 20% [133:1 as against 189:1] and for the top 100 CEOs vis-à-vis the average worker [39:1 as against over 1000:1] (Dahl 2006: 84). Joseph Stiglitz contrasted 1979 and 2010 average incomes for the *top* 0.1% and the *bottom* 90% [50:1 as against 164:1] (Stiglitz 2012: 294/295 n. 3). Thomas Piketty calculated that the *top* 10% share of national income had "increased from increased from 30 to 35%... in the 1970s to 45–50% in the 2000s—an increase of 15 points" (Piketty 2014: 295). Branko Milanovic noted that, in 2007, 81% of all US stocks were owned by the wealthiest *top* 10% of individuals (Milanovic 2016: 183).

Regarding the political ramifications of escalating economic inequality—hence ever more profoundly skewed income (and wealth) distribution -, two empirical studies by Frederick Solt and by Martin Gilens/Benjamin Page have presented complementary results:

- Due to "declining political engagement of non-affluent citizens with rising inequality", issues "on which a consensus exists among richer individuals, such as redistribution", even if in the interest of poorer citizens, "become increasingly unlikely even to be debated within the political process" (Solt 2008: 57).

- Should majorities of less well-to-do citizens nevertheless arrive at engaging in favor of political change, they are prone to face the problem of limited responsiveness or, more pointedly, of "democracy by coincidence". In America's contemporary political system, "ordinary citizens get what they want from government only when they happen to agree with [economic] elites or [business-oriented] interest groups" (Gilens and Page 2014: 573).

Solt correlated data from the cross-national Luxembourg Income Study (started in 1983; see Buhmann et al. 1988) with material from Eurobarometer and comparable surveys (Solt 2008: 50/51). Breaking down political engagement into the categories of political interest, discussion of political issues, and electoral participation, he tested several theories about possible relationships between economic inequality and citizen engagement in a multilevel model including 22 industrialized democracies. He found the results of his analysis only consistent with the relative power theory, according to which economic inequality "increases the relative power of richer citizens" and thereby "undermines political equality" (Solt 2008: 57).

The Gilens/Page study, which focused on the American political system, was grounded in 20 years' data (1981–2002) from national surveys collecting pro/con responses about proposed policy changes, including income breakdowns for respondents (Gilens and Page 2014: 568). Four theoretical approaches were tested, again in a single statistical model: majoritarian electoral (or median voter) theory, majoritarian interest-group pluralism, biased interest-group pluralism "with an upper-class accent", and economic-elite domination. Results obtained provided "substantial" support in favor of the latter—but not the first—two approaches, both with regard to agenda-setting and shaping policy outcomes on contested issues (Gilens and Page 2014: 565, 576).

This tallies with findings on constituents' political representation by US senators, which Larry Bartels got for the 1989–1994 period. In voting decisions, the views of millions of constituents in the bottom third of the income distribution pyramid "received no weight at all"—which Bartels considered "profoundly troubling"—and the middle third's views "about 50% less" than the upper third's. Bartels concluded that elections "are not forcing elected officials to cater to the policy preferences of the 'median voter'" (Bartels 2008: 253–255, 282, 287).[1] Those works epitomize the chance for a twenty-first-century political science with "a broader conception of practice and purpose", linking "scientific and public credibility" (Isaac 2014: 558). Reviewers attested that Bertels' book was "thoughtful, provocative, analytically rich", "easy to follow", "exemplary" with regard to its "judiciously employed" statistical data, its "balance between not over-reaching and asserting a clear, controversial, important thesis", provoking "the kind of big picture questions with which we need to be engaged" (Shaw 2008: 1; Hochschild 2009: 145). Gilens' and Page's article resulted in a six and a half minutes' TV interview (Isaac 2014: 557): Subsequent to already extended media coverage (*BBC*, *The New Yorker*, *U. S. News and World Report*), the piece was taken up by Comedy Central's award-winning *The Daily Show (DST) With Jon Stuart* (meanwhile *Trevor Noah*). According to 2014 DST ratings, as many as 2.5 million viewers may have watched the talk with the two political scientists.

Restricting the professional and communication skills displayed by Bartels, Gilens et al. to mere analyses of the political price paid for increased economic inequality would constrain our discipline to painting a starkly resigned picture. Rather, political science should devote the same resource-

---

[1] A study entitled: *Systematically Distorted Decisions? Responsiveness in German Politics from 1998-2015*, commissioned by the German Labor and Social Affairs Ministry from the University of Osnabrueck's Center for Research on Democracy and submitted in 2016, found a very similar pattern. Headed by Armin Schäfer, the research team analyzed (a) degrees of support within different social groups for 252 detailed survey questions posed between 1998 and 2013, covering political decisions debated at the time, and (b) whether or not, or to what degree, the policy changes addressed in these questions had been enacted by the German Federal Parliament during the next two to four years. The study's most pertinent result deserves to be quoted in full: "Not only do German citizens with different incomes participate in politics to a very unequal degree, but there is clearly a non-level playing field, to the detriment of the poor, in political decision-making. With that, there is the threat of a vicious circle of unequal participation and unequal responsiveness: Socially disadvantaged groups may find that their concerns get no hearing, and therefore turn their backs on politics—which, consequently, may follow even more the interests of the more affluent" (Elsässer et al. 2016: 43; cf. also 9, 16 ss., 35).—Meant to be included in the German (Grand Coalition) government's *5th Report on Poverty and Wealth*, these findings were watered down or omitted following interdepartmental consultations (for a comparison, see German Federal Government 2017: 46).

108   R. EISFELD

ful approach to the vexing question: Which policies may serve to slow, to stop, even to reverse the present trend?

Such a searching look would entail reaching out for "a renewed and reinvigorated political economy" (Eisfeld 2011: 221), a suggestion that will be pursued here and in Chap. 9, and which Thomas Piketty has backed up by determinedly singling out the term's—and the field's—historical, normative, and individual implications (Piketty 2014: 574/75):

- *Normative* inquiry for institutions and policies designed to attain a better, if not the "good", society remains an indispensable effort—as it does in the present book.
- *History* provides a principal, if imperfect, source of knowledge for attempted policies and their results. The lessons of twentieth-century history, in particular, are of "inestimable" value.
- *Taking a personal stance* "in regard to specific institutions and policies", including involvement in political confrontations, counts among a social scientist's necessary virtues.

As an aside, the current rank of political economy in the context of political studies may be indicated by the differences in members' numbers, which several European Consortium for Political Research (ECPR) Standing Groups have attracted. Established in 1970, ECPR may easily be regarded as the discipline's most important European association in terms of promoting cross-national cooperation. The organization's four dozen and more Standing Groups mostly grew out of workshops or general conferences. According to current figures, Political Economy has a membership of 213. The European Union Group comprises nearly three times that number (575), followed by Gender and Politics (521), Political Parties (471) and International Relations (466). Even Comparative Political Institutions (352) or Elites and Political Leadership (281) have outstripped Political Economy.

Economists cited in this chapter are agreed that no monocausal explanation for increasing income inequality exists. According to Milanovic, an interplay of economic forces and political decisions has been at work; resorting to "naïve 'economicism'" would be misplaced (Milanovic 2016: 73). Stiglitz—who also briefly worked for the World Bank which, like the International Monetary Fund (IMF), he views critically—and Krugman were more peremptory. Acknowledging that market forces "help shape the degree of inequality", Stiglitz contended that "government policies shape those market forces" (Stiglitz 2012: 28). Krugman added an ironical aside when he wrote that "institutions, norms and the political environment" mattered a lot more for the distribution of income "than Economics 101 might lead you to believe" (Krugman 2009: 8).

On the economic side, the most commonly advanced explanations have been (a) accelerating technological change biased in favor of highly skilled (highly paid) jobs and (b) globalization-induced openness for imported low-skilled, low-paid labor, plus for a broadening of international production networks, in practical terms the outsourcing of production (Milanovic 2016: 109/110, 112). Both were rejected by Piketty, because they did not account for national differences. The crucial relationship, according to his contention, is rather that of the average annual rate of return on capital—profits, dividends, interest, rents—and the annual growth rate of the economy: If, for an extended period of time, the former exceeds the latter substantially, past wealth "takes on disproportionate importance", and—in Piketty's restrained language—"the risk of divergence in the distribution of wealth is very high" (Piketty 2014: 25, also 430/431; Pressman 2016: 172/173).

The political side of the process may be conveniently summarized in a single sentence:

> With regard to both redistributive and regulatory functions, governments have been restricting their performance, and pro-market state intervention has been on the increase.

Deregulation will be the subject of Chap. 9. For their impact on increasing inequality, Milanovic pinpointed reductions both of marginal tax rates on the highest incomes and of taxes on capital. Krugman, Stiglitz, and others added the powerful effect of governmental action on the steep decline of trade unions in membership and bargaining strength as another important factor (Milanovic 2016: 107; Krugman 2009: 149–151; Stiglitz 2012: 64/65).

During the Thatcher, Reagan, and Bush II Administrations (late 1970s to early 2000s), marginal rates in the top income tax bracket were successively cut in the United Kingdom from 83 to 40%, and in the United States from 70 to just over 30%. Estate (inheritance) taxes were reduced (UK), or phased out (US), taxes on dividends and capital gains were also lowered. The Reagan and Thatcher governments' responses to the 1981

110 R. EISFELD

air traffic controllers' and the 1984/1985 miners' strikes prefigured the trade unions' subsequent descent in both countries.

Reagan fired over 11,000 controllers—who, it should be noted, were legally prohibited to strike—banning them from federal civil service for life (a ban which would only be lifted by President Clinton 12 years later); their union was decertified by the Federal Labor Relations Authority. Reagan's action, Federal Reserve Board Chair Alan Greenspan remarked, "gave weight to the legal right of private employers, previously not fully exercised, to use their own discretion to both hire and discharge workers" (Greenspan 2003). Within little more than two decades, union membership rates in the United States were halved (20.1% of the labor force in 1983, 10.7% in 2016). In the private sector, union "density" stood at 6.4%, *reduced to pre-New Deal levels.*

During the same period, trade union membership in the United Kingdom fell from 11 to 7 million. Even if the unionization rate—25% of the workforce—compares favorably to that of the United States, the private/public sector ratio just about matches that of the latter country, *meaning that unions are virtually absent from corporate America and corporate Britain.* (For the United States, it should be added that, according to Department of Labor data, they are also *virtually absent from almost the entire South and Southwest.*) The defeat of the miners' strike—which had been called without a previous ballot, and thus was clearly problematic— by Margaret Thatcher's government preceded several increasingly complex strike laws. These stipulated ballots, subjected walkouts to numerous procedural requirements, and made unions liable for unlawful industrial action.

The unions' declining fortunes not merely reduced their economic bargaining power. They also weakened the political and the norm-shaping strength of organized labor.

- Deterioration of union membership has figured as a crucial factor in US minimum wage policies, "contribut[ing] greatly to the decline in the real value of the minimum wage" (Bartels 2008: 226, 240).
- Because unions "mobilize beyond their membership", US 2004 voter turnout of the bottom and the middle third of the income distribution would *each* have increased by 3.5 percentage points, provided union strength had remained at 1964 levels. Turnout of the top third, in contrast, would have expanded by only 2.5% (Leighley and Nagler 2007: 438, 440).

- Culturally, politically, and institutionally embedded norms of equity had, over time, generated a "moral economy" prescribing "the fairness of a standard rate for low-pay workers and the injustice of unchecked earnings for managers". Promoted by organized labor across countries, that moral economy has gradually eroded with union membership. The process included a "deterioration of the labor market as a political institution", contributing significantly to the rise in earnings' inequality (Western and Rosenfeld 2011: 517–519, 528, 533).

Unsurprisingly, "revitalizing unions"—easier said than done—figures high on the list of measures proposed by Krugman, Milanovic, Piketty, and Stiglitz to redress escalating inequality. Further mutually supportive policy options which have been suggested include a progressive tax on capital levied, for a start, on regional levels—with a global tax as a reference point; ensuring high standards of international financial transparency and introducing an array of additional laws aimed at curbing excesses of the banking sector; targeting a "more widely spread ownership of capital" by combining high inheritance taxes with corporate taxes favoring a distribution of shares to lower- and middle-income employees; raising the quality of schools and colleges through increased public funding to move toward equalizing qualified secondary and higher education (Krugman 2009: 263; Milanovic 2016: 221/222; Piketty 2014: 486/487; ch. 15; Stiglitz 2012: ch. 10).

None of these policies may be easily implemented. The most far-reaching proposal, a global tax on capital, was qualified by its author as "hard" to imagine "anytime soon" (Piketty 2014: 515). Debate on the broadest possible level would seem the more essential. Chapter 2 already quoted from a 2011 American Political Science Association (APSA) Task Force Report which had picked inequality, along with diversity and inclusiveness, as analytical categories that should "inform each unit of study, rather than be seen as a separate or supplementary unit in the curriculum" (APSA 2011: 3). More than half a decade earlier, APSA's Task Force on Inequality and American Democracy had pressed for a "vigorous campaign" by perturbed citizens and alarmed political scientists "to expand participation and make our government responsive to the many, rather than just the privileged few" (APSA 2004: 20).

However, even at the time the signs did not bode well. According to several disillusioned Task Force members, past responses to appeals that

112   R. EISFELD

the discipline ought to offer a "sustained and critical consideration of larger questions about the nature of American democracy" had been "meager". A number of others invoked the parable of "the blind men and the elephant"—while certainly exploring "parts of the puzzle", researchers had "mostly failed to take in the larger picture" (Bartels et al. 2004: 4/5; Hacker et al. 2004: 5). *Unless, as argued in this book's first chapters, the discipline's incentive structure is revamped, current forms of research governance put under scrutiny, and the role of "big" issues emphasized in academic education, that predicament will hardly change.*
Not a single economist considered in this chapter failed to refer

- to deficiencies in public education as a major determinant of inequality,
- and to improvements in the quality and universal accessibility of such—particularly secondary and higher—education as a signal factor in transcending the present quandary.

Time after time—in the 1980s, the 1990s, the 2000s, and the 2010s—educational attainment has been identified as *the* political resource with the strongest impact on political interest, political participation, and acquisition of politically relevant skills (Dahl 1982: 171; Verba et al. 1993: 457; Solt 2008: 55). Taking into account the challenges posed by further societal pluralization due to continuing immigration that were discussed in Chap. 7, an additional relationship becomes particularly relevant: *educational level as a determinant of ethnic prejudice.* Even acknowledging the existence of significant cross-national variances, specific educational effect "remains strong" across Europe, as it does in the United States. Highly educated individuals exhibit less ethnically grounded prejudice than poorly educated (Hello et al. 2002: 5/6, 20; Kalmijn and Kraaykamp 2007: 563, 567/568).

Education, as John Kenneth Galbraith has written, is "decisive" in many ways—not just as an investment in economic betterment, but also in social peace, intelligent self-government, last but far from least, in the enlargement of life. Denying that opportunity may well be considered a particularly "brutal form of social discrimination" (Galbraith 1996: 73; ch. 9). A political science not shying away from normative judgments ought to include these aspects along with the familiar "occupational qualification" argument. Two decades after Galbraith, Robert Putnam forcefully reminded his readers then, when equality of opportunity has deteriorated into a fleeting vision "even for talented and energetic kids", our *basic moral code* is being violated (Putnam [2]2016: 240, 242).

But even if the economic productivity ("human capital") argument should remain central to the discussion, a recent assessment by Joel Klein, former chancellor of the New York City public school system (the largest in the United States), cautioned about emerging educational divisions which, paralleling the disturbing trends in income inequality, "tea[r] at the very fabric of our society". Echoing the alarm sounded by Benjamin Disraeli even before the Gilded Age about Britain's "two nations", the deprived many and the privileged few, Klein warned that a rapid move toward "two Americas" was under way—"a wealthy elite, and an increasingly large underclass that lacks the skills to succeed" (Klein 2011: 3). Vividly portraying the arrival of "class-based educational segregation" and the diminishing prospects of American children born into poverty since the 1970s, Robert Putnam conveyed the same ominous message in no less stark terms (Putnam [2]2016: 39; ch. 4, esp. 160 ss., 183 ss.).

Several telling statistics were provided by Piketty, Stiglitz, and other researchers. Over a 40-year period, from 1970 to 2010, the proportion of college degrees—hence, life chances—earned by children from families in the US income pyramid's *top* quartile rose from 40 to 80%; it stagnated between 10 and 20% for those from families in the *bottom* two quartiles. A 2011 summary of research results noted that just about 30% of *low*-income US middle school students (eighth graders, more precisely) with *high* test scores completed college, as compared with, again, 30% of *high*-income students who had scored *low*, yet earned a college degree. There is, of course, a connection to exorbitant tuition fees charged by elite universities—but also, as Piketty has pointed out, to admission policies: donations by high-income parents to American universities have been found to be "strangely concentrated in the period when the children are of college age" (Piketty 2014: 485; Stiglitz 2012: 307 n. 79, 80).

Regarding the lower end of the income hierarchy, a 2013 paper published under the auspices of the American Psychological Association stressed that, much too often, poor students with substandard educational environments—such as housing, nutrition, and other family resources—are additionally attending underequipped urban public schools offering outdated textbooks, outdated computers, inadequate science equipment as additional barriers. Low student motivation and disengagement are among the consequences (Hudley 2013: 1, 2). The combination of lacking social resources and inadequate school equipment has been particularly

114   R. EISFELD

working to the disadvantage of Hispanic adolescents. On the one hand, as shown in Chap. 7, Hispanics are the fastest growing population group in the United States. On the other hand, they continue to have "the lowest rates of high school and college attainment"—indeed, one more "cause for national concern" (Schneider et al. 2006: 179; Ryan and Bauman 2016: 3).

Comparative analyses have demonstrated that a pronounced similarity between the United States and the United Kingdom in the magnitude of income inequality increases, emphasized earlier in this chapter, is about equaled by both countries' "uniquely high levels of educational inequalities" (Reardon and Waldfogel 2016: 4). In cooperation with other researchers, Sean Reardon—a Stanford specialist in the causes, trends, and consequences of educational disparities—and Jane Waldfogel—a Columbia expert in child welfare, poverty, and social mobility working on the United States and Great Britain—found substantially widened educational achievement gaps related to parents' high or low incomes in the two societies. As in the United States, tuition fees play an outstanding role in unequal access to British higher education: Since 1998, the English tuition fee cap was increased ninefold—from £1000 to £9000. The 2010 share of such fees in the resources of British universities was "almost as high as in the 1920s and close to the U. S. level" (Piketty 2014: 632 n. 34).

Political scientists should take up the demand for equalizing access to "meaningful" education—in the sense of the quality of the schooling offered—hence, for a reemphasis on state-funded education (Milanovic 2016: 221). Such equalization could form an important segment of a restructured twenty-first-century welfare state, as proposed by Piketty and Milanovic. However, programs for reducing widening gaps in educational attainment would, as convincingly argued by Robert Putnam, need to be more multi-faceted and comprehensive than that. Efforts at reducing residential segregation rooted in income inequality, at reducing current paternal incarceration rates, and at improving links between schools and local communities (e.g., by expanding mentoring programs) are other salient factors for which allowance should be made (Putnam [2]2016: 247, 251, 259).

Even if the present chapter, like others in the book's "Issues" Section, highlights merely a few exemplary problems, it seems evident that income distribution and educational attainment are inseparably linked to any conceivable success of the "engaging the public" role envisioned here for political science. Audiences whose energies are largely exhausted by the struggle for existence, additionally having experienced a lack of educational opportunities that would stimulate intellectual abilities, will be ill-equipped to value any sustained efforts by our discipline's members at publicly spreading fact-inspired analytical, let alone normative, reasoning.

REFERENCES

APSA [American Political Science Association] (2004): *American Democracy in an Age of Rising Inequality.* Report of the Task Force on Inequality and American Democracy. http://www.apsanet.org/portals/54/Files/Task%20 Force%20Reports/taskforcereport.pdf, accessed August 7, 2017.

APSA [American Political Science Association] (2011): *Political Science in the 21st Century.* Report of the Task Force on Political Science in the 21st Century. Washington DC: APSA, www.apsanet.org/portals/54/Files/ TaskForceReports/TF_21stCentury_AllPgs_webres90.pdf, accessed Sept. 14, 2016.

Atkinson, Anthony B. (2015): *Inequality. What Can Be Done?* Cambridge/ London: Harvard University Press.

Bartels, Larry M. (2008): *Unequal Democracy. The Political Economy of the New Gilded Age.* Princeton/Oxford: Princeton University Press.

Bartels, Larry M. et al. (2004): *Inequality and American Governance.* Memorandum, APSA Task Force on Inequality and American Democracy. http://www.apsanet.org/portals/54/Files/Memos/governancememo.pdf, accessed August 7, 2017.

Beddoes, Zanny Minton (2012): "For Richer, For Poorer". Special Report, *The Economist,* October 13. http://www.economist.com/node/21564414, accessed June 16, 2017.

Berry, Jeffrey M./Wilcox, Clyde (^{5rev}2009 [^{1}1984]): *The Interest Group Society.* New York: Pearson Longman.

Buhmann, Brigitte et al. (1988): "Equivalence Scales, Well-Being, Inequality, and Poverty: Sensitivity Estimates Across Ten Countries Using the Luxembourg Income Study (LIS) Database." *Income and Wealth,* Vol. 34, 115–142.

Conference Board of Canada (2017): "Income Inequality – Canada and World Results". http://www.conferenceboard.ca/hcp/details/society/income-inequality.aspx, accessed May 31, 2017.

Dahl, Robert A. (1961): *Who Governs?* New Haven: Yale University Press.

Dahl, Robert A. (1967): *Pluralist Democracy in the United States. Conflict and Consent.* Chicago: Rand McNally.

Dahl, Robert A. (1982): *Dilemmas of Pluralist Democracy.* New Haven: Yale University Press.

116   R. EISFELD

Dahl, Robert A. (2006): *On Political Equality*. New Haven: Yale University Press.
Egerton, John (1974): *The Americanization of Dixie. The Southernization of America*. New York: Harper's Magazine Press.
Eichler, Alexander/McAuliff, Michael (2011): "Income Inequality Reaches Gilded Age Levels, Congressional Report Finds". *Huffington Post*, December 26. http://www.huffingtonpost.com/2011/10/26/income-inequality_n_1032632.html, accessed June 16, 2017.
Eisfeld, Rainer (2011): "How Political Science Might Regain Relevance and Obtain an Audience: A Manifesto for the 21st Century". *European Political Science*, Vol. 10, 220–225.
Elsässer, Lea/Hense, Svenja/Schäfer, Arnim (2016): *Systematisch verzerrte Entscheidungen? Die Responsivität der deutschen Politik von 1998 bis 2015*. Berlin: Bundesministerium für Arbeit und Soziales.
Galbraith, John Kenneth (1996): *The Good Society*. Boston: Houghton Mifflin.
German Federal Government (2017): *Life Situations in Germany. 5th Report on Poverty and Wealth. Executive Summary*. http://www.bmas.de/SharedDocs/Downloads/EN/PDF-Publikationen/a306e-the-german-federal-government s-5th-report-on-poverty-and-wealth.pdf?_blob=publicationFile&v=1, accessed November 30, 2017.
Gilens, Martin/Page, Benjamin I. (2014): „Testing Theories of American Politics: Elites, Interest Groups, and Average Citizens". *Perspectives on Politics*, Vol. 12, 564–581.
Greenspan, Alan (2003): "The Reagan Legacy." Speech Given April 9, 2003 at the Ronald Reagan Library. https://www.federalreserve.gov/boarddocs/speeches/2003/200304092/default.htm, accessed July 10, 2017.
Hacker, Jacob et al. (2004): *Inequality and Public Policy*. Memorandum, APSA Task Force on Inequality and American Democracy. http://www.apsanet.org/portals/54/Files/Memos/feedbackmemo.pdf, accessed August 7, 2017.
Hello, Evelyn/Scheepers, Peer/Gijsberts, Mérove (2002): "Education and Ethnic Prejudice in Europe: Explanations for Cross-National Variances in the Educational Effect on Ethnic Prejudice." *Scandinavian Journal of Educational Research*, Vol. 46, 5–24.
High Pay Commission (2011a): *More for Less*. http://highpaycentre.org/img/High_Pay_Commission_More_for_Less.pdf, accessed May 31, 2017.
High Pay Commission (2011b): *Cheques With Balances: Why Tackling High Pay is in the National Interest*. http://highpaycentre.org/files/Cheques_with_Balances.pdf, accessed May 31, 2017.
Hochschild, Jennifer L. (2009): Review of *Unequal Democracy* by Larry M. Bartels. *Perspectives on Politics*, Vol. 7, 145–147.
Hofstadter, Richard (1966): *Anti-Intellectualism in American Life*. New York: Alfred Knopf.

Hudley, Cynthia (2013): "Education and Urban Schools." *American Psychological Association, SES (Socioeconomic Status) Indicator*, May. http://www.apa.org/pi/ses/resources/indicator/2013/05/urban-schools.aspx, accessed June 19, 2017.

Isaac, Jeffrey C. (2014): "Rethinking American Democracy?", Editorial. *Perspectives on Politics*, Vol. 12, 557–562.

Kalmijn, Matthijs/Kraaykamp, Gerbert (2007): "Social Stratification and Attitudes: A Comparative Analysis of the Effects of Class and Education in Europe". *British Journal of Sociology*, Vol. 58, 547–576.

Klein, Joel (2011): "The Failure of American Schools". *The Atlantic*, June 2011, https://www.theatlantic.com/magazine/archive/2011/06/the-failure-of-american-schools/308497, accessed June 19, 2017.

Krugman, Paul (2007): "Gilded Once More." *New York Times*, April 27. http://www.nytimes.com/2007/04/27/opinion/27krugman.html, accessed May 31, 2017.

Krugman, Paul (2009): *The Conscience of a Liberal*. New York/London: W. W. Norton.

Krugman, Paul (2011): "Oligarchy, American Style". *New York Times*, Nov. 4, 2011, A 31. http://www.nytimes.com/2011/11/04/opinion/oligarchy-american-style.html, accessed May 19, 2017.

Leighley, Jan E./Nagler, Jonathan (2007): "Unions, Voter Turnout, and Class Bias in the U. S. Electorate, 1964–2004". *Journal of Politics*, Vol. 69, 430–441.

Lindblom, Charles E. (1977): *Politics and Markets*. New York: Basic Books.

Mickey, Robert/Levitsky, Steven/Way, Lucan Ahmad (2017): "Is America Still Safe for Democracy?" *Foreign Affairs*, Vol. 96 No. 3, 20–29.

Milanovic, Branko (2016): *Global Inequality*. Cambridge: Harvard University Press.

Phillips, Kevin (2002): *Wealth and Democracy*. New York: Broadway Books.

Piketty, Thomas (2014): *Capital in the Twenty-First Century*. Cambridge/London: Belknap Press of Harvard University Press.

Piketty, Thomas (2017): "Inequality in France". *Le Blog de Thomas Piketty*, April 18. http://piketty.blog.lemonade.fr/2017/04/18/inequality-in-france, accessed May 31, 2017.

Piketty, Thomas/Saez, Emmanuel (2013): "Top Incomes and the Great Recession: Recent Evolutions and Policy Implications". *IMF Economic Review*, Vol. 61, 456–478.

Pressman, Steven (2016): *Understanding Piketty's Capital in the Twenty-First Century*. London/New York: Routledge.

Putnam, Robert D. (^{2}2016): *Our Kids. The American Dream in Crisis*. New York/London: Simon & Schuster.

Putnam, Robert D./Campbell, David E. (2010): *American Grace*. New York: Simon & Schuster.

118   R. EISFELD

Reardon, Sean/Waldfogel, Jane (2016): "International Inequalities: Learning from International Comparisons." Sutton Trust *Research Brief* # 16 (December). http://www.suttontrust.com/wp-content/uploads/2016/12/International-inequalities_FINAL.Pdf, accessed August 23, 2017.

Ryan, Camille L./Bauman, Kurt (2016): "Educational Attainment in the United States: 2015". U. S. Census Bureau: Current Population Reports. https://www.census.gov/content/dam/Census/library/publications/2016/demo/p20-578.pdf, accessed August 23, 2017.

Schneider, Barbara/Martinez, Sylvia/Owens, Ann (2006): "Barriers to Educational Opportunities for Hispanics in the United States". In: Marta Tienda/Faith Mitchell (eds.): *Hispanics and the Future of America*. Washington DC: National Academies Press, 179–227.

Shaw, Daron (2008): *Review of Unequal Democracy* by Larry M. Bartels. *The Forum*, Vol. 6, Issue 3, Article 10. https://doi.org/10.2202/1540-8884.1266, accessed June 19, 2017.

Shibley, Mark A. (1991): "The Southernization of American Religion: Testing a Hypothesis". *Sociological Analysis*, Vol. 52, 159–174.

Skocpol, Theda (2004): *Diminished Democracy: From Membership to Management in American Civic Life*. Norman: University of Oklahoma Press/Arthur H. Clark.

Solt, Frederick (2008): "Economic Inequality and Democratic Political Engagement". *American Journal of Political Science*, Vol. 52, 48–60.

Stiglitz, Joseph E. (2011): "Of the 1%, by the 1%, for the 1%." *Vanity Fair*, March 31, 2011. http://www.vanityfair.com/news/2011/05/top-one-percent-201105, accessed May 19, 2017.

Stiglitz, Joseph E. (2012): *The Price of Inequality*. New York/London: W. W. Norton.

Verba, Sidney/Schlozman, Kay Lehman et al. (1993): "Race, Ethnicity and Political Resources: Participation in the United States". *British Journal of Political Science*, Vol. 23, 453–497.

Western, Bruce/Rosenfeld, Jake (2011): "Unions, Norms, and the Rise in U. S. Wage Inequality". *American Sociological Review*, Vol. 76, 513–537.

Wuthnow, Robert (2004): "Bridging the Privileged and the Marginalized?". In: Robert D. Putnam (ed.): *Democracies in Flux. The Evolution of Social Capital in Contemporary Society*. Oxford/New York: Oxford University Press, 59–102.

CHAPTER 9

Robust Regulatory Policies for Capitalism

Twenty-First-Century Political Science's Political Economy

> *Deregulatory state intervention and determined governmental underperformance with regard to public services have (a) been eating into the capacity of legislatures to allocate resources and (b) have deepened, if not triggered, persistent financial crises. The entrenched neo-liberal discourse has made governments and market players alike rival each other in reorganizing states as quasi-enterprise associations bent on cutting outlays. Citizens' loyalty to the state and grassroots commitment to the democratic process are thus being weakened. The pro-market trend needs to be reversed, and political science must visibly intervene in the political debate.*

During the 1980s and 1990s, a neo-liberal (actually, largely laissez-faire, or "Manchester"-liberal) discourse bent on cutting welfare expenditures and government supervision of the capitalist economy became increasingly hegemonic. Under its impact, government and market players alike pushed for the realization of recipes aimed at "slimming down" the role of states.

Neo-liberalism stands for a set of supply-side economic policies which include tax cuts, the downsizing of social security, deregulation, privatization, and free trade. Administrations led by social democratic parties joined their liberal-conservative counterparts in opting for these policies. "Cognitive capture" (Stiglitz 2012: 47/48) by the beliefs of the potentially regulated—corporate and banking executives—shaped the mindsets

© The Author(s) 2019
R. Eisfeld, *Empowering Citizens, Engaging the Public*,
https://doi.org/10.1007/978-981-13-5928-6_9

120   R. EISFELD

of players promoting deregulation. The label "modernization" came to serve as a catchword for "reforms" whose retrenchment and commodification features belied the term's traditional progressive connotation.

Some awareness that capitalist economies, definitely including banking institutions, require "tough", internationally coordinated regulation (Eisfeld 2011: 223) only began to return when a financial capitalism running "amok" (Piketty 2014: 474) triggered the 2007–2009 Great Recession. However, a caveat is indicated: Different from what might have been expected due to the severity of the global crisis, research has suggested that the Recession did *not* "significant[ly] change policy and policy thinking". Neo-liberalism proved largely resilient to calls for more efficient regulation (Wilson and Grant 2012: 7, 9, 12, 13).

In the ongoing discussion, a reinvigorated political economy needs to intervene—the more if Paul Krugman was right when, in his 2011 EEA Presidential Address, he judged that macroeconomics had entered a "Dark Age", during which "much of the profession had lost its former knowledge". The paramount reason, Krugman asserted, was that academic success had increasingly resulted from publishing "hard" papers using "rigorous and preferably difficult mathematics". Having achieved tenure, academics thus trained had "closed off" promotion to anyone who "questioned" the mainstream approach (Krugman 2011: 310, 311). That should sound familiar to political scientists.

The trend of "pro-market", deregulatory state intervention on the increase (Cerny 1999: 13, 19) was epitomized by the strategies of the Clinton ("New Democrats"), Blair ("New Labour"), and, in Germany, Schröder ("New Center") administrations. During Bill Clinton's incumbency, US government and congress pioneered the deregulatory push in major respects:

- The Gramm-Leach-Bliley Act of 1999 permitted combinations of banking, securities, and insurance services under the same conglomerate roof. Removing restrictions on affiliations between commercial (deposits and loans) banking and investment (securities) banking, the law repealed the relevant provisions of the 1933 Glas-Steagall Act. A key part of the New Deal's legislation in response to the Great Depression, the separation had been enacted as much to protect bank customers' deposits from speculative use, as to curb the volume of excessively speculative, therefore risky, operations. By failing to give authority to the US Securities and Exchange Commission—also

ROBUST REGULATORY POLICIES FOR CAPITALISM 121

created during the New Deal—or to any other federal agency to supervise investment bank conglomerates, the Gramm-Leach-Bliley Act moreover "created a significant regulatory gap" (Cox 2008).

Culminating in "a $300 million lobbying effort" (Stiglitz 2008; Sanati 2009, quoting then-Senator Barack Obama) to influence Congress, the banking community had long sought repeal of the Glass-Steagall Act. The invoked rationale, successfully imparted to the Clinton administration, was "modernization" and "competitiveness". Clinton's Treasury Secretary Lawrence Summers praised the 1999 law, officially labeled "Financial Services Modernization Act", as an "update" that would allow American companies "to compete" in the twenty-first century; the President's Chief of Staff John Podesta dismissed Glas-Steagall as "out of date", even while acknowledging that the new law would allow banks "to engage in riskier activities" (Sanati 2009; Roberts 2014).

Glas-Steagall's provisions had, by that time, already been hollowed out by regulatory interpretation. But the repeal, not unlike the earlier-discussed trade unions' defeat at the hands of Reagan and Thatcher, "changed an entire culture": When commercial and investment banks started merging into complex financial conglomerates, "the investment-bank culture came out on top" (Stiglitz 2008). The "appetite" grew for resorting to leverage (borrowing) in conjunction with the use of derivatives, financial instruments based on—derived from—the expected price movement of an underlying asset or transaction. Such contracts, which may include options, futures contracts, or credit-default swaps, promise large returns, but are highly speculative and risk-prone. Eventually, when the credit bubble resulting from "reckless" lending (Stiglitz 2012: 202) burst, they were to lead to enormous losses. Discussions of the extent to which the repeal of Glass-Steagall caused the Great Recession have remained controversial. The argument that it made the crisis "broader, deeper and more dangerous" has been markedly less contested (Ritholtz 2012; Sanati 2009; Elson 2017: 12, 30).

- The 1999 statutory rule was fatally reinforced by a further "modernizing" law relating to financial products, the 2000 Commodity Futures Modernization Act. It removed effective regulation of derivatives—including credit-default swaps—traded over-the-counter (OTC), rather than on standardized exchanges. The legislation was pushed over the objections of the Commodity Futures Trading

122   R. EISFELD

Commission chair (who resigned) by President Clinton's Working Group on Financial Markets (PWG) which included the chairs of both the Federal Reserve Board and the Securities and Exchange Commission in addition to the Treasury Secretary. In the group's report to the House and the Senate, magic words such as "U. S. leadership", "innovation", "competition", "efficiency", even "transparency" (!), abounded (PWG Report 1999). Before the final vote, a "compromise" on the bill between the Treasury Department and Republican Senator Phil Gramm—who had already spearheaded the drive for the 1999 law—resulted in even stricter provisions exempting derivatives from oversight (Blumenthal 2009).

In the wake of the Great Recession, the 2010 Dodd-Frank Wall Street Reform and Consumer Protection Act, enacted during the Obama presidency, largely overturned the 2000 law. Implementation of these changes has been hindered, however, by industrial and Republican opposition (Wilson 2012: 55/56), and they will be rolled back in their turn, should the Financial Choice Act, passed by the House in 2017 during the early months of the Trump presidency, become law. At the time of writing, the Senate was working to forge a bipartisan version of the bill.

- In his 1992 presidential campaign, Clinton had pledged to cut welfare benefits, "end[ing] welfare as we know it". Asserting that it trapped "too many people" in an alleged "cycle of dependence", he had held out the prospect of replacing it by a system that emphasized "work and independence". Due to the bitter struggle over health insurance reform, which eventually killed the president's proposed Health Security Act, and to conflicts within the administration, Clinton failed to pursue the issue early during his first term, and found himself "forced to react" to Republican initiatives demanding deeper cuts than he had envisaged (Noble 1997: 128, 131, 133). After vetoing two bills passed by Republican congressional majorities, he signed a third version in 1996 on the eve of his re-election campaign. According to Clinton, in spite of "serious flaws" the bill offered the "best chance we will have in a long, long time" to deliver on his pledge (Harris and Yang 1996: A01).

The Personal Responsibility and Work Opportunity Act imposed time limits and work requirements. General eligibility for federal cash benefits was limited to five years, and to two years for family heads who had in the meantime found no work. States might opt for stricter requirements or shorter time frames. After two months, they could require adults to perform community services. Generally, the law's focus was on work, rather than on vocational training and education. State discretion and "experimentation" were emphasized throughout. Individual entitlements under Aid to Families with Dependent Children provisions were replaced by federal block grants, which were also administered by the states and had to be supplemented by state funds under a "maintenance of effort" rule. Legal immigrants who had not become citizens were made ineligible for welfare benefits during their first five years in the United States.

Six years after adoption of the law, state policies were judged to differ "dramatically". No consensus on best practices had emerged (Weaver and Gais 2002). When the national unemployment rate doubled during the Great Recession, "robust evidence" was found by Berkeley economist Hilary Hoynes and her team—specializing in the study of economic disparities and anti-poverty programs—that welfare reform, mainly because of the loss of cash assistance, was "not responsive" regarding the "most disadvantaged". Compared to prior downturns, the group suffering greatest hardship in the recession were those in "extreme poverty", with incomes below 50% of the poverty threshold (Bitler and Hoynes 2016: 437; Hoynes 2017).

The Brookings Institution proposed that, during periods of high unemployment, Congress should give vocational training more weight (as "most experts believe the unemployed should expand their skills through job training during recessions"), and should also considerably extend time limits for becoming employed—because during downturns "the average period of job search increases sharply" (Brookings 2014). In an impassioned appeal published six months before his death, former New York Mayor Ed Koch pleaded for "decency and fairness" in treating the very poor. Rejecting "arbitrary" time limits, he concluded: "Mr. President, you must speak for the poor. No one else seems willing, or effective" (Koch 2012).

- In addition to deregulating financial institutions and reducing welfare benefits, promotion of free trade and protection of foreign investment provided a final cornerstone to the neo-liberal policy pattern. Adopted by Canada, Mexico, and the United States in 1993, the North American Free Trade Agreement (NAFTA) did indeed

124   R. EISFELD

create the world's largest continental free trade zone. When entering into force, NAFTA is said to have encompassed the impressive production output of 6.5 trillion US dollars (Grimm 1998: 179).

However, the treaty also killed the traditional agricultural production of Mexico's Mayan Indians' impoverished descendants: The Mexican government abolished the constitutional guarantee for indigenous communal landholdings, considered an investment barrier incompatible with NAFTA provisions. In addition, by opening these lands for privatization and sale, it wished "to encourage U. S. style agri-business and new latifundios designed for export-economy mass production". The act led directly to the 1994 Chiapas (Zapatista) rebellion which, symbolically, erupted on the day (January 1, 1994) of NAFTA's entry into force (Vargas 1994: 1, 12/13, 19–21).

Like the bills discussed before, the NAFTA Implementation Act was passed by the US Congress as a bipartisan law. (The treaty had been negotiated by the Republican administration of George H. W. Bush. President Trump demanded a renegotiation, which commenced in August, 2017.) Yet, the legislation also—like the 1996 Welfare Act—split the Democrats' congressional vote down the middle. Trade unions and environmental groups had mounted strong opposition against a project which, they feared, would favor the transfer of investment outlays and production facilities to low-wage labor and unregulated manufacturing conditions in Mexico.

Clinton, who strongly supported NAFTA, needed to blunt that opposition, while also maintaining business support. He therefore made signing the implementation bill contingent on the negotiation of environmental and labor cooperation side agreements (NAAEC, NAALC) which required the three member countries to enforce their *own* environmental and labor relations standards. The strategy worked, not least against the backdrop of the prevailing anti-union climate described in Chap. 8. While resulting in "rather shallow" (Charnovitz 1994: 32) agreements lacking international enforcement powers, NAAEC and NAALC at least established both an "oversight mechanism" (Compa 1994: 109) and a "public forum" where violations or abuses might be—and have been—exposed by claimants (Kay 2011: 130).

During the subsequent two decades, NAFTA inspired three similar trade agreements—in fact, trade-and-investment treaties (it is the investment part on which the subsequent discussion will focus). None, however, has reached the stage of ratification by all signatory countries.

In January 2017, President Donald Trump issued a memorandum withdrawing the United States from the Trans-Pacific Partnership (TPP) agreement signed a year earlier by 12 countries including Australia, Canada, Japan, Malaysia, Mexico, Singapore, and Vietnam. TPP had also faced strong opposition within the Democratic Party. Congressional minority leaders Nancy Pelosi (House), Harry Reid (Senate), Democratic nominee Hillary Clinton, and Vermont Senator Bernie Sanders had, during 2016, distanced themselves from the Obama Administration's project.

Negotiations on a companion agreement, the Transatlantic Trade and Investment Partnership (TTIP) between the United States and the European Union, were being halted indefinitely after Trump's 2016 election. Leaks of proposed TTIP contents had earlier kindled a major controversy in Europe over issues such as environmental standards, foreign investment protection, and consumer and labor rights.

Similar protests were also triggered by the Comprehensive Economic and Trade Agreement (CETA) between Canada and the European Union signed in 2016. In the end, these—and the Canadian government's experiences with NAFTA—resulted in the safeguarding of much larger regulatory space (de Mestral 2015: 641, 649). Subsequent to approval by the European Parliament in early 2017, and pending ratification by the EU's 28 national legislatures, major parts of the agreement may be provisionally applied from the autumn of 2017. The extent of the temporary arrangement is subject to an October, 2016 ruling by Germany's Federal Constitutional court which, for instance, expressly excludes CETA's clauses on foreign investment protection from provisional application (Bundesverfassungsgericht 2016).

There have been attempts to demonstrate the continuity of such protection over the past, if not several past centuries (e.g., Tietje and Baetens 2014, 15 ss.). Actually, practices of investment protection underwent a distinct change of purpose since the 1960s: *From safeguards against expropriation they became corporate instruments to try and prevent or escape regulation.* This inserts them squarely into the neo-liberal pattern and requires some in-depth discussion.

- NAFTA's Chapter 11, allowing foreign investors to file suits against host states (Investor-State Dispute Settlement, ISDS), contributed heavily to the "explosion" (van Harten 2014) of such claims since the 1990s. The provision has been judged the first "sophisticated" regime for settling investment disputes between developed countries (Côté 2014: 60). Because of damage incurred by an alleged breach of a treaty obligation, an enterprise may submit a claim against a state for arbitration by "an impartial tribunal" established under the rules of either the 1965 International Center for the Settlement of Investment Disputes (ICSID) or the 1976 United Nations Commission on International Trade Law (UNCITRAL). The tribunal comprises three arbitrators—two appointed by the disputing parties and a third (presiding) appointed by agreement.

State-to-state settlement of investment and other business disputes had "persisted until the mid-twentieth century" (Tietje and Baetens 2014: 19). The first post-World War II bilateral treaty specifically focusing on "the promotion and protection" of foreign direct investment was concluded between (West) Germany and Pakistan in 1959. An document of just 9 pages and 14 articles, it included arbitration by a tribunal of three (analogous to the later NAFTA formula) as one possibility in the case of disputes. The spate of investment agreements which followed was signed between developed and developing countries, which explains the initial focus—noted above—on protection against expropriation (the 1959 agreement, for instance, devoted a separate article to that contingency). The subsequent creation in 1965, by the Convention on the Settlement of Investment Disputes and, under the auspices of the World Bank, of the ICSID served as a "key step" (Côté 2014: 58) in forging a procedural framework for the shift from state-to-state negotiation to investor-state arbitration.

Two decades after the Center's inception, ICSID Secretary-General Ibrahim Shihata in a telling statement voiced his expectation that the institution would "'depoliticize' the settlement of investment disputes" (Shihata 1986: 4). Shihata, who held two law degrees, continued to serve as a legal counsel to the World Bank (he died in 2001). His view was quite typical for the emphasis on "technical", supposedly "unpolitical" solutions long popular among many World Bank and IMF jurists and economists who continued to consider themselves "unbiased" experts. Events would prove that it could hardly have been further off the mark.

- By the end of the twenty-first century's first decade, some 2600 bilateral investment treaties plus another 250 bilateral investment-related economic agreements were in effect—again, a virtual "explosion" since the 1990s (Wellhausen 2016: 121). NAFTA's comprehensive provisions on investment dispute regulation became the model for subregional agreements, sparking hypotheses about an "emerging global regime for investment", where decision-making— as by arbitral tribunals—was increasingly being "privatized" (Salacuse 2010: 427/428, 466). According to data collected by Rachel Wellhausen, the number of publicly known annual investor-state dispute settlement filings approximately doubled every five or six years between 1991 and 2014. Evolving from 0 to over 20 in 1997, to some 50 in 2002 and over 100 in 2012—nearly hitting that mark again in both 2013 and 2014—the total amounted to 676 arbitrations during 25 years (Wellhausen 2016: 120 [database], 121 Figure 1, 122 Table 1).

These unexpected and "unprecedented challenges to Mexican, Canadian and U. S. regulatory measures" raised "the spectre of regulatory chill in the areas of health, safety and the environment" (Côté 2014: 60/61). The "chill" notion implies that a government refrains from adopting or enforcing specific "bona fide"—that is, not intentionally discriminatory—policies because of a perceived risk (not necessarily an actual threat) of an investor-state dispute and the ensuing expensive legal battle (Tienhaara 2011: 607/608; Tietje and Baetens 2014: 40/41). Particularly in the case of developing countries, anticipation may be compounded (a) by a lack of legal expertise and financial resources, (b) by concern over "treaty shopping", under which multinational corporations may resort to varying legal ownership structures—for example, by establishing a subsidiary—to benefit from "multiple nationality claims" and optimal investment protections under particular treaties (Gaukrodger and Gordon 2012: 55; Wellhausen 2016: 125). That misgivings such as these are no mere theoretical constructs is illustrated by the following two cases.

During 2010 and 2011, the Philip Morris multinational tobacco company—in keeping with strategies pursued by the tobacco industry generally and Philip Morris specifically, as portrayed earlier in Chap. 4— filed complaints against Uruguay and Australia. The corporation sought $25 million in compensation from Uruguay and unspecified "billions of dollars" from Australia for "substantially diminishing" the value of the claimant's investments by effects of the two countries' anti-smoking legislation. The 2010 claim was initiated under the Switzerland-Uruguay, the 2011 claim under the Hong Kong-Australia bilateral investment treaty;

128   R. EISFELD

the first arbitration was conducted by the World Bank's ICSID, the second under UNCITRAL rules (see above). Including decisions on costs, litigation took six years. Both tribunals in the end ruled against Philip Morris.

The contention based on the outcomes of earlier arbitrations under NAFTA Chapter 11 that concerns about regulatory chill "might have been premature" (Côté 2014: 64) seemed to be borne out by the results of these two investor-state disputes. That, however, would be the wrong conclusion to draw.

- A 2012 OECD Working Paper reported that, according to publicly available information, costs in recent ISDS cases had averaged $8m (occasionally exceeding $30m), with counsels' fees (at billing rates for the arbitration lawyers of large law firms running to $ 1000 per hour) estimated to cover 82% of that amount (Gaukrodger and Gordon 2012: 19, 20). Specialized corporate law firms thus emerge as "the real winners" (Olivet and Villareal 2016) from the proliferation of dispute arbitration. As was widely reported (and publicly acknowledged by the government of President Tabraré Vásquaz, an oncologist), Uruguay—whose GNP is substantially lower than the Philip Morris company's annual net revenue—would have been forced to renege on its tobacco-control policy, had the country not received funding from Bloomberg Philanthropies, the charitable organization founded by former New York mayor Michael Bloomberg, partnering with the Melinda & Bill Gates Foundation. While the tribunal shifted some costs, ruling that Philip Morris must reimburse Uruguay $7m to defray part of its judicial expenses, the country was still left with another $2.6m in legal costs to pay (Olivet and Villareal 2016).

Available data on arbitration outcomes collected by Rachel Wellhausen (Wellhausen 2016: 128/129) provide no reason for optimism, either. Of 461 concluded ISDS cases, the state won in 174 (37.7%), the investor in 134 (29.1%), and a settlement was reached in 153 (33.1%). Because "settlement" implies that governments will either pay some amount of compensation, or change policies, investors may be said to have scored in 62.2% of claims entered. This is illustrated by the case of Canada, which so far paid out $150m in compensation, the "bulk" by way of settlement. The country's legal costs until January 1, 2015 by "conservative" estimate totaled over $50m. During the same period, Mexico paid more than

$204m to investors. The United States lost no case (Dattu and Pavic 2017; CCPA 2015: 31).

- Philip Morris found itself unable to challenge Australian anti-tobacco legislation under the 2005 Australia-United States Free Trade Agreement (AUFTA): While largely modeled on NAFTA, AUFTA lacks any ISDS provisions, due to Australia's insistence that these were not required because of both countries' robust domestic legal systems and rule-of-law tradition. The multinational company therefore "rearranged its assets to become a Hong Kong investor" and take advantage of a clause in the earlier Australia-Hong Kong Bilateral Investment Treaty (AFTINET 2012). This was, of course, a perfect case of "treaty shopping". Duration of the Australia and Uruguay litigations caused noticeable policy chilling, "put[ting] a brake" on planned anti-tobacco legislation in Costa Rica, Paraguay and New Zealand and causing Canada to backpedal, settling for "watered-down" control measures (Olivet and Villareal 2016; CCPA 2015: 37).

Like Australia in the case of AUFTA, Canada drew its consequences. During current NAFTA renegotiations, the Canadian government seeks to reform Chapter 11. CETA, which provides for an independent investment court system, consisting of a permanent tribunal as a first instance and an appellate tribunal, might serve as a model. Canada and the European Union have moreover agreed to campaign for a permanent Multinational Investment Court (MIC).

- International unease over ISDS procedures has been growing to an extent that dispute settlement may be entering a transition phase (to speak of a turning point would be premature) where modifications and alternatives are debated in earnest. During TTIP negotiations, German Economics Minister Sigmar Gabriel, in a March 2014 letter to EU Trade Commissioner Karel de Gucht, embraced Australia's AUFTA argument: Between countries with proven legal systems, he wrote, foreign investment arbitration is "not necessary" (AFP 2014). The present dispute settlement regime demonstrably poses problems of financial constraints—primarily for developing countries—and of policy chilling due to uncertainty (Tienhaara 2011: 615). In particular, however, because it has been emerging (as also briefly indicated

130   R. EISFELD

earlier in this chapter) as a form of *private* international governance, it raises issues of accountability and hence legitimacy.

Normatively and empirically, legitimacy as the justification of authority and the basis of consent is a core concept of political science: Should private international players indeed continue to be entrusted with authoritatively reviewing "actions of governments, decisions of national courts, laws emanating from parliaments?" (Fernández-Armesto 2012. The author is a renowned Spanish arbitrator). The issue, involving the roles of private interests and public interest in international investment agreements, should figure prominently in a newly invigorated political economy. ANU-based scholar Kyla Tienhaara (Tienhaara 2011: 606, 627) noted a dearth of present studies by political scientists in a field "which is dominated by legal analysis" (as well she might: hers was the sole "view from political science" in a 28 essay-volume on global investment dispute and arbitration). Her assessment bears repeating: Political scientists need to become significantly "more involved" in debates about lessons from present and perspectives for future issues of power, conflict, and procedure in a crucial domain of policy-making mired too long in "relative obscurity" (Tienhaara).

The recent texts by Côté (2014) and Wellhausen (2016) indicate directions in which empirical and normative inquiries could be moving. It might be added that there is in fact a field, namely sustainable forestry management through forest certification, where political scientists have been paying detailed attention to regulatory regimes constructed through agreements by market players, and to issues of their legitimacy (e.g., Cashore et al. 2004: chs. 1, 8). However, the Forest Stewardship Council considered by that work is an environmental-group conceived sector program, hardly comparable to the authoritative *private* resolution of disputes between international *private* economic players and elected *public* policy-makers.

To turn now to the emulation of Clinton's deregulatory push by the Blair and Schröder administrations: With Labour still in opposition, Tony Blair had early looked to Clinton for inspiration regarding his own election campaign (King and Wickham-Jones 1999: 65–69). The 1992 "New Democratic" Party Platform had announced a "radical" shift to a more efficient and "flexible" government, had rejected "big" government "hamstring[ing] business", had affirmed belief in "the power of market forces" and vowed "to create a far better climate for business", and had finally "offered" people on welfare "a new social contract", including the two-year time limit for benefits mentioned earlier. The 1997 "New Labour" Manifesto signed by Blair echoed those tenets. A "commitment to enterprise" was included alongside the "commitment to justice". Changes in industrial relations legislation under Thatcher (referred-to in Chap. 8), which had weakened trade unions, would be left intact. A "modern" welfare state would be designed, based on "rights" balanced by "duties". And the processes of government would be "simplified" and made more "effective". That would include reforming the Bank of England.

The Democratic Platform was, as has been seen, adopted by the Clinton Administration. Things were no different in the case of the Labour Party Manifesto and the Blair government.

During that government's first 100 days, Chancellor Gordon Brown in 1997 gave the Bank of England its independence, ceding control over monetary policy (the setting of interest rates), while transferring banking supervision from the Bank to the newly established Financial Services Authority (FSA). The FSA was to pool coverage of banking, insurance, and investment services, with the "proclaimed intention" to set up "a regime of 'light-touch' regulation that would support the City of London's pre-eminence as a financial center". The light touch failed dismally during the financial crisis that started in 2007 (Daripa et al. 2012: 1, 15 ss.). Subsequent legislation creating a new regulatory framework in 2012 abolished the FSA.

Again taking their hint from the US Democrats, modifying the welfare state by adding a compulsory, presumed "welfare to work" component was a second focal point of the New Labour government's approach (King and Wickham-Jones 1999: 62/63, 70/71). Because of high youth unemployment at the end of the Thatcher era, measures were initially targeted at those aged between 18 and 24 and out of work for six months or longer. Subsequent to mandatory "gateway" counseling, they were offered four options: Subsidized job placement for 6 months with private employers, including on-the-job training; voluntary community service work (6 months); voluntary environmental task force work (again, 6 months); vocational training, or further education, up to 12 months. Failing to respond to these offers "without good cause", claimants would lose their benefits for four weeks (or longer periods in case of successive violations). The scheme subsequently came to include single parents, the disabled, and finally long-term unemployed (for 18 months or more) aged over 25.

In contrast to the program for young unemployed, these latter programs were means-tested: eligibility was dependent on existing income and savings. The extent to which ensuing reduction in unemployment was due to New Labour's programs or to returning economic growth during the decade before the Great Recession remains controversial. In any event, when it came to those not easily employable, Labour's rhetoric "failed to realize" that, *due to the changing character of work in the United Kingdom and elsewhere*—increasingly "low-paid and insecure"—many of those on welfare were "not long-term scroungers, but casualties of the low-end jobs market". Political culture was also following the adoption of get-tough language by the government: "Public attitudes shifted decisively towards the idea that being on benefits made you a blight to society" (Asato 2011: S183). That was the very trend which New York's former Mayor Ed Koch, cited earlier in this chapter, had denounced in the United States.

Blair gained an academic godfather in Anthony Giddens (*The Third Way*, 1998), who added London School of Economics (LSE) laurels to Labour's "more business-friendly" attitude but who would, in retrospect, lambaste the Blair-Brown governments for their "fawning dependence" on the City of London (Giddens 2010: 35). And the prime minister found a conceptual ally in German chancellor Gerhard Schröder, whose Social Democrats had carried national elections in 1998 (one year after the British conservatives' "bloodbath") and who, with Joschka Fischer, formed a Red-Green coalition, but who would part ways with Blair over the Iraq invasion. The programmatic impact of the Blair/Schröder *Europe: The Third Way/Die Neue Mitte [The New Center]* manifesto which both signed in 1998 was ephemeral. However, it did sum up "what they were already doing" (Atkins 2016), or would shortly embark on, and it expressly referred to "ever more rapid globalisation" as *the* decisive factor to which government and society alike would have to adapt.

In fact, "adaptability" and "flexibility" emerged as the magic words which dominated the manifesto's approach. To an extent unimagined two decades earlier, the document—taken as an example—bore out an early (1971) prediction in the pages of the *Journal of Conflict Resolution*. The authors had singled out the multinational enterprise as a normative agent of political culture—"not bound by notions of constituency, responsiveness, and accountability"—which would profoundly reshape world-wide values and behavior patterns. These would definitely include "the range of possible forms and content that politics may assume", quite possibly entailing formidable social costs for large parts of the globe (Osterberg and Ajami 1971: 460, 467, 469).

The Blair/Schröder text saw no need for the forces of global capitalism to be "resisted or even restrained" by governments (Taylor 1999: 411). Quite the contrary, its authors held that their "new politics", whose economic, supply side-focused aspects were summed up by Australian economist Flavio Romano as "neither 'new' nor social democratic" (Romano 2006: 79),

- should promote "a new entrepreneurial spirit at all levels of society", celebrating successful entrepreneurs "just as it does artists and footballers";
- should cut corporation tax rates; neither should companies "be gagged by rules and regulations";
- should transform the welfare state into a "springboard to personal responsibility", although the labor market also "need[ed] a low-wage sector in order to make low-skill jobs available" (Blair and Schröder 1998: 5, 6/7, 10, 11/12).

An overhaul of Germany's welfare system, labeled Agenda 2010, took effect between 2003 and 2005. Exhibiting many features familiar from the British case—such as cutbacks, time limits, sanctions for non-compliance with job center appointments or job offers, and means-tested non-contributory benefits (for an overview, see Keitel 2015)—it had profound economic and some unexpected political consequences. While no consensus has emerged—again, as in the United Kingdom—concerning the Agenda's effect on the fall of high unemployment, the policy definitely increased the share of precarious (low-paid, part-time) jobs, and it accelerated income inequality. According to a 2012 OECD report, Germany was the only OECD country between the mid-1990s and the late 2000s where, due to the weakening power of trade unions and the 2003/2005 cuts, increasing labor earnings inequality drove growing income disparity in the bottom half of the income distribution (Bonesmo Frederiksen 2012: 9).

Politically, the Agenda 2010 cost Schröder the chancellorship in the 2005 federal elections. Wide-spread sustained anger had led to formation of the WASG (*Wahlalternative für Arbeit und soziale Gerechtigkeit*, Electoral Alternative for Labor and Social Justice). An electoral alliance concluded by the "alternative" with the PDS (Party of Democratic Socialism), whose mainstay was the former GDR, obtained nearly 9% of the national vote. Both parties merged two years later to the new party The Left (*Die Linke*), depriving—as subsequent elections would show—the Social Democrats of its traditional role as Germany's center-left omnibus party.

The Blair/Schröder manifesto had signaled that the German government would lower corporation taxes. The Red-Green coalition's Finance Minister, after Oskar Lafontaine had unceremoniously stepped down, was former Hesse Governor Hans Eichel, a politician who possessed "extensive networks within the worlds of business and finance" (Lees 2000: 127). Eichel's state secretary Heribert Zitzelsberger, who drafted the 2000 Tax Reduction Act, had previously headed the Bayer multinational corporation's tax department.

The law not just cut the corporation tax to 25%, but made corporations' capital gains from sales of shares tax-exempt for 15 years. The provision included retained profits from the past two years on which, if distributed to shareholders, companies might reclaim the difference between the higher previous and the new tax rate from fiscal authorities. The German weekly ZEIT labeled the provision "the biggest gift of all time" (Herz 2005): The loss in corporation tax revenue resulting from the law amounted to no less than 24.1 billion euros in 2001 (showing a balance of −0.5 billion euros), as against 2000. In his autobiography, Michael Naumann—former CEO of Rowohlt and Henry Holt publishers, 1998–2001 the Federal Government's first Commissioner for Cultural Affairs, presently Rector of the Barenboim-Said Academy in Berlin—narrated how the bill had passed the cabinet without discussion. Neither Eichel nor Schröder had mentioned the exemption clause for capital gains (Naumann 2017: 306).

The Tax Reduction Act proved a mere prelude to the 2002 and 2004/2006 Financial Market Promotion and Investment Modernisation Acts. The derivatives trading spree touched off in the United States (as described earlier in this chapter) by the Gramm-Leach-Bliley Act of 1999 now caught up with Germany. The laws first authorized derivatives transactions and subsequently removed caps for investment in these highly risk-prone instruments. Asset management companies, pooling investors' funds, were exempted from liquidity rules; capital adequacy requirements for such firms (regardless of investment fund size) eased; hedge funds—with a limited clientele, pronounced opaqueness, and an intense aversion to regulation—were also authorized. It had been "the evolution of the legal landscape since the 1990s", Germany's Central Bank would observe after the Great Recession, which had "radically transformed [the larger German banks'] entire business operations." The Bank report did not mince words either about the consequences: Deregulation had acted as a "catalyst" for a "not altogether sustainable" expansion in market-based transactions by not a few large German banks which had invested in securitized assets to such an extent "that they were jeopardizing their solvency" (Deutsche Bundesbank 2015: 38, 39).

The preceding review of downsizing and deregulatory policies in the United States, the United Kingdom, and Germany substantiates the assertion that democratic regimes have been mutating into "competition states", whose pro-market interventionism has played a "fundamental" role in promoting globalization. Increasingly bent on "dismantling and disarming" economic and financial policy instruments in the name of global competitiveness, consequently "underperforming" with regard to regulation, delivery of public services, and redistribution, these minimal welfare and regulatory states with their will lose their capacity "equitably to provide welfare and public goods". The loss undermines both the effectiveness and the legitimacy of democratic processes—"the sense of citizenship and the notion of public interest" (Cerny 1999: 5, 13, 14/15, 19).

Even in the mid-run, the issues associated with a weakening of legitimacy—social passivity, depoliticization, alienation, for lack of a "stake in society" (Kellner 2011: S161), from the core ideas of democracy—may present the most serious threat. Shirley Williams (Baroness Williams), the *grande dame* of the British Liberal Democrats, who has also lived and taught in the United States, warned about the "rounding on government itself ", the "level of tribalism" which she had observed in that country as a result of the perceived "failure of democratic government in continuing to deliver prosperity to most of the American people" (Williams 2011: S191). The Norwegian Study on Power and Democracy, commissioned in 1997 by that country's parliament, found—as the power and the accountability of democratic governments are literally bleeding away, as welfare states are being "traded down to minimal safety nets", and as resources for allocation by representatives to constituents become unavailable—that the reasons for "active commitment to the democratic process" are disappearing fast (Hirst 2004: 155; Putzel 2005: 12; also Haugsvær 2003; Ringen 2004).

136   R. EISFELD

There has been more empirical corroboration: A robust statistical examination assessing the effects of globally mobile capital and enterprise on democracy in a large sample (127 countries, 1970 to mid-1990s) concluded that, due to reduced democratic accountability and constrained space for public policies, globalization not merely erodes the *prospects* for democracy. The evaluation of empirical data in a cross-sectional model also showed that, *already now*, compliance with the demands of both international investors and inter-state competitive pressures is "beginning to cause a decline in national democratic governance" (Li and Reuveny 2003: 30, 53).

These implications ought certainly, as the authors write, "cause concern for both policy makers and academicians" (Li and Reuveny 2003: 53). As of this writing, they may be considered established wisdom, which political scientists should be driving home. No new insights need to be presented in order to argue, as Quan Lee and Rafael Reuveny have done (ibid.: 53/54), that regulating governments might, for instance, design new tax and subsidy policies, work to reduce "excessive volatility" of capital movements, curtail by law "excessive rent-seeking" by multinational firms.

That globalization, in a word, may be harnessed is precisely what Chap. 3 of this book insisted on, when it urged that political scientists should help citizens

- judging change according to norms of equity and social justice, and shaping such change through political participation,
- insisting on being offered meaningful choices, rather than resignedly submitting to the preferences of international economic players and national politicians caught in the vise of "cognitive capture".

Joseph Stiglitz cut to the heart of the issue when he maintained, in concluding his forceful book on the price of inequality, that market forces *can be reshaped* by politics (Stiglitz 2012: ch. 10, esp. 266, 285/286)—by alternative policy paradigms, by laws and regulations, by the behavior of players and agencies and, in the final instance, by vibrant and responsive political systems prevailing over present tendencies toward mendocracy and plutocracy. As an illustration, it might be mentioned that, in Canada, neo-liberal moves toward banking deregulation in the 1990s were "incremental" rather than "dramatic". They left banks more committed to meeting capital adequacy requirements and balancing their risks. The Canadian government's more restrained deregulatory policy enabled the country's financial system to largely, if not fully, contain the spread of the 2007/2008 crisis to other market sectors (Puri 2013: 156, 179, 182). Canada's regulatory regime had, in other words, remained stronger than in the United States, the United Kingdom, or Germany. In the latter countries, as indicated at this chapter's outset, merely "the first tentative steps" have been made toward reversing market deregulation (Deutsche Bundesbank 2015: 35). Prevailing neo-liberal orthodoxies have been "dented, but not replaced"; regulatory institutions thus far "not significantly strengthened" (Wilson and Grant 2012: 249, 258). Elections— again excepting Canada—have mirrored citizens' perplexed anger and anxiety, rather than political trust and confidence. No "alternative vision of economic management" (Wilson 2012: 59) has emerged.

The necessary public debate on tough regulation ought to be pushed by a reenergized political economy. More research ought to be devoted to the effort of getting behind "technocratic discourses on market efficiency", laying bare "the interests being served" by ostensible expertise (Morgan 2012: 85). Such engagement by a discipline bent on improving the human condition should emphatically be promoted by the realization that a lack of regulatory constraint has facilitated and deepened a recession that has spelled "disaster for millions of people who have lost jobs, homes, and savings" (Wilson and Grant 2012: V).

Intense research efforts and public policy debate are likewise warranted on a terrain where large-scale individual and corporate tax evasion place a morally absolutely unjustifiable burden on ordinary citizens. British urban geographer Gareth Jones has labeled that terrain—which two leaked datasets, the 2016 *Panama* and the 2017 *Paradise Papers*, finally thrust into the public spotlight—**spatial political economy**—more precisely, the economic geography of globally mobile capitalism. In what may arguably be the most important contribution to the volume *After Piketty*, Jones criticized the inattentiveness to space of Thomas Piketty's approach to political economy. He contended that the geographical mobility of capital implied by the term "globalization" has involved, to an accelerating degree, locating in "offshore and onshore jurisdictions" which "serve to decouple the economy from democratic politics", minimizing companies' "moral obligations and fiscal responsibilities" (Jones 2017: 282/283, 284). Some 70 tax havens and some 4000 (by 2006) zones/enclaves governed by trusts or agencies, but actually by resident corporations, combine organizational complexity via different jurisdictions, secrecy, private security, absence of democracy and of trade unions in order to promote "tax avoidance on an industrial scale", often along with money laundering and/or illegal trade in arms, drugs, and other repugnant goods or services (Jones 2017: 285/286, 287, 289/290).

Berkeley economist Gabriel Zucman has calculated from available records that 11.5% of the world's GDP, a staggering amount in the vicinity of $8.7 *trillion*, is held in lowtaxed or untaxed offshore accounts. *Accounting for these hidden assets would "significantly" affect assessments of the extent of inequality discussed in Chap. 8* (Zucman 2017; id. 2014: 140). A 2015 OECD Report estimated the corporate tax revenue *annually lost* to the G-20 countries at $240 *billion* (Jones 2017: 283).

Tax havens and extralegal zones are, again, *the result of deliberate policies*, the work of governments in places such as in Ireland, Luxembourg, the Netherlands, the United Kingdom (Bahamas, Bermuda, Cayman Islands, Virgin Islands, Channel Islands), Malta, Hong Kong, Singapore, a number of US states such as Delaware and, of course, Switzerland. As a comprehensive step toward international transparency, Piketty and Zucman have demanded a world financial registry, along the lines of present property registries for land and real estate, but identifying true beneficial owners—rather than shell companies—of financial assets such as bonds, derivatives, equities, and mutual fund shares (Piketty 2014: 520 ss.; Zucman 2016; id. 2017). Zucman and his international collaborators have also called for stiff punitive legislation that would deprive banks and law firms (e.g., Appleby, Mossack Fonseca; *vide Panama* and *Paradise Papers*) found helping tax evasion of their licenses, and for putting tax cooperation, rather than investment protection, at the center of future free-trade negotiations (Alstadsæter et al. 2017).

The US 2010 Foreign Account Tax Compliance Act (FATCA) requiring foreign banks to provide information about assets held abroad by US taxpayers is a first step in the direction of more transparency, even if deficiencies are notable (Piketty 2014: 522/523). While a considerable number—over 100—of intergovernmental agreements regarding FATCA's international implementation has meanwhile been concluded, Republican opposition to FATCA has resulted, so far unsuccessfully, in the introduction of bills to repeal the law in the US Senate and House of Representatives. A legal challenge to FATCA, also led by Republicans, was also rejected in 2018 by the US Supreme Court.

The lesson should be obvious: It's the politics, stupid! Public policies may enact the first timid legal measures to constrain the offshore movement of corporate assets and earnings which exacerbates inequality.

"Public" policies may also reverse these tentative reforms, refusing to address practices yielding such enormous benefits to individual and corporate profiteers. Political scientists should, they indeed ought to, visibly emerge as an ally of the first kind of strategies. For how may our discipline expect citizens who feel helpless in view of the quasi-officially sanctioned reemergence of "two nations" in their countries to harbor sympathy for action meant to contain any discrimination of arriving immigrants? And why should citizens whose lives appear to them as warped by the effects of stark inequality not submit to fatalism when it comes to efforts intended to protect their environment from the consequences of climate change?

References

AFP [Agence France Presse] (2014): "German Stumbling Block to Transatlantic Trade Talks." *Digital Journal*, March 27. http://www.digitaljournal.com/business/business/german-stumbling-block-to-transatlantic-trade-talks/article/378521, accessed November 15, 2017.

AFTINET [Australian Fair Trade & Investment Network] (2012): "Australian High Court Rules Against Big Tobacco on Plain Packaging". Media Release. http://aftinet.org.au/cms/node/519, accessed November 15, 2017.

Alstadsæter, Annette/Johannesen, Niels/Zucman, Gabriel (2017): "Tax Evaders Exposed: Why the Super-Rich Are Even Richer Than We Thought." *The Guardian*, June 14, 2017. http://gabriel-zucman.eu/tax-evaders-exposed/, accessed December 16, 2017.

Asato, Jessica (2011): "Why Did Labour's Public Sector Reforms Fail to Transform Communities?" In: Patrick Diamond/Michael Kenny (eds.): *Reassessing New Labour. Market, State and Society under Blair and Brown*. Chichester: Wiley-Blackwell in Association with *The Political Quarterly*, S177–S186.

Atkins, Curtis (2016): "The Third Way International." *Jacobin Magazine*, November 2. https://www.jacobinmag.com/2016/02/atkins-dlc-third-way-clinton-blair-schroeder-social-democracy, accessed December 6, 2017.

Bitler, Marianne/Hoynes, Hilary (2016): "The More Things Change, the More They Stay the Same? The Safety Net and Poverty in the Great Recession." *Journal of Labor Economics*, Vol. 34, 403–444.

Blair, Tony/Schröder, Gerhard (1998): *Europe: The Third Way/Die Neue Mitte*. Working Documents No. 2. Johannesburg: Friedrich Ebert Foundation.

Blumenthal, Paul (2009): "How Congress Rushed a Bill that helped Bring the Economy to Its Knees." *Huffington Post*, May 11, 2009. https://www.huffingtonpost.com/paul-blumenthal/how-congress-rushed-a-bil_b_181926.html, accessed October 16, 2017.

140   R. EISFELD

Bonesmo Frederiksen, Kaja (2012): "Income Inequality in the European Union". OECD Economics Department Working Paper No. 952, April. Paris: OECD Publishing. http://library.bsl.org.au/jspui/bitstream/1/3251/1/Income%20 inequality%20in%20the%20european%20union.pdf, accessed December 10, 2017.

Brookings Institution (2014): "Reformed Welfare Program Effective During Great Recession". Brookings Economic Studies, https://www.brookings. edu/wp-content/uploads/2016/06/TANF_in_recession_release.pdf, accessed October 20, 2017.

Bundesverfassungsgericht (2016): "Applications for a Preliminary Injunction in the 'CETA' Proceedings Unsuccessful." Press Release No. 71/2016, October 13. https://www.bundesverfassungsgericht.de/SharedDocs/Pressemitteilungen/ EN/2016/bvg16-071.html, accessed Nov. 2, 2017.

Cashore, Benjamin/Auld, Graeme/Newsom, Deanna (2004): *Governing Through Markets. Forest Certification and the Emergence of Non-State Authority.* New Haven/London: Yale University Press.

CCPA [Canadian Centre for Policy Alternatives] (2015): "NAFTA Chapter 11 Investor-State Disputes to January 1, 2015." https://www.google.de/search? q=canada+isds+arbitration+nafta+legal+fees&ie=utf-8&oe=utf-8&client=firefoxb&gfe_rd=cr&dcr=0&ei=fmoJWogtrqDzB_3PhJgN, accessed November 13, 2017.

Cerny, Philip G. (1999): "Globalization and the Erosion of Democracy." *European Journal of Political Research*, Vol. 36, 1–26.

Charnovitz, Steve (1994): "The NAFTA Environmental Side Agreement: Implications for Environmental Cooperation, Trade Policy, and American Treatymaking." *Temple International and Comparative Law Journal*, Vol. 257, 1–62, http:// www.wilmerhale.com/uploadedFiles/WilmerHale_Shared_Content/Files/ Editorial/Publication/charnovitznaftaenvironment.pdf, accessed October 30, 2017.

Compa, Lane (1994): "American Trade Unions and NAFTA". In: H. Totsuka et al. (eds.): *International Trade Unionism at the Current Stage of Economic Globalization and Regionalization.* Tokyo: Friedrich Ebert Foundation, 97–117. http://digitalcommons.ilr.cornell.edu/cgi/viewcontent.cgi?article= 1009&context=conference, accessed October 30, 2017.

Côté, Christine (2014): *A Chilling Effect? The Impact of International Investor Agreements on National regulatory Autonomy in the Areas of Health, Safety and the Environment.* PhD Thesis submitted to LSE. etheses.lse.ac.uk/897/8/ Cote_A-Chilling_Effect.pdf, accessed October 30, 2017.

Cox, Christopher (2008): "Securities and Exchange Commission Chairman Cox Announces End of Consolidated Supervise Entities Program". September 26. https://www.sec.gov/news/press/2008/2008-230.htm, accessed October 1, 2017.

ROBUST REGULATORY POLICIES FOR CAPITALISM   141

Daripa, Arup et al. (2012): "Labour's Record on Financial Regulation". Birkbeck College (University of London) Faculty Papers. http://www.bbk.ac.uk/ems/faculty/wright/pdf/oxrep, accessed November 21, 2017. Later published in *Oxford Review of Economic Policy*, Vol. 29 (2013), 71–94.

Dattu, Riyaz/Pavic, Sonja (2017): "Canada Seeks to Reform NAFTA's Investor-State Dispute Settlement Chapter." OSLER Resources, August 23. https://www.osler.com/en/resources/cross-border/2017/canada-seeks-to-reform-nafta-investor-state-disp, accessed November 15, 2017.

Deutsche Bundesbank (2015): "Structural Developments in the German Banking Sector", in: *Monthly Report*, April, 35–60.

Eisfeld, Rainer (2011): "How Political Science Might Regain Relevance and Obtain an Audience: A Manifesto for the 21st Century". *European Political Science*, Vol. 10, 220–225.

Elson, Anthony (2017): *The Global Financial Crisis in Retrospect. Evolution, Resolution, and Lessons for Prevention*. New York: Palgrave Macmillan.

Fernández-Armesto, Juan (2012): Quoted in: Corporate Europe Observatory: "Who Guards the Guardians?", November 27. https://corporateeurope.org/trade/2012/11/chapter-4-who-guards-guardians-conflicting-interests-investment-arbitrators, accessed November 15, 2017.

Gaukrodger, David/Gordon, Kathryn (2012): "Investor-State Dispute Settlement." *OECD Working Papers on International Investment*. 2012/03. Paris. http://www.oecd.org/investment/investment-policy/WP-2012_3.pdf, accessed November 12, 2017.

Giddens, Anthony (2010): "The Rise and Fall of New Labour." *New Perspectives Quarterly*. Summer Issue, 32–37.

Grimm, Nicole L. (1998): "The North American Agreement of Labor Cooperation and Its Effects on Women Working in Mexican Maquiladoras." *American University Law Review*, Vol. 48, 179–228.

Harris, John F./Yang, John E. (1996): "Clinton to Sign Bill Overhauling Welfare". *Washington Post*, August 1. http://www.washingtonpost.com/wp-srvw/politics/special/welfare/stories/wf080196.htm, accessed October 18, 2017.

Haugsvær, Steinar (2003): "The Norwegian Study on Power and Democracy: Main Conclusions." August 26. www.oecd.org/norway/33800474.pdf.

Herz, Wilfried (2005): "Das größte Geschenk aller Zeiten." DIE ZEIT No. 37 (September 8). http://www.zeit.de/2005/37Steuern, accessed December 7, 2017.

Hirst, Paul (2004): "What is Globalization?" In: Fredrik Engelstad/Øyvind Østerud (eds.): *Power and Democracy*. Aldershot: Ashgate, 151–168.

Hoynes, Hilary (2017): "Interview." *The Region*, Federal Reserve Bank of Minneapolis, June 1. https://www.minneapolisfed.org/publications/the-region/interview-with-hilary-hoynes, accessed October 20, 2017.

142   R. EISFELD

Jones, Gareth A. (2017): "The Geographies of 'Capital in the Twenty-First Century': Inequality, Political Economy, and Space." In: Heather Boushey/J. Bradford DeLong/Marshall Steinbaum (eds.): *After Piketty. The Agenda for Economics and Inequality.* Cambridge/London: Harvard University Press 2017, 280–303.

Kay, Tamara (2011): *NAFTA and the Politics of Labor Transnationalism.* Cambridge/New York: Cambridge University Press.

Keitel, Jannika (2015): "Germany's Welfare System: An Overview." *Policy in Practice*, April 14. http://policyinpractice.co.uk/the-welfare-system-in-germany/, accessed December 10, 2017.

Kellner, Peter (2011): "The Death of Class-Based Politics": Patrick Diamond/Michael Kenny (eds.): *Reassessing New Labour. Market, State and Society under Blair and Brown.* Chichester: Wiley-Blackwell in Association with *The Political Quarterly*, S152-S164.

King, Desmond/Wickham-Jones, Mark (1999): "From Clinton to Blair: The Democratic (Party) Origins of Welfare to Work". *Political Quarterly*, Vol. 70, 62–74.

Koch, Ed (2012): "It's Time to Reexamine the Welfare Reform Law of 1996." https://www.huffingtonpost.com/ed-koch/welfare-reform_b_1428284.html, accessed October 20, 2017.

Krugman, Paul (2011): "The Profession and the Crisis". *Eastern Economic Journal*, Vol. 37, 307–312.

Lees, Charles (2000): *The Red-Green Coalition in Germany.* Manchester/New York: Manchester University Press.

Li, Quan/Reuveny, Rafael (2003): "Economic Globalization and Democracy: An Empirical Analysis". *British Journal of Political Science*, Vol. 33, 29–54.

Mestral, Armand de (2015): "When Does the Exception Become the Rule? Conserving Regulatory Space under CETA." *Journal of International Economic Law*, Vol. 18, 641–654.

Morgan, Glenn (2012): "Constructing Financial Markets: Reforming Over-the-Counter Derivatives Markets in the Aftermath of the Financial Crisis." In: Wyn Grant/Graham K. Wilson (eds.): *The Consequences of the Global Financial Crisis. The Rhetoric of Reform and Regulation.* Oxford: Oxford University Press, 67–87.

Naumann, Michael (2017): *Glück gehabt. Ein Leben.* Hamburg: Hoffmann & Campe.

Noble, Charles (1997): *Welfare As We Knew It.* Oxford/New York: Oxford University Press.

Olivet, Cecilia/Villareal, Alberto (2016): "Who Really Won the Legal Battle between Philip Morris and Uruguay?" *Guardian*, July 28. https://www.the-guardian.com/global-develop-ment/2016/jul/28/who-really-won-legal-battle-philip-morris-uruguay, accessed November 15, 2017.

ROBUST REGULATORY POLICIES FOR CAPITALISM   143

Osterberg, David/Ajami, Fouad (1971): "The Multinational Corporation: Expanding the Frontiers of World Politics". *Journal of Conflict Resolution*, No. 15, 457–470.

Piketty, Thomas (2014): *Capital in the Twenty-First Century*. Cambridge/London: Belknap Press of Harvard University Press.

Puri, Poonam (2013): "Canada: 'Bank Bashing' Is a Popular Sport." In: Suzanne J. Konzelmann/Marc Fovarque-Davies (eds.): *Banking Systems in the Crisis: The Faces of Liberal Capitalism*. London/New York: Routledge, 155–185.

Putzel, James (2005): "Globalization, Liberalization, and Prospects for the State." *International Political Science Review*, Vol. 26, 5–16.

PWG Report (1999): *Over-the-Counter Derivatives Markets and the Commodity Exchange Act*. Report of the President's Working Group on Financial Markets. Accompanying Letters to the Speaker of the House and the President of the Senate, 1–2. https://www.treasury.gov/resource-center/fin-mkts/Documents/otcact.pdf, accessed October 16, 2017.

Ringen, Stein (2004): "Wealth and Decay. The Norwegian Study of Power and Democracy." *Times Literary Supplement*, February 13, 3–5.

Ritholtz, Barry (2012): "Repeal of Glass-Steagall: Not a Cause, But a Multiplier." *Washington Post*, August 4, 2012. https://www.washingtonpost.com/repeal-of-glass-steagall-not-a-cause-but-amultiplier/2012/08/02/gJQAuvvRXX_story.html?utm_term=.689105f8d05a, accessed October 16, 2017.

Roberts, Dan (2014): "Wall Street Deregulation Pushed by Clinton Advisers, Documents Reveal". *The Guardian*, April 19. https://www.theguardian.com/world/2014/qpe/19/wall-street-deregulation-clinton-advisers-obama, accessed October 2, 2017.

Romano, Flavio (2006): "Clinton and Blair: The Economics of the Third Way." *Journal of Economic and Social Policy*, Vol. 10, No. 2, 79–94.

Salacuse, Jeswald W. (2010): "The Emerging Global Regime for Investment". *Harvard International Law Journal*, Vol. 51, 427–473.

Sanati, Cyrus (2009): "10 Years Later, Looking at Repeal of Glass-Steagall." *New York Times*, November 12. https://dealbook.nytimes.com/2009/11/12/10-years-later-looking-at-repeal-of-glass-steagall/, accessed October 16, 2017.

Shihata, Ibrahim (1986): "Towards a Greater Depoliticization of Investment Disputes". *ICSID Review – Foreign Investment Law Journal*, Vol. 1, No. 1, 1–25. https://academic.oup.com/icsidreview/article/1/1/1756171, accessed November 8, 2017.

Stiglitz, Joseph E. (2008): "Capitalist Fools." *Vanity Fair*, December 9. https://www.vanityfair.com/news/2009/01/stiglitz200901-2, accessed August 26, 2017.

Stiglitz, Joseph E. (2012): *The Price of Inequality*. New York/London: W. W. Norton.

Taylor, Robert (1999): "Some Comments on the Blair/Schroeder 'Third Way/*Neue Mitte*' Manifesto". *Transfer: European Review of Labour and*

144 R. EISFELD

Research, Vol. 5, 411–414. www.journals.sagepub.com/toc/trsa/5/3, accessed December 6, 2017.

Tienhaara, Kyla (2011): "Regulatory Chill and the Threat of Arbitration: A View from Political science". In: Chester Brown/Kate Miles (eds.): *Evolution in Investment Treaty Law and Arbitration*, Cambridge: Cambridge University Press 2011, 606–627.

Tietje, Christian/Baetens, Freya (2014): "The Impact of Investor-State-Dispute Settlement (ISDS) in the Transatlantic Trade and Investment Partnership". Study Prepared for the Dutch Ministry of Foreign Affairs, June 24. http://media.leidenuniv.nl/legacy/joint-public-hearing.pdf, accessed November 5, 2017.

Van Harten, Gus (2014): "Investor-State Arbitration." https://blog.oup.com/2014/01/van-harten-q-a-investor-state-arbitration/, January 20, accessed October 28, 2017. [OUP: Oxford University Press].

Vargas, Jorge A. (1994): "NAFTA, the Chiapas Rebellion, and the Emergence of Mexican Ethnic Law". *California Western International Law Journal*, Vol. 25, 1–79.

Weaver, R. Kent/Gais, Thomas (2002): "State Policy Choices Under Welfare Reform". Brookings Institution, April 2. https://www.brookings.edu/research/state-policy-choices-under-welfare-reform/, accessed October 19, 2017.

Wellhausen, Rachel L. (2016): "Recent Trends in Investor-State Dispute Settlement." *Journal of International Dispute Settlement*, Vol. 7, 117–135.

Williams, Shirley (2011): "Shirley Williams in Conversation with Tony Wright." In: Patrick Diamond/Michael Kenny (eds.): *Reassessing New Labour. Market, State and Society under Blair and Brown*. Chichester: Wiley-Blackwell in Association with *The Political Quarterly*, S187-S191.

Wilson, Graham K./Grant, Wyn (2012): "Preface", "Introduction" and "Conclusion". In: Wyn Grant/Graham K. Wilson (eds.): *The Consequences of the Global Financial Crisis. The Rhetoric of Reform and Regulation*. Oxford: Oxford University Press, V-VII, 1–14, 247–260.

Wilson, Graham K. (2012): "The United States: The Strange Survival of (Neo) Liberalism". In: Wyn Grant/Graham K. Wilson (eds.): *The Consequences of the Global Financial Crisis. The Rhetoric of Reform and Regulation*. Oxford: Oxford University Press, 51–66.

Zucman, Gabriel (2014): "Taxing across Borders: Tracking Personal Wealth and Corporate Profits." *Journal of Economic Perspectives*, Vol. 28, 121–148.

Zucman, Gabriel (2016): "Sanctions for Offshore Tax Havens, Transparency at Home." *New York Times*, April 7, 2016. http://gabriel-zucman.eu/sactions-for-offshore/, accessed December 16, 2017.

Zucman, Gabriel (2017): "How Corporations and the Wealthy Avoid Taxes (and How to Stop Them)." *New York Times*, November 10, 2017. http://gabriel-zucman.eu/how-corporations-avoid-taxes/, accessed December 16, 2017.

CHAPTER 10

Global Warming, Power Structures, and Living Conditions

Climate Politics and Twenty-First-Century Political Science

The activities of veto players among economic and political elites constraining climate policy changes in, for example, the United States, China, Russia, or India have overshadowed a more fundamental problem which is that the improvement of living conditions for hundreds of millions of poor implies, at present, an increase in CO_2 emissions. Any effective emission reduction will depend on decoupling population growth and income rise from increasing pollution.

In the concluding part of Chap. 4, this book discussed sustained corporate campaigns for discrediting scientific evidence by spreading disinformation, propelled in the United States by business lobby groups', think tanks' and individual scholars' deep-seated aversion against restrictions of any kind to free-market capitalism. One prominent instance the chapter referred to was planetary warming and its impact on climate change.

In what way did these concerted drives affect policy-makers' decisions about how to deal with the crisis identified by the international community of climate scientists? May not the incalculable—in terms of social misery—dimensions of environmental disruption involve "potentially devastating" implications for democracies, for their capacity to withstand such duress (Fischer 2017: 1)? Need not political science, if for no other reason, intervene in the debate on a much broader and more determined scale than hitherto?

© The Author(s) 2019

145

R. Eisfeld, *Empowering Citizens, Engaging the Public*,

https://doi.org/10.1007/978-981-13-5928-6_10

146   R. EISFELD

Chapter 4 demonstrated that what corporate disinformation campaigns were really about was averting governmental regulation. Originating, as they did, from the conservative camp, the attacks had an effect first on the US Congress and on successive Republican administrations from the Bush to the Trump presidencies. Subsequently, they began to shape part of the American public's creed.

One initial result was that the United States did not ratify the 1997 Kyoto Protocol committing the signatory states to reduce greenhouse gas emissions. Subsequent bipartisan negotiations on a projected "Clean Energy and Security" bill—which would have placed caps on carbon emissions—collapsed, as anti-regulatory/anti-tax elites' demagoguery and supporting grass roots Tea Party activism (sketched in Chap. 3) permeated the Republican Party. Republican support "melted away", and because Republican votes would have been needed to offset opposition by Democrats from oil and coal states, effective Congressional action to mitigate global warming was precluded (Skocpol 2013: 2/3, 9, 56, 61).

A 2011 sociological study additionally showed how initial widespread public sympathy with anti-climate change policies in the United States began to split along partisan lines since the mid-1990s. As more and more Republican Congressional leaders jumped on the band-wagon of climate change denial, a "bifurcated flow of conflicting information" on global warming from political elites, lobby groups, academic "contrarians", and media began to inundate American society. To a much larger extent than in European societies, a "cacophony of competing voices" succeeded in impressing citizens with an appearance of the issue's supposed ambiguity. After Congress, the American public became polarized, *with a growing percentage prepared to also deny scientific evidence* (McCright and Dunlap 2011: 158/159, 171, 178, 180).

The US example illustrates the diagnosis that in a policy arena which desperately requires an internationally coordinated approach, domestic politics determine the extent to which major greenhouse gas emitters—hence, key players—are "willing and able to engage in climate change mitigation" (Bang et al. 2015a: 1). However, even after Donald Trump's election, US climate politics have not entirely evaporated into thin air.

On the one hand, Trump announced that the United States would by 2020 (the earliest possible date) withdraw from the 2015 Paris Agreement—signed by the Obama administration—on targets for limiting global temperature rise. Trump also began rolling back, by executive order, US environmental regulations, and he proposed steep budget cuts for the Environmental Protection Agency which the (Republican) Nixon administration had created in 1970.

On the other hand, the governors of 15 US states (at the time of writing) and Puerto Rico took the unprecedented step, following Trump's announcement, of forming the bipartisan United States Climate Alliance, committing themselves to continue pursuing the goals of the Paris Agreement within their states' borders. The coalition's members (which include, e.g., California, Colorado, Connecticut, Maryland, Massachusetts, Minnesota, New York, Oregon, and Washington) presently account for just over one-third of both US population and GDP. Seven further governors (five Republicans, three Democrats) averred their states' support for the Paris Agreement without joining the Alliance.

The Climate Mayors association of US mayors, founded in 2014 and now representing nearly 400 cities—including the 10 most populous—has also pledged that it will support the objectives of the Alliance. In its first annual report, the states' coalition (presently co-chaired by the California and Washington governors) affirmed its intent to launch "cross-state collaborative initiatives" to "help transform markets nation-wide" (U. S. Climate Alliance 2017). Participating in a November 2017 United Nations conference on climate change held in Germany, the Alliance became visible internationally.

The policies developed by the Climate Mayors/Climate Alliance array of states and cities could start a cumulative "knowledge-building process". Spreading to broader segments of both the public and the state and federal law-makers, the coalition's engagement may result in a positive "change [of] preference structures" (Bang 2015: 175/176), *including an abatement of the refusal to accept evidence on climate change.*

The association may also serve as an example-in-the-making of what the late Elinor Ostrom—whose name already surfaced prominently in this book—in a seminal background paper to the World Bank's 2010 *World Development Report*, proposed as a **polycentric approach** of addressing climate change on multiple scales and levels. Involving local, regional, and national players linked by information networks and effective monitoring—and consequently the certainty that other identifiable citizens and agencies are taking similar action—such an effort would be likely to build a badly needed "core of trust and reciprocity".

The approach might therefore send the *social* messages that have been found to be "more effective in changing behavior" than messages centered on *factual* information: "We're a city/province/state of problem

148   R. EISFELD

solvers! We haven't had a problem that we haven't been able to roll up our sleeves and fix. We need to do that now with..." (Joslyn 2016). Moreover, it would encourage experimentation to cope with the multi-level problem which anti-climate change strategies have turned out to be (Ostrom 2009: 4, 35, 38/39).

Once again, as in Chap. 9, the principle and the extent of regulation are at stake. They provide the backdrop, against which the debate on climate change is being conducted not just in the United States. In his final book *Inequality—What Can Be Done?*, the late "Tony" Atkinson, distinguished British pioneer in studies on income and wealth distribution quoted earlier in this book, included an assessment of the abortive Transatlantic Trade and Investment Partnership (TTIP) agreement by John Hilary, Executive Director of the UK-based charity War on Want. According to Hilary, some of the United Kingdom's most highly regarded environmental regulations would have been among the "regulatory barriers" whose removal the treaty sought. Atkinson himself ranked mitigating climate change among the foremost policy objectives of the twenty-first century, along with reducing the extent of inequality (Atkinson 2015: 274).

When Harvard political economist/sociologist Thomas Nixon Carver laid down the core principle of governmental intervention a century ago, he contended that "government and government alone" prevented economic self-interest from leading to "destructive as well as to productive activity" (Carver 1915: 108). Evidently, the *extent of government intervention* ought to be determined by the *degree of destructivity*. Already at the outset of the 1970s, K. William Kapp, in his seminal work *The Social Costs of Private Enterprise* (first published, but largely overlooked, in 1950), was unequivocal in assessing environmental disruption *resulting from present production, transportation, and consumption patterns* as among "the most fundamental and long-term issues" ever faced by mankind, bearing directly on "human survival" (Kapp [2]1971: VIII; also XII/XIII).

During the four and a half decades since Kapp's diagnosis, it should have become palpably obvious that stemming, let alone reversing, that disruptive trend requires a "fundamental conversion of the entire global energy supply system" (Bernauer 2013: 424). The necessary measures by public agencies need to be enacted—to use terminology from a recent study by a Western Oregon University political scientist (Dickinson 2017: 128)—on a "massive", if not a "colossal", scale. Dickinson painted three potential scenarios, depending on the way the world's states would set their priorities (Dickinson 2017: 130–134):

GLOBAL WARMING, POWER STRUCTURES, AND LIVING CONDITIONS 149

- Causes and immediate dangers of climate change continue to be downplayed or denied by decisive political players. Widespread inaction in the Global North is followed "by the tragedy of the global commons".
- Untrammeled population growth, increasing emissions, rising sea levels, droughts, fires, hurricanes, famines, and pandemics trigger negative feedback loops. Markets crash, states fail, nuclear weapons spread, and armed conflicts increase. The Global North resorts to armed force to repel the attempted mass exodus out of the Global South.
- Alternatively, the threat of global collapse intensifies international cooperation, leading to an "age of reason", from which new international norms emerge with regard to environmental protection, recourse to renewable energy sources, population control, the slashing of military budgets, mitigation of economic exploitation and grossly unequal wealth distribution, health care, peace education and, eventually, free international migration which "minimizes ethnic tension over time". By the next generation, nuclear weapons programs are converted into deep space exploration projects. "Inevitably", men will one day proceed to "migrate off planet", setting out "in search of new worlds" with an "insatiable curiosity".

No less inevitably, that scenario recalls the 1936 Alexander Korda film *Things to Come*, written by H. G. Wells, where global economic and political consolidation is followed by the first manned flight around the moon. After the projectile has been launched, carrying a female and a male pilot, the former's father, Oswald Cabal, delivers a monologue to his friend Raymond Passworthy about mankind's unending quest for knowledge that will lead it to the stars. His passionate statement concludes with the rhetorical flourish: "All the universe, or nothing. Which shall it be, Passworthy? Which shall it be?"

Much like H. G. Well's prediction quoted in the prologue to this book, the starkly black-and-white alternative seems of doubtful value. Moreover, a political science with change as its primary focus may no doubt include realistic future scenarios. Mendocracy and plutocracy, discussed in the present work, are such fact-based visions. Political scientists might also occasionally want to tap into observations made by science fiction authors, as exemplified in this work by brief references to J. G. Ballard and Chad Oliver. But they should refrain from appropriating some of the more

150   R. EISFELD

speculative trappings of that genre, such as a benign "age of reason" or even humanity "migrating off planet".

By contrast, Dickinson's gloomy second scenario may not have been overdone. The *MIT Technology Review* magazine (whose coverage received numerous awards over the years, and which is not noted for sensationalism) reported that, significantly, carbon emissions in India and China had increased during 2017, more than offsetting a modest pollution decline in the United States. Summarizing several recent studies, the author—the magazine's senior energy editor—identified 2017 as the year global warming may have begun "to spin out of control". Not unlike Dickinson in his book, the article emphasized the emergence of feedback loops, which made worst-case scenarios look "increasingly likely": rising emissions, higher temperatures, hyperactive hurricanes, shrinking sea ice, thawing permafrost, massive wildfires—and higher emissions still (Temple 2018).

The preceding references to several global warming-related political science works with strong normative touches may, in one important sense, convey a slanted picture. In 2013, the outgoing editors of *Global Environmental Politics* noted that, from 2003 to 2011, the proportion of the journal's authors from political science had declined by over 20% to just under 40% (Dauvergne and Clapp 2016: 9). Over the following three years, further disquieting facets were added to their portrayal. During her research on climate change adaptation, Debra Javeline (Notre Dame) found that political scientists were "largely absent" from that "crucial" interdisciplinary field. Javeline's work was informed by the premise that, while mitigating efforts remain indispensable, current emissions are presently *and inevitably* causing climate change, compelling societies to additionally develop strategies of reducing vulnerability to its impact. Javeline argued that, like mitigation, adaptation is fundamentally dependent on politics, and that political scientists could therefore make "tremendous" contributions to addressing the issue. Continuing lack of such expertise, in contrast, would represent a definite obstacle for the realization of adaptive strategies (Javeline 2014: 420/421, 424).

When Robert Keohane (Princeton) received the American Political Science Association's (APSA) James Madison Award in 2015, he noted—referring to Javeline's article—that, with respect to mitigation, the situation so far had been "not been much better". Engaging global warming politics is, Keohane maintained, the discipline's responsibility. It is also, as emphasized by him, "a great opportunity" for a political science committed to meeting current challenges (Keohane 2015: 19, 26).

The coincident emergence of Elinor Ostrom's conceptual framework for multi-level climate policy dynamics, the formation of the Climate Mayors/U. S. Climate Alliance coalition and of similar initiatives to be discussed subsequently *offers political science a unique window for combining responsibility and opportunity:* As in the case of the national-regional-local pacts for integrating immigrants reviewed in Chap. 7 (designed not least, it will be remembered, like Ostrom's model for the purposes of building trust and reciprocity), the discipline ought to offer substantial support in the development of action programs, the assessment of results, the design of monitoring programs.

Climate politics may indeed—slowly, "but surely", as contended by Thomas Bernauer—be making "its way into mainstream political science research" (Bernauer 2013: 422). Yet it would do well to remember at this point that three years after the Swiss political scientist made his statement, the founding editor of *Global Environment Politics* (*GEP*), Peter Dauvergne, and his successor Jennifer Clapp professed surprise at "how few of [*GEP*'s] articles take a critical political economy approach" (Dauvergne and Clapp 2016: 8). Their related observation—cited in Chap. 1—that in the field of environmental politics, too, method-oriented approaches have been crowding out problem-driven approaches should additionally qualify Bernauer's pronouncement.

However, as has also become apparent, that is a far cry from saying that no salient work on climate change politics has been produced by political science. The more such work reflects cutting edge research, the more disquieting are the substantial results. A 2015 comparative politics volume on the domestic politics of global climate change may serve as an outstanding example here. Like Elinor Ostrom's proposal, it invites further in-depth study. The volume was edited by three Norwegian political scientists. Several scholars from Norway, the Netherlands, and Japan, mostly based at the Fridtjof Nansen Institute Oslo, participated in its compilation.

Analysis of the climate policy trajectories of seven key players—the European Union, the United States, Brazil, India, China, Japan, and Russia—made the authors arrive at a sobering conclusion: Under present conditions, both a coalition of these pivotal actors or of a smaller subgroup would, in the short to medium term, fail "by fairly wide margins" to achieve a mitigation effort successful in the only sense that would seem to carry weight: to arrive at preventing "dangerous anthropogenic interference with the climate system" (Bang et al. 2015b: 203).

152   R. EISFELD

Moreover, prospects for the emergence of any such coalition remain severely constrained (Bang et al. 2015b: 187/188, 190–192, 197–199). The researchers found fossil fuel dependency high in China, India, Russia, the United States and the EU's Central/Eastern European member states. In these otherwise strongly diverging political systems, interlinked demands by both policy-makers and public for energy supply security, low energy prices, and continuous economic growth curb mitigation policies.[1] Public engagement in climate change issues varies between virtually non-existent (Russia) to barely emerging (China), weak (India, Japan), declining (Brazil), or divided (the US, West/East European Union societies). Additionally, effective interest groups in the United States, Russia, Brazil, and Japan work in the direction of maintaining the status quo.

Yet even these hurdles may prove not the biggest stumbling blocks. Societies such as, most extremely, India, but Brazil and, to a decreasing extent, China, too, grapple with reducing poverty, while projected population growth and urbanization continue. They exemplify the plight of countries in large parts of Africa and Asia (but also including, for instance, Mexico), where the improvement of living conditions remains a "political imperative". Climate change mitigation would require to decouple greenhouse gas emissions from the combined effect of population growth, urban concentration, and rise in income levels. For the world at large, decoupling at present remains "a remote prospect" (Bang et al. 2015b: 184, 201).

---

[1] Andrea Lenschow and Carina Sprungk have identified a narrative, which emerged during the late 1990s and early 2000s, by which the European Union would proclaim itself a global climate policy leader capable of "improving the world we live in". Both authors equated that narrative with a "functional myth" used to generate added legitimacy (identity, solidarity) for the European project. As regards the claim's factual basis, Lenschow and Sprungk found it, even at the time (2009/2010), "ambiguous" and only "vaguely positive", raising doubts whether the member states' "sluggishness" in effectively implementing environmental policies might not endanger the narrative's sustainability (Lenschow and Sprungk 2010: 134/135, 139, 141, 148/149, 150). Not quite five years later, Oxford economist Dieter Helm, agreeing on the emergence of the European Union's claim to climate change policy leadership, offered the harsh judgment that such leadership was "in tatters" (Helm 2014: 29, 32). Part of the explanation is provided in a chapter of the study by Bang and her co-authors which depicts the substantial climate policy concessions the West European EU member states had to accept to accommodate their Central/East European counterparts, "with Poland in the lead" (Skjærseth 2015: 86).

GLOBAL WARMING, POWER STRUCTURES, AND LIVING CONDITIONS   153

To achieve substantial progress in that field, two prerequisites must be met. Climate change mitigation objectives need to be integrated in development strategies on communal, regional, and national levels. And the effort must focus on the megacities of every continent, whose projected stupendous further expansion (1 million people *per month* for the next 35 years in India's urban areas alone) is bound to have the most far-reaching consequences for energy consumption and, hence, greenhouse gas emissions. "Cities account for most of the world's carbon emissions. Today, more than half of the world lives in cities, and by 2050, two thirds will. How that growth takes shape will determine whether we can avoid the worst impacts of climate change" (Bloomberg et al. 2016. Bloomberg was a three-term Mayor of New York who, in 2007, launched PlaNYC to push carbon reduction in the city. Hidalgo is Mayor of Paris. Paes is the recent Mayor of Rio de Janeiro).

The US-based Climate Mayors initiative has not remained the only cities' alliance focusing on the advancement of emission-minimizing urban growth. It was even preceded by the C40 Cities Climate Leadership Group, launched on the initiative of Ken Livingstone, then Mayor of London, by 18 megacities in 2005. A year later, after partnering with the Clinton Foundation's climate initiative, the number of participating cities had grown to 40—hence the acronym; at present, the network comprises 90 participants. Current C40 Chair is Paris Mayor Anne Hidalgo. Boston, Copenhagen, Dubai, Durban, Hong Kong, London, Los Angeles, Mexico City, Milan, Seoul, and Tokyo are presently represented on the Steering Committee. Joint workshops to exchange on best practices, technical assistance, and research across sectors and areas such as public health, transport, electricity supply, housing development, involvement of citizens' groups are among the chief services provided by the group.

A recent C40 initiative is the Coalition for Urban Transitions, which aims at bringing together and establishing partnerships with research institutes, foundations, urban planning agencies, and multilateral organizations to explore policy tools, to structure and finance sustainable urbanization, and to attract innovative research. Such research is exemplified by a comprehensive case study (Colenbrander et al. 2017) evaluating an environmentally and socially beneficial development model for Kolkata (formerly Calcutta), India's third most populous metropolitan area with an estimated 15 million inhabitants, one-third of whom live in extreme poverty.

The study was conducted by an 11-person research team from Kolkata's Jadavpur University and the University of Leeds/LSE Center for Climate Change Economics and Policy (funded by the UK Economic and Social Research Council). Focusing on available mitigation options, rather than on protracted structural changes, the study identified an assortment of low-emission measures (mostly in the transport, electricity production, and waste management sectors) which would, until 2025, allow Kolkata "to avoid emission increases at no net cost". Moreover, these options could—relative to conventional urban planning, and *by working closely with affected low-income communities*—"reduce urban poverty", along with the vulnerability of the marginalized poor (Colenbrander et al. 2017: 142, 148, 154/155).

Research on sustainable urban development is still overwhelmingly conducted by trained economists. Once again, inquiries on participatory "eco-localism" (Fischer 2017) can only benefit from more participation by political scientists.

Economists building on the Keynesian approach have described twenty-first-century macroeconomics as a discipline aimed at the *avoidance*, in addition to recession or inflation, *of environmental degradation*, and the *advancement* of sustainability, distributional equity, education, and health care (Harris 2009: 183).

Twenty-first-century political science, as outlined in Chap. 1, may similarly be depicted as a discipline *incorporating ecological sustainability in its canon of basic values* along with the advancement of liberty, equality of political resources, accountability of democratic government, and cultural multiplicity.

As a major part of its commitment to combating mendocracy, political scientists should stand up, with high public visibility, against climate change disinformation strategies "camouflaged as science" (Oreskes and Conway 2012: 262). Engaging the public in the context of global warming further implies that the discipline ought to explore methodically tangible medium- or even short-term benefits of mitigation and adaptation policies, and convey them to the public in a plausible manner.

Contributing to efforts at framing climate change issues and potential solutions more effectively—sending, for instance, social rather than factual messages, as suggested by Elinor Ostrom and explained earlier in this chapter—the discipline's scholars should seek to increase societal support for effective political action. "Building public understanding of climate change, and the political will to address it, is arguably the most important science translation effort of the century" (FrameWorks Institute 2015).

And there exist further topics, to whose in-depth exploration political scientists ought to address *normative and positive* analyses. An incomplete list would include (cf. also Bernauer 2013: 428/429, 430/431, 441/442; Javeline 2014: 426/427; Keohane 2015: 24/25):

- political theory: how the challenges involved in understanding and mastering global warming might be used to reinvigorate democratic processes, breaking paths toward "ecological" citizenship (Fischer 2017) and a more "ecological" democracy committed to sustainable development;
- political economy: how the political clout of corporate disinformation drives representing important economic sectors might be constrained;
- political sociology: how grassroots climate coalitions might be formed transcending value polarization between political groups, and "beneficial" citizens' initiatives might be built to press for global warming policy agenda-setting, legislative action, and bureaucratic implementation;
- political culture: how voters' emotions and expectations emphasizing a sense of intergenerational community with our societies' children and grandchildren might be formed and maintained;
- comparative politics: how different societies and political systems might evolve ways toward generating more constructive political discourses on climate issues;
- international regimes: how polycentric climate policy networks involving the contentious issues of linking participation, burden-sharing transfer payments and enforcement of commitments might be designed.

As briefly highlighted above (Colenbrander/Gouldson/Roy et al. 2017: 155), urban low-carbon development concepts should be "participatory", aimed at integrating issues of "equity and inclusivity", avoiding to exacerbate poverty and social conflict. On the international level, equity considerations, which have surfaced during negotiations between Global North and Global South countries, are proving even more complex. Equity criteria for conceivable transfer payments, not to mention amounts, remain contested.

When the German Political Science Association chose the theme: "Politics in a Changing Climate" for its 2009 Congress, it added the skeptical subtitle: "No Power for Equitable Solutions?" Contributions were, unsurprisingly, often no less skeptical (Schüttemeyer 2011). But the prevalent view was also that it befits political science to insist on such equity, exploring possible perspectives, providing citizens and policy-makers with empirical knowledge and normative guidance.

REFERENCES

Atkinson, Anthony B. (2015): *Inequality. What Can Be Done?* Cambridge/London: Harvard University Press.

Bang, Guri (2015): "The United States: Obama's Push for Climate Policy Change." In: Guri Bang/Arild Underdal/Steinar Andresen (eds.): *The Domestic Politics of Global Climate Change.* Cheltenham/Northampton: Edward Elgar, 160–181.

Bang, Guri/Underdal, Arild/Andresen, Steinar (2015a): "Introduction". In: Guri Bang/Arild Underdal/Steinar Andresen (eds.): *The Domestic Politics of Global Climate Change.* Cheltenham/Northampton: Edward Elgar, 1–24.

Bang, Guri/Underdal, Arild/Andresen, Steinar (2015b): "Comparative Analysis and Conclusions." In: Guri Bang/Arild Underdal/Steinar Andresen (eds.): *The Domestic Politics of Global Climate Change.* Cheltenham/Northampton: Edward Elgar, 182–204.

Bernauer, Thomas (2013): "Climate Change Politics." *Annual Review of Political Science,* Vol. 16, 421–448.

Bloomberg, Michael R./Hidalgo, Anne/Paes, Eduardo (2016): "A New Coalition for Urban Transitions to Help Cities Thrive." *Huffington Post,* May 5. www.huffingtonpost.com/michael-bloomberg/a-new-coalition-for-urban-transitions-to-help-cities-thrive_b_9844682.html.

Carver, Thomas Nixon (1915): *Essays in Social Justice.* Cambridge: Harvard University Press.

Colenbrander, Sarah/Gouldson, Andy/Roy, Joyshree/Kerr, Niall/Sarkar, Sayantan/Hall, Stephen/Sudmant, Andrew/Ghatak, Amrita/Chakravarty, Debalina/Ganguly, Diya/Mcanulla, Faye (2017): "Can Low-Carbon Urban Development be Pro-Poor? The Case of Kolkata, India." *Environment and Urbanization,* Vol. 29, 139–158.

Dauvergne, Peter/Clapp, Jennifer (2016): "Researching Global Environmental Politics in the 21st Century". *Global Environmental Politics,* Vol. 16 No. 1, 1–12.

Dickinson, Eliot (2017): *Globalization and Migration.* Lanham/Boulder: Roman & Littlefield.

FrameWorks Institute [McArthur Foundation] (2015): "Climate Change." http://www.frameworksinstitute.org/climate-change-and-the-ocean.html, accessed February 10, 2018.

Fischer, Frank (2017): *Climate Crisis and the Democratic Prospect: Participatory Governance in Sustainable Communities.* Oxford: Oxford University Press.

Harris, Jonathan M. (2009): "Ecological Macroeconomics: Consumption, Investment and Climate Change." In: Jonathan M. Harris/Neva R. Goodwin (eds.): *Twenty-First Century Macroeconomics.* Cheltenham/Northampton: Edward Elgar, 169–186.

Helm, Dieter (2014): "The European Framework for Energy and Climate Policies." *Energy Policy*, Vol. 64, 29–35.

Javeline, Debra (2014): "The Most Important Topic Political Scientists Are Not Studying: Adapting to Climate Change." *Perspectives on Politics*, Vol. 12, 420–434.

Joslyn, Heather (2016): "Words that Change Minds." *Chronicle of Philanthropy*, FrameWorks Institute [McArthur Foundation], September. http://www.frameworksinstitute.org/assets/files/PDF/chroniclephilanthropy_wordsthatchangeminds_2016.pdf, accessed February 10, 2018.

Kapp, K. William ([2]1971): *The Social Costs of Private Enterprise.* New York: Schocken Books.

Keohane, Robert O. (2015): "The Global Politics of Climate Change: Challenge for Political Science." *PS: Political Science and Politics*, Vol. 48 No. 1, 19–26.

Lenschow, Andrea/Sprungk, Carina (2010): "The Myth of a Green Europe." *Journal of Common Market Studies*, Vol. 48, 133–154.

McCright, Aaron M./Dunlap, Riley E. (2011): "The Politicization of Climate Change and Polarization in the American Public's Views of Global Warming, 2001–2010." *Sociological Quarterly*, Vol. 52, 155–194.

Oreskes, Naomi/Conway, Eric M. (2012): *Merchants of Doubt.* London. Bloomsbury.

Ostrom, Elinor (2009): "A Polycentric Approach for Coping with Climate Change." Policy Research Working Paper 5095 (Background Paper to the *World Development Report 2010: Development in a Changing Climate*). Washington D.C.: World Bank. http://www20.iadb.org/intal/catalogo/pe/2009/04268.pdf, accessed January 20, 2018.

Schüttemeyer, Suzanne S. (2011, ed.): *Politik im Klimawandel. Keine Macht für gerechte Lösungen?* Baden-Baden: Nomos.

Skjærseth, Jon Birger (2015): "EU Climate and Energy Policy: Demanded or Supplied?" In: Guri Bang/Arild Underdal/Steinar Andresen (eds.): *The Domestic Politics of Global Climate Change.* Cheltenham/Northampton: Edward Elgar, 71–94.

Skocpol, Theda (2013): "Naming the Problem: What it Will Take to Counter Extremism and Engage Americans in the Fight Against Global Warming." Symposium on *The Politics of America's Fight Against Global Warming*, Harvard University, February 14. https://www.scholarsstrategynetwork.org/sites/default/files/skocpol_captrade_report_january_2013_0.pdf, accessed January 15, 2018.

Temple, James (2018): "The Year Climate Change Began to Spin Out of Control." *MIT Technology Review*, January 4. https://www.technologyreview.com/s/609642/the-year-climate-change-began-to-spin-out-of-control/, accessed January 12, 2018.

U. S. Climate Alliance (2017): *Alliance States Take the Lead.* 2017 Annual Report, Executive Summary. https://static1.squarespace.com/static/5936b0bde4fcb5371d7ebe4c/t/59bc4949914e6b6f10ffe219/1505511753953/USCA_Exec-Summary-V2-Online-RGB.PDF, accessed January 18, 2018.

CHAPTER 11

Radicalization, Terrorism, Subversion of Civil Liberties

Conundrums of Twenty-First-Century Political Science

A twenty-first-century political science that focuses on peaceful conflict settlement may be facing a number of domestic and international security dilemmas. These dilemmas might not least be cast in terms of the need to develop concepts of "soft" policing and de-radicalization strategies against millennialist violence, rather than relying solely on repressive measures which threaten fundamental democratic values, without actually offering prospects of success.

"Innocent lives" would be put at risk, Theresa May, then UK Home Secretary, told the House of Commons in January 2015, unless new legislation would give the security agencies "the capabilities they need" in the surveillance of email, social media, and other communications data (May 2015a). Her statement came one week after the terrorist attacks on the satirical magazine *Charlie Hebdo* and a kosher supermarket in Paris, which had evoked worldwide solidarity with the attacked ("Je suis Charlie"). In the face of "such threats" to the United Kingdom, May reaffirmed five months later, there was a "duty" to ensure that security services had the powers they needed "to keep us safe" (May 2015b).

May's second comment responded to a report which had just been submitted by the Independent Reviewer of Terrorism Legislation— dubbed "the U. K.'s terror watchdog" in the media—a position which had evolved during the conflict over Northern Ireland and been put on a

© The Author(s) 2019

R. Eisfeld, *Empowering Citizens, Engaging the Public*,

https://doi.org/10.1007/978-981-13-5928-6_11

159

statutory basis after 9/11. Prepared by David Anderson QC [Queen's Counsel], the report was titled "A Question of Trust". A more fitting title, however, would have been "Minimize No-Go Areas", which was the first of five principles governing Anderson's recommendations (Anderson 2015: 245), and which would serve as blueprint for the 2016 Investigatory Powers Act (IPA).

In an attempt at "balancing" (Anderson 2015: 248) the intrusive authority accorded to government under the first principle, Anderson listed "limited powers" as a second proposition, expressing disapproval of no longer exotic devices such as drone-based blanket surveillance or CCTV facial recognition software. As a further verbal concession, he added compliance "with internationally guaranteed rights and freedoms". But he left no doubt that, under the "minimizing no-go areas" concept, the issue was "when it should be lawful" to intercept any particular communication, not whether the state's power to do so "should exist at all" (Anderson 2015: 247).

The IPA 2016, which went into force by the end of the same year, took up that approach. Civil and human rights groups severely criticized the law; Amnesty International's UK Section lambasted its provisions as "a beacon for despots everywhere" (Griffin 2016)—in fact, China had, by December 2015, invoked the UK bill in defense of its own intrusive anti-terror legislation. The National Council for Civil Liberties (established in 1934, "Liberty" for short) commenced preparation of legal action against the law. In mid-2015 and early 2018, both the UK High Court and the Court of Appeal had already ruled mass digital surveillance regimes unlawful under the preceding 2014 Data Retention and Investigatory Powers Act, which had inspired IPA: The law did not restrict interference with communications to investigating serious crimes and also lacked adequate safeguards.

Under the new legislation, telecommunications operators were required, upon receipt of an official notice, to retain communications data for 12 months. Access to these records without a warrant would have been allowed, in the law's original version, not just to law enforcement and intelligence services, but in excess of 30 other government agencies ranging from the Departments of Health, of Work and Pensions, and of Transport to the Financial Conduct Authority, the Food Standards Agency, and the Gambling Commission. By late 2017, in anticipation of the above-quoted court rulings, authorization to access without oversight was removed. Requests now require approval from the Investigatory Powers Commission (IPC), also created by the law.

The 2016 Act's primary content, however, related to direct governmental interception of private communication. IPA permitted intelligence agencies—the Government Communications Headquarters (GCHQ), the Security Service (MI5), and the Secret Intelligence Service (MI 6)

- to intercept (listen in on) transmitted communications under a warrant, and
- to interfere with (to hack) electronic "equipment" also under a warrant. That capacity was formerly referred to, in less "neutral" language, as Computer Network Exploitation (CNE).

IPA authorized warrants to be issued by a Secretary of State, subject to review by a Judicial Commissioner on the IPC. The Act allowed interception of and interference with electronic devices to include

- either a *targeted* focus on specific persons (or groups of persons), organizations, and locations,
- or the acquisition and collection of *bulk* personal datasets (BPD) on a wide range of individuals amounting, in practice, to mass surveillance.

Powers for *targeted* interception and equipment interference were also given to the police forces and to Revenue & Customs. Because a "targeted" focus may cover multiple persons or even organizations, dividing lines between "targeted" and "bulk" remain fluid. Moreover, UK intelligence agencies, according to a later report by David Anderson, have made "little attempt precisely to assess the extent to which the use of bulk interception achieves or fails to achieve the desired goal". He had the impression, the "watchdog" wrote, "that *the utility of bulk interception may have seemed so self-evident to the [agencies] that they had not seen a need to assess its value or failure rate*" (Anderson 2016: 89; emphasis added).

This chapter will return to the issue of effectiveness below. Anderson's observation comes hardly as a surprise. As revealed by whistleblower Edward Snowden in 2013, the great majority of legalized programs were already jointly practiced for years by GCHQ and National Security Agency (NSA), who shared results with, for example, Canadian, Dutch, French, and German intelligence services. Documents leaked by Snowden were initially published by the *Washington Post* and the *Guardian*. When the UK government threatened the *Guardian* with legal action, which might freeze the newspaper's reporting, editors and senior officials thrashed out a compromise: The *Guardian* would not surrender Snowden's files, but would in a surreal—because largely symbolic—gesture, supervised by GCHQ agents, destroy the hard drives. Reporting would and did continue from the United States, where the Supreme Court decision in the *Pentagon Papers* case, referred to in Chap. 6, made any government attempt at obtaining an injunction highly improbable (Borges 2013).

In his 2015 report, "terror watchdog" Anderson chose to summarize the most prominent mass surveillance activities disclosed by Snowden. Carefully avoiding identifying himself with the "limited selection of published documents", he reasonably argued that to omit reference to the leaks, as if they "had never been made or could be politely ignored", might "corrode public confidence" in his review. From the programs listed in Anderson's report (Anderson 2015: 125, 330–333), three—code-named MUSCULAR, PRISM, and TEMPORA—will be briefly reviewed here to provide an idea of the scope and methods of what must be classified as *global* surveillance based on *blanket* data interception and acquisition.

- Jointly run by GCHQ and NSA, the MUSCULAR program taps into fiber-optic cable traffic between Yahoo and Google data centers, daily storing millions of records for decoding, filtering, and selectively exploiting at data "warehouses" in Fort Meade (Maryland), the NSA headquarters—in 2012/2013, for instance, more than 180 million during a 30-day period. Unlike the PRISM program (which also involves Google and Yahoo), MUSCULAR surveillance has proceeded without authorization by warrants obtained from the United States Foreign Intelligence Surveillance Court (FISC), as it is conveniently presumed to target only non-US persons. In quantitative terms, the MUSCULAR project has been reported to employ more than twice the number of "selectors"—search terms—compared to PRISM (Gellman and Soltani 2013). FISC has itself come under criticism, because it meets in secret, hears no testimony opposing the government's case prior to its rulings, and has no enforcement capabilities. Still, NSA (and GCHQ) "prefer to avoid restrictions where [they] can" (Gellman and Soltani 2013).
- PRISM is the sole NSA program (conducted once again in partnership with GCHQ) whose existence was, subsequent to Snowden's disclosures, acknowledged by the US and UK governments. Legal interception (because pursued under Section 702 of the Foreign

Intelligence Surveillance Amendment Act and supervised, if deficiently,[1] by FISC), covers email, audio, video and video conferencing, VoIP (internet phone calls including Skype), and other data such as photos or transferred files from the servers of internet companies. The program involves no less than nine US corporations: Microsoft, Yahoo, Google, Facebook, PalTalk, AOL (America Online, now a division of Verizon), Skype, YouTube, and Apple.

Former US President Barack Obama attempted to downplay PRISM as, purportedly, "a circumscribed narrow system" (Madison 2013). By January 2018, when Section 702 would have expired, both houses of the US Congress voted to extend the provision, and thereby PRISM, for another six years, without inserting new privacy safeguards.

- TEMPORA is a GCHQ operation collecting data for storage and analysis by—again—accessing fiber-optic cables carrying internet traffic. Data stored by the TEMPORA system are shared with NSA. Based on documents provided by Snowden, the *Guardian* (MacAskill et al. 2013) reported that, by 2012,

  - GCHQ had intercepted, "under secret agreements with commercial companies", more than 200 transatlantic fiber-optic cables, was able to process data from at least 46 of them at a time, and was increasing its operations;
  - 300 analysts from GCHQ and 250 from NSA had been assigned to sort the millions of records;
  - 40,000 search terms ("selectors", as under MUSCULAR) had been chosen by GCHQ and another 31,000 by NSA;
  - a total of 850,000 NSA employees and US private contractors with top secret clearance (intelligence "professionals", such as Edward Snowden) had access to GCHQ data.

In 2018 as in 2016, chances were squandered, following Snowden's disclosures, to constrain the bulk collection of data. From a mixture of

---

[1] Former Washington District Judge James Robertson, who had served on FISC from 2002 to 2005, criticized in 2013 that the court had "turned into something like an administrative agency", not least because it was ruling on "entire surveillance systems" (Braun 2013).

"deference to the executive", including the intelligence establishment (Rudenstine 2016: 5), and fears of terrorist attacks, both the UK House of Commons and the US Congress—against a backdrop of revived widespread apathy—voted in favor of continued sweeping surveillance.

Home Secretary May, quoted at this chapter's outset, had earlier evoked continuing terrorist threats that would put "innocent lives at risk", unless new laws provided intelligence services with "needed" capabilities. US Homeland Security Secretary John Kelly had, before Section 702 came up for extension, asserted that the threat of terror, perpetrated "by generally the same groups", is "everywhere… It's nonstop… It can happen here almost anytime" (Green 2017). According to US editor and writer Thomas Engelhardt, Kelly's statements aimed at keeping American citizens "in a fear-filled psychic lock-down mode" by dramatically spotlighting the dangers of one single peril (Engelhardt 2017).

May's and Kelly's contentions in fact tie in with the discourse of threat and fear whose pursuit by political decision-makers and whose consequences were briefly discussed in Chap. 4. In the context of terrorism, one of the unmistakable intentions is to win support for curbing civil liberties and expanding intrusive measures. Raising the level of societal nervousness (Secretary Kelly: "The American public would 'never leave the house' if they knew what he know about terrorist threats"), the discourse of fear facilitates and legitimizes thinking in stereotypes and aggressive projections which allow "slick leaders to gain leverage over [citizens'] perceptions, values, votes, and tax dollars" for their policies (Altheide 2006: 18).

Constantly repeated messages about the severity of terrorist threats also correlate with widespread perceptions and attitudes acquired during the Cold War period. These understandings may be presumed to be still deeply ingrained in Western societies' collective memories, due to a mere decade's interval between the collapse of the Soviet Union and the 9/11 attacks. Echoed by political players and compliant media throughout the West, the US National Security Council (established in 1947) and successive US governments had preceded present administrations in invoking "militant subversion from within", even a "worldwide Fifth Column", as a major part of the Communist threat to the Western way of life. Already at the time, these messages had contributed to an "autistic trap" of demonizing political enemies. A dynamic of ever more "sophisticated" armament capacities, largely self-produced and *internally* determined by "autistic hostility", shaped ensuing mutual threat politics (Senghaas 2013: 39, 42, 47).

For militant subversion, one may read today "disguised fanatical Islamism"; for worldwide Fifth Column "Islamist networks around the globe". Continuities are unmistakable. Then as now, narratives of domestic threats serve to elicit unreasoning fears of being "victimized". Concomitantly, again in the past no less than today, these narratives are aimed at inspiring uncritical reliance on leaders "who know what's best", strengthening the power of the executive, reducing governmental accountability (Altheide 2006: 6/7, 16, 129). At this point, the notion of trust enters the debate. When the UK Reviewer of Terrorism Legislation titled his June 2015 report *A Question of Trust*, he contended that "public consent to intrusive laws depends on people trusting the authorities" (Anderson 2015: 245). That, it should be emphasized, is not the Lockean concept of government as trust, which implies that the people shall be the judge whether their elected representatives are acting according to the trust consigned in them. Rather, "trust" now implies faith in the assertion that even broad restrictions merely need to be written in law to inspire confidence in citizens that no act performed by executive players is happening needlessly. What the model fails to consider is the danger that, once such legislation is in place, "the exceptional becomes normal, the extraordinary routine. The new standard then can become a fresh point of departure"(Atanassow and Katznelson 2017: 101).

Analysis of recent security-related US and UK legislation, which included the just quoted warning, led Ewa Atanassow (Bard College Berlin) and former APSA President (2005–2006) Ira Katznelson (Columbia) to a harsh inference: The very measures taken to blunt the terrorist threat were "compromising constitutional and ethical principles", resulting in nothing less than "democratic subversion" (Atanassow and Katznelson 2017: 96, 109). In substance, that conclusion does not differ from the assessment that—as counter-terrorism has become an "encompassing domestic policy paradigm"—the security state of the Cold War period has mutated into the twenty-first century's "security constitution" (Glaser 2017a: 11. Glaser is Director of the German-Southeast Asian Center of Excellence for Public Policy and Good Governance). The term designates an array of arrangements following the overriding principle that security measures should take precedence over civil liberties.

Pleading in favor of reversing the subversion of democratic core values and institutions, Atanassow and Katznelson maintained (ibid.: 105, 106, 109) that

166 R. EISFELD

- the distinction between exceptional legislation and permanent policies must be preserved;
- like the latter, the former must be grounded "in normative goals beyond state security";
- emergency measures must therefore be fixed in time and subject to oversight;
- capacities for timely evaluation and retrospective appraisal must either be created or, where in existence, strengthened.

Atanassow's and Katznelson's forceful intervention does not, however, stand exemplary for sustained engagement by an array of political scientists with the dangers posed for the viability of democratic regimes by presently prevailing ways of attempting to blunt the threat of terrorist attacks. Rather, so far their voices have remained a rather isolated call in the wilderness. *But if not now, when should be the time for the discipline's scholars to start blowing the whistle, alerting the public, as the term was used in Chap. 6? The security constitution is not a distinct sector, to be scrutinized by special expertise only. Rather, it provides an underlying restrictive matrix on which mendocracy, liars' rule, flourishes more easily, and which aids in pushing the political system faster toward oligarchy.*

As a mere first step, the situation requires that political scientists commit all the institutional imagination they can muster toward devising robust measures for constraining and overseeing intelligence agencies. Such work should benefit from having regard to the views of NGOs such as Liberty or the Open Rights Group (both mentioned in this chapter, associated with other British and European privacy and digital rights groups in a temporary coalition campaigning against the passing of IPA), or of their US counterparts.

Atanassow's and Katznelson's case is made the more compelling by the fact that it is far from clear how effective blanket surveillance measures have proved to be in averting terrorist acts. The fundamental considerations advanced so far should, of course, rank paramount: The lesson of history, if not of ethics, is that ends do *not* justify any means. However, it would be doubly misplaced to rely on instruments deeply questionable in moral, but at most modestly successful in efficiency terms.

During the debate on PRISM following Edward Snowden's 2013 disclosures, Democratic Senators Mark Udall (Colorado) and Ron Wyden (Oregon) called into question NSA statements that surveillance programs had helped avert "dozens of terrorist attacks". Both were then serving on the US Senate Select Committee on Intelligence. The plots mentioned, Udall and Wyden contended, "appear to have been identified using other [i.e., less intrusive] collection methods". A "key measure of the effectiveness of the bulk collection program" would be whether it did provide intelligence that could *not* be obtained in other ways (Udall and Wyden 2013).

When the investigative powers bill came up, Theresa May promised, as quoted at this chapter's outset, that the broad capabilities involved would provide intelligence services with the powers needed "to keep us safe". A report by the UK-based Open Rights Group published in early 2016, while the British parliament was discussing the bill, maintained that the government had not shown "any demonstrable link between their calls for surveillance powers and the specific problems investigating the criminals" in recent terrorist atrocities (Open Rights Group 2016: ch. 9, p. 1). After the law had taken effect, four acts of terrorism were carried out on British soil during 2017, claiming 35 dead and nearly 400 wounded victims. The attackers' age ranged from 52 (Westminster attack, March) to 22 (Manchester Arena bombing, May), 22/27/30 (London Bridge attack, June), and finally 18 (London tube bombing, September). Several had criminal records. One had been monitored by Italian authorities, who had informed the United Kingdom. One had even been involved with the PREVENT de-radicalization program, on which we have more below. Even a cautious assessment might presume that nuanced intelligence gathering may have been neglected because of misplaced confidence in the results of blanket surveillance.

A slightly differently focused study of post-Bataclan counter-terrorism strategies in France, with an emphasis on home searches by police without warrants under state of emergency provisions, and related practices conveyed a hardly different picture. Neither these measures, nor extended video and communications surveillance prevented the 2016 stabbings of two police officers and an 86-year old priest, nor finally the Bastille Day mass murder in Nice with 86 dead and over 400 injured. In preparation, the attacker had driven his 19 ton cargo truck 11 (!) times along the same Nice promenade prohibited for trucks, without being stopped and interrogated (Jobard 2017: 594, 595).

The article just quoted did neither downplay nor exaggerate the real danger. Rather, as will be seen in a moment, it suggested priorities for confronting that danger that were different from those which currently prevail.

A French parliamentary report preceding the essay provided several crucial facts. It listed some 4300 police raids on homes and mosques for the year between November 2015 and November 2016. Of these, 61 or not quite 2% led to court proceedings because of "facts connected to terrorism", which in two thirds of the cases meant expressing sympathy for terrorist acts. The report consequently ranked the contribution, which the thousands of police raids had made to the fight against home-grown terrorism, as "modest" (Assemblée Nationale 2016: 37, 49, 120). What these raids did succeed in, according to juridical critics and exonerated suspects, was upgrading flimsy, sometimes anonymous intelligence; tending to reverse the burden of proof; and reinforce Muslims' feelings of being collectively stigmatized (Chassany 2017).

During his election campaign, Emmanuel Macron had referred to the report and had stated that he would let the emergency provisions expire. As president, he reversed his stance. In 2017, a counter-terrorism law retaining most features of the previous state of emergency decree (relating, e.g., to security zones, identity checks, house arrests) went into effect. Home searches by police now require a warrant. The law will be up for review in 2020. However, by the time, the extraordinary—as predicted by Atanassow and Katznelson—may have become routine.

Rather than relying on the ever more pervasive, at best moderately expedient restriction of civil liberties, a different approach may take its inspiration from the manner French police were alerted to the identities and hideouts of two jihadist murderers (Jobard 2017: 596/597). Following the 2012 Toulouse/Montauban shootings which claimed seven victims, a motorcycle mechanic phoned the police, pointing them to a client who was identified as the perpetrator. After the 2015 Bataclan (and other Paris) murders, police were led to the hideout of the suspected plot ringleader, his female cousin, and another attacker by a tip from a female witness who had been enlisted by the cousin to help carry food supplies.

Put in a nutshell: In the two cited cases, neither blanket surveillance nor police searches produced results. It was "social control" (Jobard 2017: 597), input from civil society, that did the trick. Even at first glance, this strongly suggests more investment, *as a core element of counter-terrorism policies*, in building social capital; in recruiting police with minority roots; in reducing, rather than reinforcing, existing resentment between police and minorities; and eventually in forging consensual ties between police and local communities. Substantial affinities with the development and

RADICALIZATION, TERRORISM, SUBVERSION OF CIVIL LIBERTIES   169

implementation of well-considered programs for the societal inclusion of immigrants, as set out in Chap. 7, are evident.

These contentions are borne out by two recent (2008 and 2010) studies on counter-terrorism policing among culturally diverse—specifically Muslim—communities in New York City and Melbourne (Australia). Both resulted from empirical projects designed to explore under what preconditions members of the researched communities would be willing to cooperate with law enforcement in preventively alerting police to terrorism-related threats. (The Australian study also included interviews with police forces.) Outcomes were, for all practical purposes, identical (Pickering et al. 2008: 91, 94/95, 96–98, 104; Tyler et al. 2010: 367/368, 369/370, 371/372, 385/386):

- Procedural justice in the sense of *fair* police procedures—consistently and neutrally applying legal rules, treating people respectfully, explaining actions, seeking input from community members—emerged as *the* major determinant for perceiving police as a *legitimate* authority. Legitimacy may be defined as goodwill and trust, smoothing the way for cooperation in efforts to prevent terrorist acts.
- "Hard power" police behavior may produce risks to security. Intrusive surveillance, ethnic or religious profiling, intensive street frisks, and needless arrests risk to be counterproductive by decreasing police legitimacy. Generating estrangement and outrage, they may prepare the ground for ideological radicalization and terrorist recruitment.

The authors of the Melbourne study stressed that sustained "soft power" approaches by the police need to be preceded by cultural training. On the law enforcement side, resources—along with a commitment to accountability and social inclusion—are of the essence. In a changing societal environment, such resources include cultural understanding as a salient component. Cultural learning should consequently become embedded in police curricula, rather than be reduced to a specialization (Pickering et al. 2008: 102, 108).

Attempts at working toward "community consent" for cooperation with police forces will, however, by necessity unfold in a complex and actually quite grim local, national, and international environment which makes such attempts "incredibly difficult" (Spalek 2010: 793, 800):

170   R. EISFELD

- On the local level, goodwill-oriented policies need to show an awareness of linkages between cultural and economic factors such as job
discrimination, economic (schooling, health, housing) deprivation,
and lack of meaningful prospects for adolescents, which are rarely
amenable to short-term betterment. Failure to effectively address the
latter, however, cannot but undermine or thwart efforts to promote
civic engagement. In the telling words of a UK local official, these
would at best remain "sticking plaster stuff" (Husband 2011: 9–11;
quote from Husband and Alam 2011: 188).
- Nationally defined, more aggressive approaches to the prevention of
terrorist attacks exhibit a tendency (often reinforced by media) to
view entire Muslim communities as "suspect". In contrast, "the July
2011 killing spree in Norway by a far-right extremist"—or the 2016
fatal stabbing of anti-Brexit Labour MP Jo Cross, or the series of
bombings and murders (nine Germans of Turkish or Greek origin,
and a policewoman), between 2000 and 2006, by Germany's self-
styled National Socialist Underground (NSU)—serve "as a stark
reminder that the perpetrators of violent extremism may be of any
ethnicity, religion, or political ideology" (Archick et al. 2011: 1).
Still, whether Muslim citizens are in toto labeled as "suspect" or
targeted as mere potential "informants", such tactics are prone to
impinge on local attempts at longer-term dialogue. This was noted
in the Melbourne study (Pickering et al. 2008: 97/98) and con-
firmed in work on different versions of the UK government's (briefly
mentioned above) PREVENT strategy. Problems include disproportionate use of "far too broad[ly]" defined police powers against
Muslim citizens; resort to comprehensive profiling, passing over the
fact that Muslim communities are anything but homogenous; stigmatizing "activities and people" without robust evidence (Awan
2012: 1163, 1165, 1177; Husband and Alam 2011: 193).
- Finally, perceptions of international politics related to the so-called
global war on terror are more than likely to strain interaction between
police and Muslim communities (Spalek 2010: 805). Such politics
notoriously include US resort to "enhanced interrogation techniques"—torture—of detainees under the Bush Administration, or
targeted killings by commandos and drones under the Obama
Administration, plus the emergence of "literally hundreds of allegations" concerning British "complicity in prisoner abuse", both by

RADICALIZATION, TERRORISM, SUBVERSION OF CIVIL LIBERTIES   171

"direct" and "indirect support" (Blakeley and Raphael 2016: 244, 246; Glaser 2017b: 325, 329).[2]

Where this book focuses on how political science might contribute to empowering citizens, that aim includes—as a matter of course—the empowerment of Muslim and other minority communities to voice their concerns, to see them discussed and addressed. The substantial impact of police behavior on public attitudes, including civic responsibility, was already referred to in the chapter on immigration. Freeing democracies from the "cul-de-sac" of present, predominantly "hard power" approaches to combating terrorism will certainly require citizens' and media's support, a determined government and widespread police commitment (Pickering et al. 2008: 106). Political scientists should buttress such efforts, in line with attempts stressed above to "rein in" intelligence agencies, offering support to communities demanding changes in police competences.

Even if these suggestions should eventually fall on fertile ground, the contention that "the idea of liberty versus security presents a false dichotomy in the realm of counter-terrorism" (Pickering et al. 2008: 103) is too glib. More realistically, it is of the essence for political science to push for reversing the present "securitization" of ethical and constitutional norms, maintaining—rather than paying mere lip service to—a robust framework of democratic core values and institutions within which "inherent conundrums of liberty and security" may be mitigated (Atanassow and Katznelson 2017: 110).

---

[2] Along with the US Senate Select Committee's on Intelligence *Committee Study of the Central Intelligence Agency's Detention and Interrogation Program.* Executive Summary (Washington 2012, Declassification Revisions and Release 2014), Blakeley's and Raphael's article provides required reading for anyone wishing to obtain a realistic picture about the dehumanizing impact of covert practices under the "war on terror" umbrella. (Ruth Blakeley is Professor of Politics and International Relations at Sheffield University. Sam Raphael works at Westminster University as Senior Lecturer in the same field.) In this context, Henning Glaser's observation on the "functional value" of the recourse to torture warrants consideration: "The systematic transgression of a taboo conveys an important message. By breaking the taboo, the perpetrator [i.e., the United States] can demonstrate the fact of a sovereign foundation of a new order" (Glaser 2017b: 325). Using a term coined by Judith Butler, Blakeley and Raphael argued that UK agencies, exploiting the international extension of sovereign US power with regard to torture, were able to emerge as "petty sovereigns" (Blakeley and Raphael 2016: 245/246, 261). Their article also reveals that the extent of the UK government's dissembling on British involvement in prisoner abuse would make a fitting addition to this book's chapter on mendocracy.

172   R. EISFELD

In this context, concepts for de-radicalization remain, according to an informed judgment, contested, understudied, even—despite a few projects in South East Asian countries, primarily Malaysia and Indonesia and, surprisingly, Saudi-Arabia—"not really well understood". In places where Islamist terrorist groups were operating, such programs have in the past involved religious counseling by Muslim clerics and scholars, psychological assistance, family support to offset hardships, job-seeking assistance and last, but far from least, Muslim community involvement (Banlaoi 2017: 92, 93, 95, 100–102. Banlaoi chairs the Board of the Philippine Institute for Peace, Violence and Terrorism Research). Engagement by Muslim communities and the participation of moderate clerics have been deemed key components (Acharya 2017: 58/59; Gunaratna 2017: 69/70). The pivotal aim consists, of course, in effecting the relinquishment of violence in favor of peaceable methods.

As long as the hegemonic international policy patterns briefly described above persist—even in superficially modified forms—"hearts and minds" efforts aimed at de-radicalization are bound to remain exceedingly difficult. That should not deter political scientists—in cooperation with sociologists, psychologists, and criminologists—to add de-radicalization efforts to that agenda of comprehensive, comparative research work which the entire field of "soft power" approaches (including present barriers) to counter-terrorism merits. In the spirit of the study by Husband and Alam on PREVENT (2011: 191), such an agenda ought to focus on posing "questions that are not adequately present" in current counter-terrorism policies—questions pointing toward societies just conceivably more civil liberties-conscious *and* more secure.

REFERENCES

Acharya, Arabinda (2017): "The Right War, the Just War? Assessing the Fight Against Terrorism Since 9/11." In: Hennig Glaser (ed.): *Talking to the Enemy. Deradicalization and Disengagement of Terrorists.* Baden-Baden: Nomos, 35–66.

Altheide, David L. (2006): *Terrorism and the Politics of Fear.* Landam/Oxford: AltaMira Press.

Anderson, David (2015): *A Question of Trust. Report of the Investigatory Powers Review.* London: Crown Copyright. https://www.gov.uk/government/uploads/system/uploads/attachment_data/file/434399/IPR-Report-Web-Accessible1.pdf, accessed February 16, 2018.

RADICALIZATION, TERRORISM, SUBVERSION OF CIVIL LIBERTIES   173

Anderson, David (2016): *Report of the Bulk Powers Review.* London: Crown Copyright. https://www.gov.uk/government/uploads/system/uploads/attachment_data/file/546925/56730_Cm9326_WEB.PDF, accessed February 28, 2018.

Archick, Kristin/Belkin, Paul/Blanchard, Christopher M. et al. (2011): "Muslims in *Europe: Promoting Integration and Countering Extremism.*" *Congressional Research Service.* http://www.fas.org/sgp/crs/row/RL33166.pdf, accessed March 26, 2018.

Assemblée Nationale (2016): Rapport d'Information sur le Contrôle Parlementaire de l'Etat d'Urgence. http://www2.assemblee-nationale.fr/documents/notice/14/rap-info/i4281/(index)depots, accessed March 16, 2018.

Atanassow, Ewa/Katznelson, Ira (2017): "Governing Exigencies: On Liberal Democracy and National Security." In: Hertie School of Governance (ed.): *The Governance Report 2017.* Oxford: Oxford University Press, 95–110.

Awan, Imran (2012): "'I Am a Muslim Not an Extremist': How the Prevent Strategy Has Constructed a 'Suspect' Community." *Politics & Policy,* Vol. 40, 1158–1185.

Banlaoi, Rommel C. (2017): "Counter-Terrorism Measures and De-Radicalization Efforts in Southeast Asia: A View From the Philippines." In: Henning Glaser (ed.): *Talking to the Enemy. Deradicalization and Disengagement of Terrorists.* Baden-Baden: Nomos, 91–104.

Blakeley, Ruth/Raphael, Sam (2016): "British Torture in the 'War on Terror'". *European Journal of International Relations,* Vol. 23, 243–266.

Borges, Julian (2013): "NSA Files: Why the *Guardian* in London Destroyed Hard Drives of Leaked Files." *Guardian,* August 20. https://www.theguardian.com/world/2013/aug/20/nsa-snowden-files-drives-destroyed-london, accessed March 1, 2018.

Braun, Stephen (2013): "Former Judge Admits Flaws With Secret FISA Court." *Associated Press/CBS News.* https://www.cbsnews.com/news/former-judge-admits-flaws-with-secret-fisa-court/, accessed March 3, 2018.

Chassany, Anne-Sylvaine (2017): "France: The Permanent State of Emergency." *Financial Times,* October 2. https://www.ft.com/content/f5309ff8-a521-11e7-9e4f-7f5e6a7c98a2, accessed March 16, 2018.

Engelhardt, Tom (2017): "'Never Leave The House': Locked In With The National Security State." https://www.huffingtonpost.com/entry/never-leave-the-house-locked-in-with-the-na-tional-security-state_us_594827b9e4b07499199dd48b, accessed March 5, 2018.

Gellman, Barton/Soltani, Ashkan (2013): "NSA Infiltrates Links to Yahoo, Google Data Centers Worldwide, Snowden Documents Say." *Washington Post,* October 30. https://www.washingtonpost.com/world/national-security/nsa-infiltrates-links-to-yahoo-google-data-centers-worldwide-snowden-documents-say/2013/10/30/e51d661e-4166-11e3-8b74-d89d714ca4dd_story.html?utm_term=.70c0239b3d1, accessed March 2, 2018.

174   R. EISFELD

Glaser, Henning (2017a): "Talking to the 'Enemy': Counterterrorism and Communication – An Introduction". In: id. (ed.): *Talking to the Enemy. Deradicalization and Disengagement of Terrorists.* Baden-Baden: Nomos, 11–34.

Glaser, Henning (2017b): "The Margin of Maneuver: Responding to the Terrorist Threat In Times of the Global War on Terror's Third Phase". In: id. (ed.): *Talking to the Enemy*, op. cit., 257–354.

Green, Miranda (2017): "Homeland Secretary: People Would 'Never Leave The House' If They Knew What I Knew." *CNN*, May 26. https://edition.cnn.com/2017/05/26/politics/john-kelly-terror-threat-people-wouldnt-leave-the-house/index.html, accessed March 5, 2018.

Griffin, Andrew (2016): "Investigatory Powers Act Goes Into Force, Putting UK Citizens Under Intense New Spying regime." *Independent*, December 31. https://www.independent.co.uk/life-style/gadgets-and-tech/news/investigatory-powers-act-bill-snoopers-charter-spying-law-powers-theresa-may-a7503616.html, accessed Feb. 16, 2018.

Gunaratna, Rohan (2017): "Fighting Terrorism With Smart Power: The Role of Community Engagement and Terrorist Rehabilitation." In: Henning Glaser (ed.): *Talking to the Enemy*, op. cit., 67–89.

Husband, Charles (2011): *British Multiculturalism, Social Cohesion and Public Security.* Warsaw: Institute of Public Affairs.

Husband, Charles/Alam, Yunis (2011): *Social Cohesion and Counter-Terrorism – A Policy Contradiction?*, Bristol: Policy Press.

Jobard, Fabien (2017): "Terrorismus – nicht nur ein Problem der inneren Sicherheit." *Leviathan*, Vol. 45, 592–599.

MacAskill, Ewen/Borger, Julian/Hopkins, Nick/Davies, Nick/Ball, James (2013): "GCHQ Taps Fibre-Optic Cables for Secret Access to World's Communications". *Guardian*, June 21. https://www.theguardian.com/uk/2013/jun/21/gchq-cables-secret-world-communications-nsa, accessed February 28, 2018.

Madison, Lucy (2013): "Obama Defends 'Narrow' Surveillance Programs." *CBS News*, June 19. https://www.cbsnews.com/news/obama-defends-narrow-surveillance-programs/, accessed March 3, 2018.

May, Theresa (2015a): "Theresa May Says 'Lives at Risk' Without Data Surveillance." *BBC*, January 14. http://www.bbc.com/news/uk-politics-30816331, accessed February 16, 2018.

May, Theresa (2015b): "Threats to UK 'considerable and evolving'." *BBC*, June 11. http://www.bbc.com/news/av/uk-33094318/theresa-may-threats-to-uk-considerable-and-evol-ving, accessed February 16, 2018.

Open Rights Group (2016): *GCHQ and UK Mass Surveillance. Report*, Chapter 9, March. https://www.openrightsgroup.org/assets/files/pdfs/reports/gchq/09-Conclusion__.pdf, accessed March 15, 2018.

RADICALIZATION, TERRORISM, SUBVERSION OF CIVIL LIBERTIES 175

Pickering, Sharon/McCulloch, Jude/Wright-Neville, David (2008): "Counter-Terrorism Policing: Towards Social Cohesion." *Crime, Law and Social Change*, Vol. 50, 91–109.

Rudenstine, David (2016): *The Age of Deference. The Supreme Court, National Security, and the Constitutional Order.* New York: Oxford University Press.

Senghaas, Dieter (2013): *Dieter Senghaas, Pioneer of Peace and Development Research.* Springer Briefs on Pioneers in Science and Practice # 6. Heidelberg/New York 2013. [Quotes are from a 1974 essay included in the volume.]

Spalek, Basia (2010): "Community Policing, Trust, and Muslim Communities in Relation to 'New Terrorism'." *Politics and Policy*, Vol. 38, 798–815.

Tyler, Tom R./Schulhofer, Stephen/Huq, Aziz Z. (2010): "Legitimacy and Deterrence Effects in Counter-Terrorism Policing: A Study of Muslim Americans." *Law & Society Review*, Vol. 44, 365–401.

Udall, Mark/Wyden, Ron (2013): "Udall, Wyden Call on National Security Agency Director to Clarify Comments on Effectiveness of Phone Data Collection Program." *U. S. Senate Press Release.* June 13. https://www.wyden.senate.gov/news/press-releases/udall-wyden-call-on-national-security-agency-director-to-clarify-comments-on-effectiveness-of-phone-data-collection-program, accessed March 14, 2018.

PART III

Partisanship

CHAPTER 12

Twenty-First-Century Political Science: Politicization of a Discipline?

A Normative Science of Democracy with Empirical Rigor

> *At a moment in history when the accountability of democratic governments is literally bleeding away, when the hybridization of democratic regimes in Central-East Europe is on the rise and democracies in Western Europe and North America are compromised by the erosion of democratic rules and values, political science as a science of democracy becomes inevitably partisan. It should acknowledge such partisanship, explaining aims and implications.*

American Political Science Association (APSA) presidential addresses were once christened "barometers of yearning and hope" by SUNY political scientist John Gunnell (1993: 268). He might as well have referred to them as benchmarks of critique and appeal.

At this book's outset, former APSA President Elinor Ostrom was quoted as reproaching the discipline for neglecting to inform citizens "of the actions they need to know and can undertake". Elected APSA President a decade after Ostrom, Ira Katznelson took the same line. Too often, he warned in his presidential address, customary political science had developed a lack of "urgency or purpose", settling instead for "the aesthetic appeal of scientific inquiry well-done". Decades ago, he reminded his audience, when many in his generation had decided to turn to political science, they had been motivated by what impressed them as the discipline's

© The Author(s) 2019
R. Eisfeld, *Empowering Citizens, Engaging the Public*,
https://doi.org/10.1007/978-981-13-5928-6_12

179

180   R. EISFELD

indeed urgent purpose: not staying aloft, but helping find the way "to a more decent politics and society under dangerous and difficult conditions". That responsibility, Katznelson concluded, not merely persists. It has become even more pronounced now that political science has evolved into an overall more robust discipline (Katznelson 2007: 4, 12).

Forty years before Katznelson, David Easton (1917–2014) responded in yet another presidential address to what he called the "post-behavioral revolution"—what Albert O. Hirschman, in a perceptive 1982 study, would refer to, more comprehensively, as the "spirit of 1968". As a pivotal ingredient of that movement of radical dissent, Hirschman[1] identified "an overwhelming concern with public issues" (Hirschman ²2002 [¹1982]: 3). Easton argued no differently. In his address, he anticipated, down to a number of details discussed in Chap. 1, the later debate about whether—and if so, by what means—the discipline needed to become more relevant, more comprehensible, and more critical (Easton 1969: 1053, 1055/56, 1057/58, 1059, 1061):

- *A shift in focus to large, immediate problems*: Easton ranked nuclear weapons, the population explosion, pollution of the environment, racial and economic discord among pressing "clear and present dangers".
- *A warning about the future*: Easton foresaw a movement toward "deepening fears and anxieties about the future", triggered by these pressures and resulting in more pronounced social conflict.

---

[1] Albert Otto Hirschman (1915–2012) should not only be remembered as an unconventional political economist, but also for contributing to the rescue of well over 2000 Jewish Germans and other refugees from being deported to Nazi concentration and extermination camps. He worked with Varian Fry (1907–1967), who during much of 1940/1941 headed the privately funded, US-initiated Emergency Rescue Committee (Centré Américain de Secours) in Marseilles. The committee provided a fig leaf for smuggling refugees across the Spanish border by clandestine escape routes or falsified documents. In shameful cooperation between the Vichy regime and the US State Department, Fry was eventually expelled. His achievements "were largely unrecognized in his own country"; his death at 59, following severe illnesses, "went almost unnoticed" (Hirschman 1992: VIII). Among those rescued by Fry and his small operation were Hannah Arendt, Alma Mahler, Anna Seghers, Heinrich Mann and his wife, Franz Werfel and his wife, Marc Chagall, Max Ernst, Lion Feuchtwanger, Arthur Koestler and Siegfried Kracauer. Varian Fry was finally, in 1994, recognized as a "Righteous Among the Nations" by Yad Vashem. A square in Marseilles and a street in the center of reunified Berlin have been named after him.

TWENTY-FIRST-CENTURY POLITICAL SCIENCE: POLITICIZATION... 181

- *A plea for relevance and action*: The discipline's acquired technical proficiency should be put to the service of prescribing and acting to "improve political life according to humane criteria".
- *Training of communicative skills*: Political scientists' knowledge would have to be transformed into "a form far more consumable for purposes of political action".
- *Revamping the discipline's incentive structure*: A shift in emphasis in the "allocation of financial and human resources" ought to occur "at once".
- *Lastly, no shying away from visions for designing and attaining a "good society"*: Striving to escape current "research myopia" in the form of uncritical, even "crippling", commitment to prevailing politics and values, political scientists ought to start formulating "broad, speculative alternatives" to current political relationships. Such change in orientation, Easton suggested, should involve more communication with racial and economic minorities, unrepresented publics at home, and the post-colonial masses of developing countries.

Easton's concerns would resurface decades later in the Perestroika and other initiatives, both in APSA and Political Studies Association (PSA). That fact alone demonstrates that the "revolution" invoked in the title of Easton's address never happened in political science. The discipline's "mainstream" continued to be shaped by quantitative and functionalist approaches informing a "science of democracy" not in the sense of a science for democratic citizens, but predominantly for academic insiders, focusing as it did on the "management" of parliamentary or presidential political systems driven by parties and pressure groups. As has been apparent throughout this book, that paradigm has shown quite considerable resilience. It has bred the "executive" type of professor who, as Harold Laski scathingly remarked in 1928 (!), "knows how to 'run' committees and conferences", has "access to a trustee here and a [foundation] director there", and has thereby come to dominate the profession—congenial, as Easton would later add, to "elites in government, business, the military" (Laski 1930: 164, 175; Easton 1969: 1059).

A continuing focus on the major players and institutions of liberal-representative democracy was favored by the fact that "actually existing" socialism—Stalinism and post-Stalinism—had discredited "radical" alternatives. Emphasizing the features that distinguished democratic regimes from authoritarian varieties seemed "called for" in political science both

182   R. EISFELD

nationally and internationally; quantitative voting studies were considered to hold more methodological promise than qualitative interviews with black ghetto inhabitants.

And the product proved suitable for export, "chart[ing] a route for the discipline in other parts of the world" (Coakley and Trent 2000: 4). That fact had been proved subsequent to 1945; it would be demonstrated again after 1990. While both instances will briefly be referred to here, the second, post-1990 case will receive more attention. It will furnish proof that in a region—Central-East Europe—where authoritarianism has lately been on an alarming rise, a political science which refrains from determined and competent intervention in public debates is on its way of becoming even more deficient in helping to counter present antidemocratic challenges than elsewhere in Europe or the United States.

Both after Nazi Germany's World War II defeat and after the Warsaw Pact regimes' collapse, there was a conviction that building liberal-democratic polities would be aided by educational reforms. Political science owed its establishment as an academic discipline in West Germany to a coalition of exiled scholars, American occupation officers, and German politicians—mostly Social Democrats, with a few Christian Democrats added. When the military government retreated from more ambitious plans for reorganizing German education along American lines, political science seemed to provide an input which might at least serve to make students more aware of social and political realities.

For two decades, West German political science stressed institutions, processes, and theories of representative democracies—with a special focus on parties and interest groups. The discipline's normative, "emphatically democratic stance" (Günther 1986: 37), was directed against "totalitarian" rule, both of the Nazi and the Communist variety. Subsequently, behavioral approaches, particularly with regard to policy studies, gained increasing ground. The discipline became "unusually fragmented" (von Beyme 1986: 23), and has remained so. As a union of determined specialists, it offers no disciplinary profile and is hardly well positioned for competently addressing the salient issues of the twenty-first century.

For discipline transfer to happen, financial support had needed to accompany academic contacts (in which scholars exiled during the Nazi period played a role). Funds amounting to DM 200,000 were provided by the US High Commissioner in Germany (HICOG), helping to add a Research Institute for Political Science to West Berlin's Free University (Stammer 1960: 175, 177). In the same year, 1950, HICOG awarded a

TWENTY-FIRST-CENTURY POLITICAL SCIENCE: POLITICIZATION... 183

grant-in-aid of DM 50,000 to the recently founded German Political Science Association for promoting academic research "including legislation, political parties, public opinion, civil liberties, personnel administration, and police policy" (Wolfgang Abendroth Papers: Folder 535).

Much larger funds flowed into the educational systems of Central and East European countries after 1990. Governmental and private players—US agencies and universities, European Union donor institutions, German foundations, the indefatigable billionaire financier and "Open Society" philanthropist George Soros—favored the emergence of political science disciplines akin to the prevailing Western model (Eisfeld and Pal 2010: 15–21, also for the following). With regard to quantity—number of academic staff employed or of professional associations newly established—the results have been impressive. In substantive terms, however, approaches once again remained largely functional, focused on institution-building, comparative politics, and international relations. In countries with new political systems, this may initially be judged quite normal. The question was: Would such nascent political science cultures "grow beyond that focus"? (Eisfeld and Pal 2010: 16).

What instead happened was that regime "hybridization" began to impact on disciplinary development processes. The term "hybrid" implies absence (or abolition) of key attributes of democracy, such as civil liberties, free and fair elections (including a level "playing field"), and accountability of governments. Hybridization has resulted in "competitive authoritarian" regimes (Levitsky and Way 2010: 4/5) or, for short, competitive autocracies. These soon came to include, for instance, Albania, Moldova, Ukraine, Belarus, and Russia. As demonstrated by country reports on the state of political science, their emergence has "constrained, even contorted" the discipline's further development (Eisfeld and Pal 2010: 12; passim).

The picture became much bleaker, as hybridization started to expand, including two European Union member states which, by 2010, had been ranked among consolidated democracies. Bent on establishing, since being voted into office, an "illiberal democracy" (Victor Orbán 2014), Hungary's Fidesz (Hungarian Civic Alliance) Party led by Orbán and Poland's PiS (Law and Justice) Party led by Jarosław Kaczyński have eroded judicial independence—and thereby the separation of powers—reduced the range of independent media, restricted dissenting nongovernmental associations, and fueled xenophobic fears.

By late 2017, in an unprecedented move, which mirrored deep concern over the perceived derailment of democracy in Poland, the EU Commission

184   R. EISFELD

launched proceedings under Art. 7 of the 2007 EU Lisbon Treaty against the country for "clear risk of a serious breach in the rule of law". The European Parliament endorsed the action, calling on the European Council to initiate the three-step process which could eventually lead to the suspension of Poland's voting rights. Such a decision would, however, require unanimity, and the Hungarian government immediately declared that it would veto any sanctions.

After the Fidesz government had again obtained a two-thirds majority in the April 2018 parliamentary elections, the Organisation for Security and Cooperation in Europe (OSCE) Observation Mission[2] noted that

- "a pervasive overlap" between state and ruling party resources, at odds with OSCE commitments, had "undermined" party competition on an equal basis, and that
- "intimidating and xenophobic rhetoric, media bias and opaque campaign financing" had "constrained" voters' ability to make a "fully informed" choice (OSCE 2018: 1).

Just three days later, a report to the European Parliament's Committee on Civil Liberties, Justice and Home Affairs diagnosed "a systemic threat to democracy, the rule of law and fundamental rights" in Hungary. Detailing contraventions in areas such as independence of the judiciary, freedom of expression, association and religion, academic freedom, minority rights (particularly regarding the treatment of Roma), and fundamental rights of refugees, the report called on the Parliament's members to submit to the EU Council, as in the Polish case, a proposal for determining a clear risk of a serious breach in the values of the European Union (European Parliament 2018: 4, 8/9, 10–14, 16–20).

The Polish Political Science Association did not join protests against the dismantlement of the judiciary's independence that were lodged, for example, by the Polish Sociological Association, or the universities of Warsaw, Poznań, and Kraków's Jagiellonian University. Unlike the Hungarian, the Serbian, the United Kingdom, Dutch, or German political scientists' organizations, the association also refrained from participating in the international solidarity displayed when Budapest's Central-European

---

[2] More precisely: OSCE Office for Democratic Institutions and Human Rights (ODIHR), Limited Election Observation Mission.

University (CEU) came under attack (see below for more detail). One possible reason may be that the analysis of public policies and their impact was singled out as a deficit of Polish political studies in a recent study (Sasinska-Klas 2010: 218).

Hungary's hybridization, which is said to have inspired Kaczyński and PiS, will be discussed at greater length, because its case may be considered exemplary in more ways than one. In Hungarian political science, no comprehensive assessment has emerged of the main tenets of Orbán's policies, as discerned by observers from the United Nations, OSCE, the Council of Europe, or the European Parliament—viz., fomenting a siege mentality, advancing a friend-enemy scenario, fueling division and distrust within civil society:

- Fomenting a siege mentality among the majority population by conjuring up the threat of hundreds of thousands of asylum seekers and migrants only waiting to be imposed on the country by United Nations and European Union, changing its culture beyond recognition
- Advancing a friend-enemy scenario by concentrating fear and hostility on a single purported menace—migration—and a single alleged international puppet master, George Soros (Hungarian Foreign Minister Szijjártó immediately dubbed the European Parliament Committee Report a work of "the Soros Empire")
- Fueling division and distrust within civil society by stigmatizing NGOs receiving funding from abroad as—according to the Preamble of the 2017 Transparency of Organisations Law—a potential "threat to Hungary's political and economic interests", possibly manipulated "by foreign interest groups".

To prevent citizens from questioning specific policies, political decisionmakers may ratchet up a public discourse of suspicion and fear. That is an insight, for which previous chapters of this book have drawn on David Altheide's studies. With its implications of "otherness", of potentially "overwhelming", "out-of-control" change, immigration was also earlier identified as an extremely "suitable" issue for mobilizing societal anxieties. The Trump campaign and "Brexit" referendum proved cases in point. In present-day Hungary, the government's and the ruling party's appeals to fears grounded in allegedly imminent *national* "victimization" by *international* forces not only dominate the political landscape, they also coincide

186   R. EISFELD

with large-scale purposeful media buyouts and a determined political capture of justice. The groundwork is thus being laid for a profoundly illiberal regime that it would be incongruous to label a democracy.

Exploring in depth this highly volatile constellation, and conveying the result of such work publicly, coherently, and persistently should be a key task of political scientists.

Present Hungarian political science, however, seems ill-suited for the job. In the mid-1990s, the discipline was judged by Attila Ágh, one of its early leading figures, not just as a "science of democracy", but "a masterplan and blueprint for democratization" (Ágh [4]1998 [[1]1995]: 197). The optimistic assessment may have had some merit at the time, when debates by intellectuals about the workings of the new political system and the potential role of political science often coincided (Arató and Tóth 2010: 151, 152, 153). During that same period, the unfortunate habit of 'editorial political science' evolved: Many political scientists continue to play the role of media commentators "who would be journalists in other countries", without being backed by robust research and commensurate professional prestige (Arató and Tóth 2010: 158; *Hungarian Spectrum* 2015).

To Ágh's credit, he went on to study and characterize, two decades after his too optimistic forecast, the Hungary of Fidesz and Orbán as a "Potemkin democracy"—the "worst case" in the region's ongoing "de-democratization and de-Europeanization process". But Ágh's brief analysis appeared in a journal which is published in the United Kingdom (Ágh 2016).

The Hungarian Political Science Association did issue a statement in support of Budapest's Central-European University (CEU), established by Soros in 1991, when that institution in 2017 became the obvious target of an amended Higher Education Act restricting the operation of foreign universities. In general, however, analytical uncertainties typical of the prevailing functional approaches have been dominating—and diluting—responses by Hungarian political scientists to the country's emerging competitive autocracy. That fact visibly surfaced in late 2015, when two prominent political scientists, András Körösényi and Zsolt Boda, both from the Hungarian Academy of Sciences' Research Department for Democracy and Political Theory, sharply dissented during a conference on "25 Years of the Hungarian Political Regime" (*Hungarian Spectrum* 2015, also for the following).

Boda made no effort to hide his conviction that the present political system needed to be understood "within the paradigm of hybrid regimes" and could no longer be called a democracy. Körösényi, in contrast, insisted on distinguishing "system" ("a stable, permanent phenomenon") from "regime" ("very temporary... might not be capable of 'consolidation'") and claimed that Orbán's "regime", while practicing "a new kind of exercise of power", had not basically altered the political "system", whereupon Boda took him to task for "beating around the bush".

Körösényi's argument, downplaying the depth and extent of the autocratic set-up's entrenchment, needs to be assessed in the light of the minimalist concept of democracy labeled "leader democracy" which he had put forward earlier (Körösényi 2005: 360). Artfully moving representation away from parliament, applying it to prime minister/chancellor/president, enabled him to redefine representation as leadership, based on "resolve", on "will/volition", and on the subsequent shaping of public opinion by the "leader". Körösényi studiously avoided Carl Schmitt's term "decision", but the implication was unmistakably there; the more, as he approvingly referred to Schmitts notion of "executive-centered" qualitative representation (Körösényi 2005: 364, 368, 372, 377).

As regards normative dimensions, Körösényi had nonchalantly remarked about Schumpeter's approach, which he likened to his own, that in his view, "as an explanatory-analytical model of democracy it does not need any normative justification". If any should be needed, it was satisfied, in his eyes, by the "right to vote", as it provides for "peaceful change" and produces, if not "responsive", at least "responsible" government, because "bad" rulers may be ousted (Körösényi 2005: 378).

Körösényi never bothered to discuss what makes a "good" ruler. He also refrained from considering the fact that, today, democratic derailment may "begi[n] at the ballot box". Citizens continue to vote, and elected autocrats thereby "maintain a veneer of democracy". Meanwhile, democracy's substance is "eviscerat[ed]": Electoral rules are rewritten, courts and regulatory agencies packed, and media bought off or intimidated (Levitsky and Zibalt 2018: 5/6, 7/8).

Regime hybridization in Central-East Europe provides the extreme case of democratic backsliding. However, democracies in West Europe and North America have also been compromised by the negative impact of those trends which have been discussed in earlier chapters of this book. To no small extent exceeding dangers already identified by David Easton, they are affecting the very core of democratic rules and values:

188   R. EISFELD

- Rapidity and extent of economic, social, and cultural changes are triggering aggression against democratic processes, born out of perplexed insecurity and fear.
- Strong touches of mendocracy have been poisoning informed political participation and eroding governmental accountability.
- Pro-market state intervention, tax cuts, and welfare state downsizing have been weakening citizen loyalty to the democratic process.
- Starkly rising disparities in social (income, wealth, education), hence in political resources, are pushing democracy toward plutocracy—a new Victorian (or, in the United States, "Gilded") Age.
- Deficiencies in public education have emerged as a major determinant not only of inequality, but also of xenophobic prejudice.
- Not least due to governmental action, trade union membership and bargaining power have drastically declined. Largely restricted to the public sector, labor unions are virtually absent from corporate America and corporate Britain.
- Societies are being polarized, and xenophobic backlashes fueled, by a lack of considered strategies for the inclusion of millions of immigrants in Western Europe and by the emergence of whites as the coming minority in the United States.
- Increasing governmental reliance on intrusive blanket surveillance and broad police powers to avert terrorist acts has resulted in security constitutions privileging counter-terrorism measures over civil liberties.
- Effective climate policy changes are being undermined by economic and political veto players, though human suffering due to aggravating environmental disruption may involve disastrous implications for democracies.

Minimalist concepts of democracy are really the last additions which the discipline needs against the backdrop of current uncertainties of how to continue living together meaningfully, with basic rights and principles of justice respected and protected. On the contrary, the sort of determined support for active citizenship, caring about democracy, which has been championed throughout this book, ought to be mandatory for twenty-first-century political science.

Bringing the many pressing challenges just specified even a few steps closer to their solution is a political project that involves many years and countless players on national and international levels. It is those challenges which political science now needs to address ahead of other issues. This book has advanced a number of suggestions for a topic-driven political science which might help citizens to orient themselves and, in some cases, may even assist in preparing possible substantive solutions. They include the following:

- Political science should help citizens to *fundamentally* accept processes of change (without anger, fear, or apathy), to carefully judge (according to norms of equity and social justice), and to insist on shaping them (through democratic participation), which may of course result in modifying or rejecting *specific* changes proposed by political players.
- The discipline needs to address, on a wide front, the political ramifications of escalating economic inequality in terms of non-affluent citizens' declining political engagement and political systems' limited responsiveness to the concerns of the less well-to-do, speaking up for significant policies to reduce disparities in political resources.
- Political scientists ought to develop capacities for alerting the public to sustained attempts at manufacturing ignorance or spreading falsehoods by politicians, governments, parties, and business corporations.
- The discipline is direly wanting a renewed political economy which should be researching and publicly expounding crucial elements of business-government relations that have surfaced in these pages, such as (1) investment protection by private international governance, to the possible detriment of regulation (including anticipatory "regulatory chill"), (2) policies that have generated absolutely unjustifiable offshore and onshore tax havens, permitting to decouple corporate fiscal responsibilities from democratic government, (3) processes of "cognitive capture" that have been shaping the attitudes of political players involved in (de)regulation. It should be noted that regulatory capture has been acknowledged by the OECD as a major issue requiring "correct institutional systems", including provisions of transparency and accountability. However, the OECD Secretariat's recommendations focus on pressures rather than ingrained beliefs (OECD 2014: 181).
- A revitalized political economy should be coming out in favor of significant tax reforms, internationally coordinated regulation (endowed with robust powers) of capitalist economies—first and foremost financial institutions—and of a reinvigorated "moral econ-

omy" involving embedded standards of fairness for keeping in check the highest and raising the lowest earnings.

- Political science should push for a re-emphasis on state-funded secondary and higher education, involving major improvements in quality and universal accessibility, as an investment both in life chances and in intelligent self-government and as an important segment of a restructured twenty-first-century welfare state.
- Political scientists should propose and offer to monitor the widespread establishment of integration pacts between national, regional, and local agencies designed to provide advice and support to immigrants concerning housing, schooling, and labor market access, with a focus on discriminatory practices. Arguing in favor of diversified hiring procedures for police officers on every hierarchical level should be a major component of such efforts.
- By forceful intervention, political science ought to try and contribute to reversing the subversion of democratic values and institutions in the name of anti-terrorist security measures. The discipline should invest substantial comparative research work into "soft power" approaches to combating terrorism (including efforts at deradicalization), building goodwill and trust among immigrant communities by policies that tie in with sustained integration programs.
- The discipline should engage in favor of the polycentric approach to climate change policies proposed by late Nobel Laureate Elinor Ostrom, involving local, regional, and national players linked by information networks and effective monitoring. Showing decidedly more presence in the fields of climate change adaptation and mitigation, political scientists should focus on the integration of emission-minimizing objectives into development strategies for megacities (e.g., by collaborating with the C40 Cities Climate Leadership Group).

On a fundamental level, twenty-first-century political science ought to incorporate in its canon of basic values the advancement of cultural multiplicity and ecological sustainability in addition to liberty, equality, democratic participation, and governmental accountability.

Operating as a relevant, citizen-oriented science of democracy certainly has not become any easier during the last decades. The above aims amply testify to that. Culled from the chapters in which they were discussed, and presented as a comprehensive list, they combine into an ambitious and

TWENTY-FIRST-CENTURY POLITICAL SCIENCE: POLITICIZATION... 191

demanding agenda. *Yet these aims represent what regaining relevance, obtaining an audience, and engaging the public with a view to empowering citizens are about. They result from the realization that appeals in general terms may no longer be considered sufficient.*

The discipline might draw encouragement from the fact that an organization which figures both as "the 'rich countries' club'" and as "the world's largest think tank"—in other words, the Organisation for Economic Cooperation and Development (OECD) (Pal 2012: XIII)—has commenced to consider strategies for attaining a less unequal, more inclusive society "giving voice to all" (OECD 2014: 1/2, 8–10, 162).

Yet even initial steps to address the necessary transformation of the discipline's "mainstream" will *require determined efforts at reshuffling present training—to acquire communication skills with non-academic audiences—research and teaching priorities, with every level involving the redirection of considerable financial resources.* Chapter 1 had several things to say about that. *Clearly, this implies a long march through the institutions—universities, foundations, journal editors' offices, and their respective reward structures.* Sociologists and a number of economists might emerge as coalition partners for the venture. In any case, it would be delusory to expect that such redirections, if they were attempted in earnest, would not touch off disputes within and beyond the discipline.

However, we may be at a crucial juncture. More perhaps than during any other period since 1945, twenty-first-century political science needs to take sides, to be partial in conflicts over major items on the discipline's suggested agenda, including conflicts between business interests and democratic government.

Basically, the discipline ought to become "New Dealish" in orientation.

Franklin Roosevelt's New Deal, the "Roosevelt Revolution" after 1935, did not restore, for the United States, prosperity in peacetime. Because of the system of imposed racial segregation, which still dominated the United States, it was also "bifurcated" rather than race-neutral (Hooker and Tillery 2016: 6). Yet it alleviated the suffering of millions of unemployed. And it did succeed in establishing organized labor and organized agriculture as junior bargaining partners alongside business. Capitalism, it appeared, might be reformed, democracy broadened. The New Deal "provided grounds for thinking that reform periods would again occur with some frequency" (Dahl and Lindblom 1976: XXX).

It did not happen that way. The "money changers" refused to flee their "high seats", as Roosevelt had surmised they would, and the Roosevelt

192   R. EISFELD

Coalition eventually came apart during the 1960s. But even recognizing its shortcomings, the New Deal continues to provide

- a vivid inspiration ("the only thing we have to fear is fear itself, paralyzing efforts to convert retreat into advance"),
- a significant symbol (while trade union rights were trampled underfoot by authoritarian regimes in Europe, with Germany in the lead, collective bargaining was legalized in the United States, and trade union membership increased tremendously),
- and a lasting perspective ("here is the challenge to our democracy: one-third of a nation ill-housed, ill-clad, ill-nourished. Understanding the injustice in it..., we are determined to make every citizen the subject of his country's interest and concern").

Still, not every political scientist may feel inclined to pursue such an approach. And even within a "New Dealish" framework, there would and should be ample room for differing assessments. Such differences may be expected to persist and will require developing a "culture" of informed, rational public intervention, that code of good practice which has also been discussed in an earlier chapter.

Suspicions that a "New Dealish" orientation might turn political science into a politicized discipline are unwarranted. To make sense, the charge of "politicization" would have to imply one of two things. The term could either mean "politically manipulated"—and history records that scholars have succumbed, and continue to succumb, to such manipulation, desired or imposed by political regimes. Or it could imply an unreflected, uncritical commitment to ongoing politics and values which, as emphasized by David Easton, have not infrequently prevailed in the discipline's recent past, leading (Easton's observation quoted at this chapter's outset bears repeating) to research myopia. Neither aspect is at issue here.

Analyzing, assessing, and publicly communicating tendencies in the theory and practice of democracy, political studies cannot renounce normative judgments, even if definitely not at the cost of empirical rigor. To make sense, these judgments must take into account the economic, cultural, and political constraints on the implementation of democratic principles identified in the chapters of this book. To be relevant for the citizens whose lives and civic engagement are affected by those constraints, the discipline needs to suggest and discuss possible solutions for attaining a society consistent with democratic rights, obligations, and promises of a meaningful life. In that, and just in that sense, a twenty-first-century political science ought to be partisan.

REFERENCES

Ágh, Attila ([4]1998 [[1]1995]: "The Emergence of the 'Science of Democracy' and the Impact on the Democratic Transition in Hungary." In: David Easton/John G. Gunnell/Michael B. Stein (eds.): *Regime and Discipline. Democracy and the Development of Political Science.* Ann Arbor: University of Michigan Press, 197–215.

Ágh, Attila (2016):"The Decline of Democracy in East-Central Europe. Hungary as the Worst-Case Scenario." *Problems of Post-Communism*, Vol. 63, 277–287.

Arató, Krisztina/Tóth, Csaba (2010): "Political Science in Hungary: A Discipline in the Making." In: Eisfeld/Pal (eds.), *Political Science in Central-East Europe,* op. cit., 149–162.

Beyme, Klaus von (1986): "Die deutsche Politikwissenschaft im internationalen Vergleich." In: id. (ed.): *Politikwissenschaft in der Bundesrepublik Deutschland. Entwicklungsprobleme einer Disziplin.* PVS-Sonderheft 1. Opladen: Westdeutscher Verlag, 12–26.

Coakley, John/Trent, John (2000): *History of the International Political Science Association 1949–1999.* Dublin: IPSA.

Dahl, Robert A./Lindblom, Charles E. (1976): "Preface." In: *Politics, Economics and Welfare* (Reissue; 11953). Chicago: Chicago University Press, XXI–XLIV.

Easton, David (1969): "The New Revolution in Political Science." *APSR*, Vol. LXIII, 1051–1061.

Eisfeld, Rainer/Pal, Leslie A. (2010): "Political Science in Central-East Europe and the Impact of Politics: Factors of Diversity – Forces of Convergence". In: id. (eds.): *Political Science in Central-East Europe: Diversity and Convergence.* Opladen/Farmington Hills, 9–35.

European Parliament, Committee on Civil Liberties, Justice and Home Affairs (2018): Doc. 2017/2131(INL) [*Sargentini Report*]. http://www.europarl. europa.eu/resources/library/media/20180411RES01553/20180411 RES01553.pdf, accessed April 16, 2018.

Günther, Klaus (1986): "Politikwissenschaft in der Bundesrepublik und die jüngste deutsche Geschichte." In: Beyme (ed.): *Politikwissenschaft in der Bundesrepublik Deutschland*, op. cit., 27–40.

Gunnell, John (1993): *The Descent of Political Theory.* Chicago/London: University of Chicago Press.

Hirschman, Albert O. ([2]2002 [[1]1982]): *Shifting Involvements. Private Interest and Public Action.* Princeton/Oxford: Princeton University Press.

Hirschman, Albert O. (1992): "Introduction." In: Varian Fry: *Assignment Rescue. An Autobiography.* New York: Scholastic Inc. (publ. in conjunction with the United States Holocaust Memorial Museum), V–VIII.

194   R. EISFELD

Hooker, Juliet/Tillery, Alvin B. (2016): *The Double Bind: The Politics of Racial and Class Inequalities in the Americas*. Report of the APSA Task Force on Racial and Social Class Inequalities in the Americas, Executive Summary. Washington: American Political Science Association. https://www.apsanet. org/Portals/54/files/Task%20Force%20Reports/Hero%20Report%202016_ The%20Double%20Bind/Double%20Bind%20Executive%20Summary.pdf? ver=2017-07-06-135548-510, accessed August 12, 2018.

Hungarian Spectrum (2015): "Orbán System or Orbán Regime. Debate on the Nature of the Hungarian Government", November 24. http://hungarianspectrum.org/tag/andras-korosenyi, accessed April 18, 2018.

Katznelson, Ira (2007): "APSA Presidential Address: At the Court of Chaos: Political Science in an Age of Perpetual Fear". *Perspectives on Politics*, Vol. 5, 3–15.

Körösényi, András (2005): "Political Representation in Leader Democracy." *Government and Opposition*, Vol. 40, 358–378.

Laski, Harold (1930): "Foundations, Universities and Research" [Harper's Monthly, August, 295–303], in: id.: *The Dangers of Obedience and Other Essays*. New York/London: Harper & Brothers, 150–177.

Levitsky, Steven/Way, Lucan A. (2010): *Competitive Authoritarianism. Hybrid Regimes After the Cold War*. Cambridge/New York: Cambridge University Press.

Levitsky, Steven/Zibalt, Daniel (2018): *How Democracies Die*. New York: Crown.

OECD (2014): *All on Board. Making Inclusive Growth Happen*. https://www. oecd.org/inclusive-growth/All-on-Board-Making-Inclusive-Growth-Happen. pdf, accessed May 6, 2018.

Orbán, Victor (2014): Full text of Speech of Viktor Orbán at Baile Tusnad, July 26. https://budapestbeacon.com/full-text-of-viktor-orbans-speech-at-baile-tusnad-tusnadfurdo-of-26-july-2014/, accessed April 16, 2018.

OSCE Office for Democratic Institutions and Human Rights, Limited Observation Mission Hungary – Parliamentary Elections (2018): *Statement of Preliminary Findings and Conclusions*. April 8. https://www.osce.org/odihr/elections/ hungary/377410?download=true, accessed April 16, 2018.

Pal, Leslie A. (2012): *Frontiers of Governance. The OECD and Global Public Management Reform*. New York: Palgrave Macmillan.

Sasinska-Klas, Teresa (2010): "Political Science in Poland: Roots, Stagnation, and Renaissance." In: Eisfeld/Pal (eds.), *Political Science in Central-East Europe*, op. cit., 207–220.

Stammer, Otto (1960): "Zehn Jahre Institut für politische Wissenschaft." In: id. (ed.): *Politische Forschung: Beiträge zum 10jährigen Bestehen des Instituts für Politische Wissenschaft*. Köln/Opladen: Westdeutscher Verlag, 175–203.

Wolfgang Abendroth Papers. Folder 535. Amsterdam: International Institute of Social History.

Index[1]

A
Affirmative action, 85, 94, 95
Ágh, Attila, 186
Agnotology, *see* Mendocracy
Aldrich, John H., 5, 8
Altheide, David, xx, 45, 46, 164, 165, 185
Anderson, David, 160–162, 165
Arendt, Hannah, 15–17, 35, 36, 180n1
Arrow, Kenneth, 41
Atanassow, Ewa, 165, 166, 168, 171
Atkinson, Anthony, 105, 148

B
Ballard, J. G., xxi, 149
Bang, Guri, 146, 147, 151, 152, 152n1
Banlaoi, Rommel, 172

Barber, Benjamin, 43, 44
Bartels, Larry, 103, 105–107, 110, 112
Bernauer, Thomas, 148, 151, 155
Bethe, Hans, 34
Blair, Tony, 70, 71, 120, 130–134
Blakeley, Ruth, 171, 171n2
Bloomberg, Michael, 66, 128, 153
Boal, Iain, 48
Boda, Zsolt, 186, 187
Bradbury, Ray, 19
Brintnall, Michael, 62
Brown, Gordon, 131
Bush, George H. W., 26, 69, 124, 146, 170
Bush, George W., 69–72

C
Carver, Thomas Nixon, 148
Chilcot, John, 70, 71

---

[1] Note: Page numbers followed by 'n' refer to notes.

© The Author(s) 2019
R. Eisfeld, *Empowering Citizens, Engaging the Public*,
https://doi.org/10.1007/978-981-13-5928-6

196 INDEX

Chomsky, Noam, 39, 44
Clapp, Jennifer, 6, 150, 151
Clinton, Bill, 69, 110, 120–122, 124, 130, 131, 153
Clinton, Hillary, 66, 74, 125
Coburn, Thomas, 4, 5
Cohen, Leonard, xxi, 5
Cold War, xvi, 10, 18, 27, 35–37, 43, 48, 164, 165
Conway, Eric M., xx, 46, 48, 49, 68, 154
Conway, Kellyanne, 62
Cooper, Gary, 55, 56
Crick, Bernard, xiv, 26, 73
Cross, Jo, 170

D

Dahl, Robert A., 30, 31, 35, 36, 47, 104, 105, 112, 191
Dale, Daniel, 65
Dauvergne, Peter, 6, 150, 151
de Gucht, Karel, 129
Dean, John, 71, 72
Deutsch, Karl W., 41
Dickinson, Eliot, 148, 150
Dilnot, Andrew, 67
Disraeli, Benjamin, 113
Douglas, Kirk, 60
Drumheller, Tyler, 70
Dudley, Susan, 49

E

Easton, David, 180, 181, 187, 192
Eichel, Hans, 134
Ellsberg, Daniel, 76, 77
Etzioni, Amitai, 33, 35, 42, 44, 74, 75, 96
Extralegal zones, 138

F

Farage, Nigel, 67
Figueiredo, António de, 4
Fischer, Joschka, 132, 145, 154, 155
Flinders, Matthew, xiv, 8, 9, 18, 35, 44, 73
Friedrich, Carl Joachim, 35, 36
Fry, Varian, 180n1
Fukuyama, Francis, 43, 44

G

Gabriel, Sigmar, 129
Galbraith, John Kenneth, 112
Gibson, Mel, 59
Giddens, Anthony, 132
Gilded Age, 105, 113, 188
Gilens, Martin, 103, 105–107
Glaser, Henning, 165, 171, 171n2
Glenn, John, 57
Gorbachev, Mikhail, 18, 56, 59
Gove, Michael, 66, 74
Gramm, Phil, 122
Great Recession, 45, 120–123, 132, 135
Green, Donald, 7
Griffith, Robert, 45
Gunnell, John, 179

H

Harper, Stephen, 75
Hawking, Stephen, 17
Helm, Dieter, 152n1
Hidalgo, Anne, 153
Hilary, John, 148
Hirschman, Albert O., 180, 180n1
Hoover, J. Edgar, 60
House Un-American Activities Committee (HUAC), 55, 56, 60

INDEX   197

Hoynes, Hilary, 123
Huntington, Samuel P., 10, 37–44, 46, 96
Hybridization, xi, 183, 185, 187

I
Integration pacts, 91, 92, 190
Iran-Contra Affair, 69
Isaac, Jeffrey, 46, 47, 107

J
Javeline, Debra, 150, 155
John, Peter, 8, 9, 35, 44
Johnson, Lyndon B., 36, 69
Jones, Gareth, 137, 138

K
Kaczyński, Jarosław, xvi, 183, 185
Kapp, K. William, 148
Katznelson, Ira, 165, 166, 168, 171, 180
Kelly, John, 164
Kennan, George F., 18
Keohane, Robert O., 150, 155
Killian, James, 34
Klein, Joel, 113
Koblitz, Ann, 40
Koblitz, Neal, 40
Koch brothers, 26, 49
Koch, Ed, 49, 123, 132
Körösényi, András, 186, 187
Korda, Alexander, 149
Krugman, Paul, 24, 103, 105, 108, 109, 111, 120

L
Lafontaine, Oskar, 134
Lang, Serge, 40–42, 44, 46

Laski, Harold J., 23, 24, 74, 181
Lenschow, Andrea, xiv, 152n1
Lindblom, Charles E., 10, 36, 104, 191
Linz, Juan, xix
Lipset, Seymour Martin, 40
Livingstone, Ken, 153

M
Macron, Emmanuel, 168
Mailer, Norman, 36
Mannheim, Karl, 24
May, Theresa, 95, 159, 164, 167
Mayer, Jane, 26, 49
McCarthyism, 41, 60, 61
McCartney, Alison Rios Millett, 62
McFarland, Andrew, 37
McGuire, Dorothy, 55
Mendocracy, xix, 11, 48, 101, 136, 149, 154, 166, 171n2, 188
Mikulski, Barbara, 5
Milanovic, Branko, 101–105, 108, 109, 111, 114
Mordaunt, Penny, 66
Mouffe, Chantal, 37

N
Naumann, Michael, 134
New Deal, 120, 121, 191, 192
Nixon, Richard, 60, 69, 71, 72, 76, 147, 148
Nye, Joseph S., 5

O
O'Connor, Sandra Day, 57
Obama, Barack, 26, 27, 65, 72, 121, 122, 125, 146, 163, 170
Oligarchy, *see* Plutocracy
Oliver, Chad(wick), 28, 149

198 INDEX

Orbán, Viktor, 183, 185–187
Oreskes, Naomi, xx, 46, 48, 49, 68, 154
Ostrom, Elinor, 3–6, 147, 148, 151, 154, 179, 190
Ostrom, Vincent, 20, 58

P
Paes, Eduardo, 153
Page, Benjamin, 103, 105–107
Peel, Robert, 92
Pelosi, Nancy, 125
Pence, Mike, 49
Pentagon Papers, 69, 76, 77, 162
"Perestroika" initiative, 8, 181
Perkins, Anthony, 56
Perlstein, Rick, 11, 68
Phillips, Kevin, 103
Piketty, Thomas, 103–105, 108, 109, 111, 113, 114, 120, 137, 138
Pinderhughes, Dianne, xiv, 7, 8
Plutocracy, x, 101, 103, 136, 149, 188
Podesta, John, 121
Preminger, Otto, 60
Proctor, Robert, 48
Putnam, Robert, 11, 44, 58, 102, 112–114

R
Rabi, Isidor, 34
Raphael, Sam, 171, 171n2
Reagan, Ronald, 18, 34, 56, 57, 59, 60, 62, 69, 109, 110, 121
Reardon, Sean, 114
Regulatory chill, 127, 128, 189
Reid, Harry, 125
Renwick, Alan, 68, 72
Rifkin, Jeremy, 83, 84
Robertson, James, 163n1

Roosevelt, Eleanor, 4, 92
Roosevelt, Franklin D., 191

S
Sagan, Carl, 16–20, 24, 33, 34, 46, 88
Said, Edward, 42, 44
Sanders, Bernie, 125
Sartori, Giovanni, 5, 96
Schäfer, Arnim, 107n1
Schröder, Gerhard, 120, 130, 132–134
Shapiro, Ian, 7
Sheehan, Neil, 69
Shihata, Ibrahim, 126
Skocpol, Theda, 7, 26, 27, 102, 103, 146
Snowden, Edward, 76, 161–163, 166
Solt, Frederick, 103, 105, 106, 112
Soros, George, 183, 185, 186
Sprungk, Carina, 152n1
Stiglitz, Joseph, 103, 105, 108, 109, 111, 113, 119, 121, 136
Stuart, Gisela, 66
Summers, Lawrence, 121

T
Talaga, Tanya, 65, 74
Teller, Edward, 33, 34, 41, 48
Thatcher, Margret, 67, 109, 110, 121, 131
Tienhaara, Kyla, 127, 129, 130
Tiomkin, Dimitri, 56
Trent, John, xiv, xv, 5, 6, 8, 75, 182
Trumbo, Dalton, 61
Trump, Donald J., xix, 26, 28, 51, 61, 62, 65, 66, 66n1, 68, 72, 74, 75, 85, 95, 101, 122, 124, 125, 146, 147, 185

INDEX 199

U
Udall, Mark, 166, 167
Ulam, Stanislaw, 33

V
Valls, Manuel, 88
van Gogh, Theo, 90
Vásquaz, Tabraré, 128

W
Waldfogel, Jane, 114
Watergate, 69, 71

Weber, Max, 10
Wellhausen, Rachel, 127, 128, 130
Wells, H. G., xix, 47, 149
Williams, Shirley, 87, 135
Wilson, Michael, 56, 59, 60, 84, 85, 120, 137
Wolpert, Julian, 40
Wyden, Ron, 166, 167
Wyler, William, 55, 56

Z
Zitzelsberger, Heribert, 134
Zucman, Gabriel, 138

Printed in the United States
By Bookmasters